David Lynch |

Contemporary Film Directors

Edited by James Naremore

The Contemporary Film Directors series provides concise, well-written introductions to directors from around the world and from every level of the film industry. Its chief aims are to broaden our awareness of important artists, to give serious critical attention to their work, and to illustrate the variety and vitality of contemporary cinema. Contributors to the series include an array of internationally respected critics and academics. Each volume contains an incisive critical commentary, an informative interview with the director, and a detailed filmography.

A list of books in the series appears at the end of this book.

David Lynch |

Justus Nieland

**UNIVERSITY
OF
ILLINOIS
PRESS**
URBANA,
CHICAGO,
AND
SPRINGFIELD

Frontispiece: David Lynch, at the William Griffin Gallery, Santa Monica, California, © Paul Jasmin.

Library of Congress Cataloging-in-Publication Data

Nieland, Justus.

David Lynch / by Justus Nieland.

p. cm. — (Contemporary film directors)

Includes bibliographical references and index.

Includes filmography.

ISBN 978-0-252-03693-4 (hardcover : alk. paper) —

ISBN 978-0-252-07851-4 (pbk. : alk. paper) —

ISBN 978-0-252-09405-7 (e-book)

1. Lynch, David, 1946– —Criticism and interpretation.

I. Title.

PN1998.3.L96N54   2012

791.4302'33092—dc23   2011034119

Contents |

Acknowledgments | ix

WRAPPED IN PLASTIC | 1

Interior Design   8

Bad Plumbing: *Eraserhead*   10

Inhuman Windows: *The Elephant Man*   20

Sexy Tchotchke: *Blue Velvet*   28

Furniture Porn: *Lost Highway*   47

The Art of Being Moved   62

Radio-Affectivity: *Wild at Heart*   65

Melodrama's Crypt: *Twin Peaks: Fire Walk with Me*   79

Moving Impersonality: *Mulholland Dr.*   94

Organism   111

On Moving Pictures: *Six Men Getting Sick*   114

Animated Humans: *The Grandmother*   119

Good Machine: *The Straight Story*   124

Vital Media: *Inland Empire*   134

INTERVIEWS WITH DAVID LYNCH | 161

Filmography | 171

Bibliography | 177

Index | 185

James Naremore has been a superb editor and provided extremely helpful advice about the argument of this book. His generosity is as broad as his learning, and his patience is seemingly infinite. Joan Capatano, once again, was terrific to work with. Danny Nasset saw the project to the end with cheer and shockingly prompt responses to my every query. And Jill Hughes did an expert job as copyeditor. How lucky I was to have an editor so familiar with the book's subject. Thanks to audiences at the Society for Cinema and Media Studies conference and at Concordia University, Montreal, where I presented portions of this book and received perceptive comments and questions. Thanks especially to Omri Moses for the invitation, and for many stimulating exchanges about this work. I also want to acknowledge Gerritt Terstiege at *form* magazine (www. form.de) and Rob Wilson at *Sight and Sound* for permission to reprint two previously published interviews with David Lynch.

I am lucky to have wonderful friends, colleagues, and students in the Department of English and the Film Studies Program at Michigan State University, many of whom heard or read parts of this book, always asking the most productive kinds of questions, and matching my own excitement about the project. Portions of the book were hatched in the classroom, and I want to thank in particular the students in my classes "An Erotics of Cinema: Surrealism and Film Theory" and "Cinemas of Affect: Hitchcock, Buñuel, Lynch." Their passion, smarts, and all-around liveliness helped me arrive at the conceptual heart of this book. Thanks to my chairperson, Steve Arch, and the College of Arts and Letters for the post-tenure sabbatical that enabled me to get writing. A special thanks to Akira Mizuta Lippit, Todd McGowan, and Jonathan Rosenbaum, all of whom have written—and continue to write—

brilliantly about David Lynch. They gave me the kind of intelligent, candid feedback that proved decisive to the final shape of the book. Jen Fay, Pat O'Donnell, and Karl Schoonover are my most valued readers and colleagues. Their friendships sustain me.

To Sarah Wohlford, my partner in life, I owe everything. Lila and Iris, our daughters, make everything real. They became obsessed with *The Wizard of Oz*, in its many incarnations, at a rather uncanny time. I dedicate this book, with love and gratitude, to my cinephilic family: my brothers, Andrew and James, and my parents, Maury and Sue Erickson Nieland. Like me, they liked *The Straight Story*. We used to live in Iowa.

David Lynch |

Wrapped in Plastic |

Wrapped in Plastic, as any fan of David Lynch will know, is the name of a long-running fanzine (1993–2005) devoted to the critical and cult phenomenon of *Twin Peaks* (1990–1992), one of the most innovative shows in the history of network television. The title refers to the state of Laura Palmer's dead body as a found object, waiting to be revived in the quirky fantasies of the living. The corpse of this high school homecoming queen and incest victim, enshrouded in semitranslucent synthetic sheeting, washes up on the shore of a river in a small, Pacific Northwest logging town. The body incarnates the inaugural secret—"Who Killed Laura Palmer?"—that spawns countless mysteries over the course of the series. Wrapped in plastic of the most everyday sort, beached as the unforeseen waste of a presumably more natural environment, Laura's embalmed body is rather like the synthetic environment of *Twin Peaks* itself: in its reanimations of absence, in its uncanny blurring of the quotidian and the strange, and in its perverse contaminations of the "nature" of small-town American "culture." Critic Andrew Ross had just this kind of plastic in mind when he referred to *Twin Peaks* as "one of our first examples of ecological camp."[1]

David Lynch's corpus has undergone its own plastic embalming. The evolution of his filmmaking career—from the midnight-movie success of *Eraserhead* (1977), his astonishing first feature, to critical darlings like *Blue Velvet* (1986) and *Wild at Heart* (1990)—dovetailed with the academic consolidation of postmodernism, a cultural logic Lynch's films came to embody for the likes of Fredric Jameson and Slavoj Žižek, both of whom have written brilliantly about Lynch.[2] The postmodern Lynch came prepackaged with its own theory of plastic, the ur-material in Lynch's aesthetic of depthlessness and superficiality, semiotic excess and cliché. Plastic named Lynch's detached emotional orientation— cold, ironic, and insincere. Plastic materialized Lynch's relationship to history and the political, at once nostalgic for a past that never was and shrink-wrapped against the realities of the present. And plastic was the medium of psychic reality, approached by Lynch chiefly through the malleable stuff of fantasy.

Rather than scrapping this story of plastic, since it accounts for much of Lynch's work, we might take plastic *even more seriously* as the prime matter of Lynch's filmmaking, essential to his understanding of cinema. This means understanding plastic not as a static substance—reified and hard, unchanging and resistant to history—but rather as pervaded by a mysterious dynamism. In 1957, for example, Roland Barthes described plastic as a properly alchemical substance, pulling off the "magical operation par excellence: the transmutation of matter."[3] For Barthes, the fascination with plastic—evident in awed crowds lined up to witness new secular gods like Polystyrene—was doubly historical. It was both the latest stage in the evolution of bourgeois "imitation materials"—that is, their prosaic fall from the domain of appearance to actual use—and the by-product of France's rapid postwar modernization.

Materializing the "very idea of infinite transformation," French plastics marked the belated arrival of the United States' own postwar dream of consumption. This arrival led to a broader makeover of the domestic interior as modern that would be satirized in films like Jacques Tati's *Mon Oncle* (1958), one of Lynch's favorites. Of course, Lynch's obsessive returns to the styles, songs, and domestic environments of the 1950s are often read as part of his nostalgia. But Lynch's own remarks about the cheery decade suggest a more thoughtful reckoning with the utopian kernel of mid-century design and its *promesse du bonheur*:

> It was a fantastic decade in a lot of ways. Cars were made by the right kind of people. Designers were really out there with fins and chrome and really amazing stuff . . . They were like sculpture, you know, that moved . . . The future was bright. Little did we know we were laying the groundwork for a disastrous future. All the problems were there, but it was somehow glossed over. And then the gloss broke, or rotted, and it all came oozing out . . . pollution was really good and started [*sic*]. Plastics were coming in, weird studies of chemicals and co-polymers and a lot of medical experiments, the atomic bomb and a lot of, you know, testing. It was like the world was so huge you could dump a bunch of stuff and it's not gonna matter, right? It just kinda got out of control.[4]

With typical gee-whiz enthusiasm, Lynch offers a rather shrewd micro-history of postwar material culture, which found itself catering to America's burgeoning middle-class consumers with all the outrageous, revolutionary new products and designs of cold war modernity. The excesses of this brave new built world—evident in Detroit's fins and chrome but also in fiberglass chairs, molded plywood, and the multifunctional furniture ensembles of mid-century modern designers—were the material fantasies of America's postwar, democratic futurity. As Lynch knows, the irrevocably changed substance of postwar material culture gave us not only the synthetic stuff of consumer fantasy—"Euphoric 1950s chrome optimism," he calls it elsewhere—but also the catastrophes of the built environment: environmental and ecological contamination, the atom bomb, and other kinds of scientific experimentation run amok.[5]

Plastic, for Lynch, may be the future's happy medium, but it is also the stuff of inevitable disaster and chaos and the too-fragile gloss of fantasy's containment. If plastic has a dominant mood or tone, it is one that merges the soul of postwar utopian sincerity and domestic security and its retrospectively ironic rejoinder: "Little did we know . . ." Positioned between the innocence and experience of America's material environment at mid-century, plastic is a fretful substance—uncanny anxiety materialized as kitsch. Epitomizing Lynch's ambivalence toward the lure of the mid-century, the promise of plastic is its material, affective, and temporal dynamism. Lynch's thing for the 1950s is a form of attentiveness to a transformed material environment. In it, nature is transfigured by technological second nature, homey euphoria is haunted by unease and intimations of disaster, and movement into a happy future is blocked by a nagging, still unprocessed trauma in the domain of human making. Given this, might we understand his films as themselves environments? They are as affectively unstable, as riddled with temporal ambiguities, as filled with hybrids of nature-culture as the postwar world that haunts his filmic imagination. In these atmospheres, spectators are wrapped in plastic.

It should not come as a surprise that Lynch would understand film-making as a way of shaping, plastically, a moving environment. He came to filmmaking, after all, following a failed European apprenticeship in painting with Austrian expressionist Oskar Kokoschka (Lynch left Europe soon after arriving, before meeting the painter). And in 1965 he enrolled at the Pennsylvania Academy of the Fine Arts in Philadelphia— then dominated by the prestige of American action painters like Jackson Pollock, Franz Kline, and Jack Tworkov. By this time, the American art world had witnessed a series of attempts to rethink aesthetic production on the model of a more dynamic experience, an ongoing situation, or a contingent Happening. This began, perhaps, with Allan Kaprow's so-called Environments in New York in the late 1950s and continued through the development of installation art in the 1960s and '70s. In 1956, for example, Kaprow suggested that the artistic movement toward assemblages, three-dimensional spaces, and his own multimedia "Environments" was inaugurated by the enlarged "arena" of action painters like Pollock.[6] Similarly, Lynch's first "film," *Six Men Getting Sick* (1967), was conceived as an attempt to extend the capacity of painting to move and, in moving, to frame a situation for an active viewer. *Six Men* is a thoughtful, multimedia investigation of cinema's relationship to the plastic arts—to materials that are capable of being shaped or molded in three dimensions. It is also the first of many of Lynch's films to understand cinema as theatrical in its orientation to the contingent situation and embodied experience of its viewer, anticipating the tendency of his films to turn into tableaux, or arenas of gestural intensity, or a proscenium for all manner of performances.

Many filmmakers have come to cinema from painting, of course, and Lynch is not the first to align processes of cinematic construction with the plastic arts. As part of its preoccupation with the ontology of the cinematic, classical film theory made similar comparisons. Take, for example, French art historian Élie Faure's 1923 essay "Cineplastics," which insists on cinema as "plastic first." By plastic, though, Faure means not "motionless, colorless forms called sculptural," but cinema as "moving architecture," one whose primary characteristic is "a living rhythm and its repetition in time."[7] Because he understands cinema as an aesthetic whole, dynamic, moving in time, and thus producing a "sudden coming to life," Faure sees the product of cineplastics as an "autonomous organism" whose skeleton is a "web of feeling." In this way, cinema materializes "the plastic" in the obsolete sense of the word, as the creative or procreative principle, bringing into being a new, surrogate form of life.

Remarks like these may strike us today as dubiously animistic or vitalistic, but they need not be. Instead, they make a strong claim for the plastic materiality of cinema and its capacity to fashion moving aesthetic environments for experience. In Lynch's case, these transient situations are occasions for an experience of human life as itself plastic, shot through with kinds of media that are life's original supplement but that over the span of Lynch's lifetime have estranged life irrevocably from itself. This, the plastic excess lodged at the very heart of life, everywhere energizes Lynch's filmmaking.

This book explores three nodal points in Lynch's plastic environments. "Interior Design" takes up plasticity's capacity for infinite transformation as an architectural and design dynamic, a feature of mise-en-scène, and a mode of fashioning, and psychologizing, cinematic space. Lynch's films imbue rooms with the erratic force of organic nature. They produce atmosphere in the fashion of unforeseen weather patterns, incipient environmental disturbances, or ecological disasters. As well-wrought climates, Lynch's interiors are made more lovely through their systematic deformations of habit and habitat—the failed boundaries of intimate life, the incursion of foreign bodies, unaccountable behavior, or eccentric textures and objects that, by not fitting the scene, further volatize it for the spectator. Discussing *Eraserhead*, *The Elephant Man* (1980), *Blue Velvet*, and *Lost Highway* (1997), I turn to Lynch's various ways of giving us a sense of an interior, both domestic and psychic. This aesthetic preoccupation has recently turned entrepreneurial in Lynch's collaboration in the fall 2011 opening of Club Silencio, a Rue Montmarte nightclub combining concert hall, restaurant, library, and cinema with moody interiors designed by Lynch himself and modeled on *Mulholland Dr.*'s mysterious venue of the same name. Exploring how Lynch's films stage interiority, for he shows insides to be emphatically theatrical, I consider how his films have always bespoken a familiarity with the cultural history and iconography of a broad range of modern design idioms, especially the mid-century domestication of modernism and its attempts to supplant avant-garde austerity with bourgeois pleasure. Lynch is a kind of constructivist, an engineer of atmosphere, and the mysteries of the inside—to which so much of his work is devoted—are plastic.

"The Art of Being Moved" explores the emotional registers of plasticity, attempting to explain a key affective paradox in Lynch's work: the way it seems both so manifestly insincere and so emotionally powerful, so impersonal and so intense. Plastic's instability as a substance raises the problem of Lynch's famously unstable tone and the nature of his artistic knowingness or sophistication. Attempting to distinguish the melodramatic sincerity of *Blue Velvet* from the forms of ironic cruelty so common in 1980s cinema, Lynch once described the film's curious sentimentalism as an attempt to capture the way "radiation had become an emotion."[8] Thus do historical mutations of the biosphere of the 1950s find their way into the unstable affective environments of Lynch's films, energizing their plastic arrangements of culture. Marked by a high degree of medial self-consciousness, Lynch's work is an archive of some of the most esteemed emotional strategies of aesthetic modernity—combining and oscillating between modes such as the lyric, the grotesque, irony, the emotional vicariousness of kitsch, the uncanny, black humor, romantic passion, trauma, melodrama, and the sensational, voyeuristic, or pornographic. But in films like *Wild at Heart*, *Twin Peaks: Fire Walk with Me* (1992), and *Mulholland Dr.* (2001), Lynch offers particular canny meditations on mediated affect. In these films, which are some of his most emotionally complex, Lynch explores the contours of feeling as it is shaped, deformed, and conditioned by particular media environments, protocols, and technologies. Exploring the problem of affect is one way Lynch performs media history.

"Organism" takes up Lynch's persistent tendency to think of forms of media and forms of life as related species. Here, plastic is useful for conceptualizing his picture of the human organism as malleable and heterogeneous. Lynch's unruly understanding of human biology, its tendency to exceed its own mortal limits and the boundaries of time and space, is often engendered through forms of media—whether cel animation, slow-moving lawn mowers, or low-grade digital images—which themselves become monstrously vital. Lynch wants art, and cinema, to animate aesthetic environments that are life-*like*; however, for Lynch, life is productive mostly for its capacity to never be simply itself but rather to spawn the unaccountable and the unforeseen. What this amounts to in films like *Six Men Getting Sick* (1967), *The Grandmother* (1970), *The Straight Story* (1999), and *Inland Empire* (2006) is a version of human nature and human culture as productive assemblages, sites of relentless activity and transformation made even more dynamic by organic nature's original contamination by the inorganic. Here, Lynch reveals himself to be a surrealist in anthropology—sharing with the historical surrealists both a sense of the organism as living in uncanny hybridity with technology and mediation and a subversive awareness of culture as a basically incoherent arrangement of norms, rules, and limits on human freedoms.

These ways of asking what it means, in Lynch's art, to be wrapped in plastic assume that in some fundamental ways plastic is the ur-substance of modern experience. And this means taking seriously the category of "experience" itself—a category some of the most compelling recent treatments of Lynch tend to dismiss as the hallmark of a retrograde myth of fullness, a form of New Age mysticism, or an anything-goes mode of aesthetic evaluation. Lynch is, of course, always insisting on cinema as a kind of unfathomable, qualitative experience—a ritual, a thing to be suffered, or a passion to be undergone. And perhaps unsurprisingly, he has increasingly linked this endeavor to his stumping for Transcendental Meditation, which, we are told, will be the subject of his next film. This does not mean we are to take his word on his art; rather, it should at least remind us that "experience" has been an indispensable category in twentieth- and twenty-first-century art and in theories of the strange vitality of the moving image in particular—as Walter Benjamin, André Breton, André Bazin, and Roland Barthes knew well. To think about the kinds of exemplary experience that Lynch's works, as singular environments, offer to their spectators is essential to any reckoning with his experimentalism and to understanding what, if anything, it offers as a way of thinking about cinema and its digital afterlife.

Interior Design

Interiors are mysterious. It is an old saw, even a tired metaphysical proposition, and yet its infinitely plastic potential everywhere propels Lynch's mise-en-scène. Consider the interior photographs of one rather famous Los Angeles home, the Beverly Johnson House, designed in 1963 by Frank Lloyd Wright Jr., the son of the even more famous modernist architect. The photos offer a series of views of the home, whose furnishings are spare, tasteful, and modern: the cheery red, armless mid-century lounge chair in the dining room; the yellow Bertoia Diamond Chair (designed in the 1950s for the Knoll furniture company) by the glowing hearth; the sturdy leather club chairs and their set of matching geometric wood and steel tables; the strategically small kitchen (fig. 1).[9] This more rational, more harmonious modern vision—in which the

Figure 1. Dreams of good design: the Beverly Johnson House

natural and corporeal are reorganized by good design—is the message of the home's signature concrete-block ornamentation, visible outside the window of the bedroom and picked up inside around the hearth. It is an abstraction of a pine tree, with chevrons as needles, squares as pinecones. In this mid-century design flourish, nature is domesticated as culture—forest-cum-concrete.

The rooms are unoccupied and seem as anonymous as *Inland Empire*'s Smithy (Smithee?) set. But the opened glass doorway in the bedroom and the roaring fire give the scene an ambivalent, transitory feeling of desertion or apprehension, of someone having recently left the scene or just on the verge of entering. Something is happening. The house may be empty, but its decor bears the unmistakable traces of its famous owner, David Lynch, who bought the home in 1986 after finishing *Blue Velvet*. Lynch, who credits Frank Lloyd Wright Sr. as one of his favorite architects, was struck by Jr.'s modern design. Its attractive combination of organicism and modern abstraction was somehow homey, recalling the piney Pacific Northwest of Lumberton and Lynch's own childhood. The two square tables in the master bedroom are similar design monsters: built by Lynch himself in the manner of Pierre Chareau, they turn warm wood into a cold, hard assemblage of nested iron squares and sharp angularity. But the most flagrant piece is the little table in the master bedroom, topped with a lace antimacassar and a curiously dead plant. Fans of *Eraserhead* will recognize this as a cinematic object, a prop central to the frightful inner workings of Lynch's first feature. There it sits abjectly next to Henry Spencer's anxious bed, in his claustrophobic apartment room (fig. 2). Materializing the film's vision of grotesque organicism, the tree, on the stage of Henry's fitful dream, assumes obscene proportions. Next to it, Henry will lose his head when something more forceful erupts within him, and the undead tree oozes rivulets of blood in an act of uncanny sympathy. This patently irrational object, so small and out of place in a photograph of a stylish modern home, poses only questions, turning a self-evident inside into an enigma. Is this a species of latent domestic horror masquerading as furniture, or one more piece of a kitschy design collection, or a canny prop in a home transformed into theater—a stage for a self that is present only in its atmospheric effects?

When asked about his preferred architects, Lynch answers with a roster of modernist heavyweights: "From Bauhaus, all the students of

Figure 2. The kitsch grotesque |

the Bauhaus school, and Pierre Chareau, he did the House of Glass in Paris, Ludwig Mies van der Rohe, all the Wright Family, Rudolf Michael Schindler and Richard Neutra. I like really beautifully designed, minimal things."[10] These investments place Lynch in a long line of modern directors (Sergei Eisenstein, Jacques Tati, Stanley Kubrick, Alfred Hitchcock, Federico Fellini, and Michelangelo Antonioni, among others) who are sensitive to the relationship between architecture and the spatiotemporal art of the moving image, of cinema as a "cineplastics," in Faure's terms. For Lynch, interior design is a similar matter of engineering atmosphere and producing dynamic, totally synthetic affective environments. At stake in Lynch's persistent psychologizing of spatial form is the problem of interiority—of a picture of psychic insides less as reservoirs of spirit than as material works, quintessentially modern products.

Bad Plumbing: *Eraserhead*

Eraserhead is Lynch's first great poem of interiority. Like period-specific ideas about domesticity and intimacy, "interiority" was invented as an ideological by-product of a nineteenth-century public world shaped by the traumas of industrialization and political revolution. The result was the notion that spatial and psychic insides might swaddle the individual in shared protections against a traumatic exterior. The interior, "defined in the early modern period as public space," now became what Diana

Fuss calls "a locus of privacy, a home theater for the production of a new, inward-looking subject."[11] Fuss's terms for such inwardness are theatrical or cinematic, but Walter Benjamin's are more specifically Lynchian. Describing this "addiction to dwelling," in which inwardness becomes material *nesting*, Benjamin famously explained how nineteenth-century modernity "conceived the residence as a receptacle for the person, and it encased him with all his appurtenances so deeply in the dwelling's interior that one might be reminded of the inside of a compass case, where the instrument with all its accessories lies embedded in deep, usually violet folds of velvet."[12]

Over the course of the nineteenth century, interiority was steadily redefined as both a psychological concept and an architectural idea, or, better, a way of understanding physical space itself as haptic and sensory, a dynamic product of experience rather than a passive container of unmoving things.[13] As Anthony Vidler has argued, this late nineteenth-century psychologizing of spatial form led to a fully modern understanding of space as "a production of the subject, and thus as a harbinger and repository of all the neuroses and phobias of that subject."[14] If one side of this modern formulation is the compensatory security of bourgeois privacy, on the other side lie the newly pathologized phobias of public life (alienation, agoraphobia) and the tendency of privacy to overgrow itself, to become phantasmagoric. In interviews, Lynch has captured the dilemma precisely: "The home is a place where things can go wrong."[15]

In *Eraserhead* the historical relationship between interiority and industrialization is staged with exaggerated clarity and built into its titular joke. While Henry (Jack Nance), the "Kafkaesque clerk," is "on vacation" from his printing job at La Pelle's factory, his dream reveals the feared culmination of his psychological trial as a grotesque putting-to-work.[16] When Henry is decapitated, his mind, which hosts a rich but fragile inner life, is materialized as brain, and the brain is quickly instrumentalized— psychic negation, Eraser-head. Perhaps more telling is the composition that frames Henry's arrival at the home of Mary X (Charlotte Stewart), where one of cinema's most astonishing dinner-table scenes is about to happen. Tipped off to Mary's dinner invitation by the alluring Beautiful Girl Across the Hall (Judith Roberts), Henry shambles through the Hopperesque terrain of melancholic concrete, abandoned train tracks, and darkness. We cut to a murky shot of a chain-link fence that opens onto some unseen industrial hell whose immaterial traces are the hiss and billow of stream. Lynch reframes the fence and clarifies its astonishing proximity to the Xs' home—so close that the fits and starts of smoke befoul its tiny front porch. (The closeness of factory and family nest will be echoed through Lynch's work, most obviously in the recurring static panel of his long-running *Los Angeles Times* comic strip, *The Angriest Dog in the World*.) To put it mildly, the adjacency has not done much for the Xs' yard. At frame left, two gangly, bloomless stalks of what once might have been sunflower plants line Henry's path to Mary X, peering expectantly at Henry through the window in the front door; at frame right, another vine seems to grow, waywardly, from the yard through the chain-link fence. Is the vine a natural tendril snaking outward through the fence, or is it an industrial pipe from the neighboring factory rooted in the front yard? It is impossible to tell, and this indiscernability anticipates the home's uncanny continuum of nature and culture, most obvious on its inside.

We might say that the home's plumbing is all wrong. Consider the strange way Mr. X (Allen Joseph) greets Henry in one of the film's more uncharacteristically prolix bits of dialogue: "I thought I heard a stranger. We've got chicken tonight. Strangest damn things. They're man-made. Little damn things. They're smaller than my fist! They're new! I'm Bill . . . Printing's your business, huh? Plumbing's mine. I've seen this neighborhood change from pastures to the hellhole it is now. I've put every damn pipe in this neighborhood. And people think pipes grow in their homes! Well. They sure as hell don't! Look at my knee! Look at my knees! Are you hungry?" Even as the patriarch conjures nostalgically a lost pastoral world, his speech attests to strange hybrids of nature and culture that are so theatrically on display in the Xs' home. The novelty of tiny, man-made chickens conjures a world whose plumbing collapses organic and inorganic processes, natural and mechanical orders, hopelessly troubling the security of the domestic interior in the process.

In other words, pipes *do* grow in people's homes in *Eraserhead*, a point Lynch makes by ironically framing Mr. X's speech with the black ventilation tube of the fireplace, which comprises the left border of the shot and extends vertically out of the frame. Shortly after Henry's grotesque carving of the tiny chickens, whose spilled guts have sent Mrs. X (Jeanne Bates) into an erotic fit, he is cornered by her in the living room, asked to divulge whether he and Mary have had "sexual intercourse," and then licked and kissed. When Mary interrupts Mrs. X's unseemly assault, the shot is divided vertically by the same black pipe. The pipe now separates Henry and Mrs. X from a horrified Mary and substitutes precisely for the internal archway dividing the living room, where Henry is trapped, from the family dining room in the background (fig. 3). The architecture of the shot corners both Henry and Mary in different states of psychological extremity. Henry's anxious spot is notably devoid of decor, as the façade of the bourgeois family is stripped bare through Mrs. X's incestuous violation of Henry's sexual privacy. Mary's horror at this spectacle of domestic obscenity is framed by the pipe against the bourgeois dining room's compensatory domestications of nature—an extravagant floral arrangement sits on a table in front of a painting of flowers affixed to a floral wallpaper pattern. Henry's and Mary's corners are both bad nests, host to families and family rooms in which nature has run amok.

In this same sequence, Mrs. X announces that there is a baby, that Henry is the father, and that he'll soon have to marry Mary. With the abrupt revelation of the baby's premature birth, the cultural machinery of bourgeois propriety kicks too quickly into gear—paternity is established, marriage is inevitable. The baby's speedy materialization poses again the problem of another improper inside within a domestic space

Figure 3. Domestic plumbing

whose inner speeds and rhythms are constantly out of synch or ill-timed. The baby is the film's most untimely gestation; its suddenness is mimicked in Henry's own bodily reaction, an involuntary nosebleed. All of this domestic havoc transpires next to the exposed fireplace tube—the uncanny infrastructure of the violated interior.

In *Eraserhead* what is proper to bourgeois privacy fails to stay inside or is violently exteriorized under the aesthetic sign of the grotesque. Henry's introduction to Mrs. X is interrupted by the noisy squeals and slurps of a litter of puppies nursing on the living room floor. In moments like this the domestic interior houses just too much animal life; in others it suffers from unsettling absences of vitality or from darkly comic incursions of mechanism into domestic rhythms. The grandmother (Jeanne Lange), secreted in the kitchen, is catatonic and tosses the salad for dinner only with the prosthetic aid of Mrs. X's arms. The rest of the family is prey to equally disturbing lurches in and out of animation: Mary is prone to seizures; Mrs. X to convulsive sexual arousal; Mr. X to numbness, non sequiturs, and frozen grimaces. *Eraserhead*'s grotesque inversions of natural and cultural orders are most obvious at the Xs' dinner table: Mr. X can't cut the man-made chickens because of his unfeeling arms, while the birds themselves are monstrously lively; they dance gamely, and then, sliced open by an obliging Henry, they spill more blood than their tiny bodies would seem to allow. Here and elsewhere, there's a lot more happening through the internal mechanisms of things than seems possible. Lynch's plumbing is excessive and irrational.

While sexual reproduction is surely horrific in *Eraserhead*, the film's meditation on "plumbing" is more than a puerile metaphor. Because its mise-en-scène positions grotesque inversion against the stability of the domestic sphere, *Eraserhead* participates in a challenge to the ideology of bourgeois privacy. Central to the early twentieth-century avant-garde's revolt against modern social forms was a grotesque denaturalization of the modern family. This was often accomplished by eschewing or estranging the kinds of sentimental emotional protocols thought to secure the distinction between private and public life. Rather than simply refusing domesticity, the avant-garde turned the home into a kind of domestic laboratory, experimenting with and remaking not just the material structures of the home but also the forms of intimacy, sexuality, and gendered behavior organized by more traditional architectural forms.

For a film about violated interiors, *Eraserhead* also spawns them compulsively. Insides reproduce and multiply. They hatch inside of each other, and in the process they become subject to strange correspondences, passages, or thresholds of energetic transfer. The apartment lobby, from hindsight recognizable as the first iconically Lynchian room, is also Lynch's first *nested* interior. The expectant openness of the lobby, its expanse of zigzagged carpet, spotlit like a vacant stage, is twice echoed: first in the rows of smaller mailboxes at frame left, most of them empty, and then more comically as Henry, inside an inside, waits forever for the elevator doors to close (fig. 4).

More telling in this regard is the decor of Henry's one-room apartment. The tubular, black metal frame of Henry's bed extends the bad plumbing at the Xs'; it will later frame Mary's spasm of jerking at the foot of the bed—a frustrated act that seems masturbatory, or a simulation of sex, but is later revealed to be an attempt to dislodge her suitcase and flee to her parents. As the failing heart of conjugal intimacy, the bed is the space of sexual frustration, troubled sleep, and boredom. Dominating Henry's room, it is something to be escaped, or transformed into a place from which to watch something more interesting in the radiator, or dissolved in a milky dream of sex with the Beautiful Girl Across the Hall.

On one side of the room, Henry's anxious bed is surrounded by an ensemble of prosthetic insides extending in row. There is, first, the

Figure 4. The nested interior |

gramophone that plays several Fats Waller recordings and so provides some of the room's scant warmth, no less soothing for being mechanical. A tinny organ snuggled in a wooden box, the gramophone is one of the film's less uncanny monsters of technology and organicism; its encasing of media in wood will later appear again in Lynch's own furniture design for *Lost Highway*. Then there is Henry's wooden dresser, whose top drawer he opens to examine a severed photograph of Mary X. Stranger still is the small, empty cabinet adjacent to the dresser in the room's darkened corner. This box seems to be a locus of secrecy itself, awaiting its role in some unknown ritual. Like many Lynchian interiors, the box does double duty as both cage and stage. In his mailbox in the hotel lobby, Henry has received yet another mysterious box, which he later opens furtively on the street, extracting the small, spermlike worm he will then enclose in the cabinet in his room that seems to have been waiting for it. Lynch later explores the force field built by this curious web of resonant interiors when Henry—abandoned by Mary to minister to the crying baby—opens the cabinet to check on the sperm-worm, his other, smaller organic charge. The opening triggers a fulsome electric hum that bridges the shot of Henry in front of the cabinet and Lynch's abrupt cut—first to the set of mailboxes in the hotel lobby and then to a close-up of Henry's empty mailbox.

The unmotivated cutaway suggests a kind of irrational sympathetic correspondence between these spatially scattered insides—the cabinet, the mailbox, the sperm's tiny container. Editing and sound build and connect insides across gaps in space and time. Cinema, for Lynch, is a relentlessly interiorizing technology. These correspondences, and their cinematic nature, will become grotesquely literal inside the radiator—the film's most famous and fragile interior. The Lady in the Radiator (Laurel Near) is only the most exaggerated version of the film's failed wish to endow furniture with the promise of better, because more profound and secret, insides. Is the radiator a kind of metaphysical plumbing? Its toasty inwardness makes literal the metaphor of bourgeois interiority as a home theater. After all, Henry watches the radiator like a virtual window—a television set or, better, a movie screen placed under his room's actual window, which frames only the claustrophobic view of a brick wall. But like all the other interiors in the film, the radiator fails to secure the metaphysical boundary between inside and outside. In the midst of the Lady's performance of "In Heaven Everything Is Fine," her stage is rained on by larger versions of the spermlike substance that has already proven its ability to travel porously between Lynch's nested boxes. And the Lady's spotlit stage itself—with its tableau-like frontality and geometrically tiled floor—is anticipated both in the mise-en-scène of Henry's lobby and later echoed in Henry's dream, when the tiny doors of his bedside cabinet open and the sperm, now itself a spotlit performer, dances before transforming itself into a mouth, which opens to swallow Lynch's camera.

The camera's movement toward the heart of a dark interior is an obsessive tool in Lynch's visual style. *Eraserhead*'s trippy opening sequence contains Lynch's first complex series of interiorizing movements and enfoldings of textural density. Its impossible series of nested insides reminds us that Lynch's interiors are always designed—their spaces made tactile by attention to textural surface and sound. The architecture of the interior, in short, is cinematic, as we see again in the conspicuous mise-en-scène of frames and enframing in Henry's room: the ripped photograph of Mary, the menacing window/wall, the radiator/theater, and the room's one piece of wall art—a framed photograph of a mushroom cloud, which, for Lynch, is the sign of postwar "plastic" gone bad.

Lynch's approach to interior design is less soulful than constructivist; the inside is not so much a romantic reservoir of feeling than an effect, a tool of feeling's formal manipulation. Cinema builds interiors; mise-en-scène imbues rooms with their particular atmosphere ("room tone," Lynch has called it elsewhere); the mysteries of the inside are plastic. Such, at least, seems to be the lesson of the film's greatest and best-kept secret, which has always been a constructivist one: how *did* Lynch make that baby? The very question still makes Lynch uncomfortable, and he is quick to shift the conversation in what he considers the properly cinematic direction—away from the question of genesis and toward the effects and affects of the well-built thing.

Eraserhead ends with the fitful death of one mysterious contraption. Henry's act of infanticide, a violent opening of a mysterious inside, precipitates the film's final sympathetic transfers of energy across interiors—of bodies and walls, proximate furniture and distant planets, lightbulbs and radiators. The electric din in Henry's room intensifies in proportion to the baby's foaming guts. Sparks shoot from inside an electrical socket, causing Henry's lamp to flicker stroboscopically, blindingly, before burning out. The burnout cracks a hole in the very planet first plumbed in the film's prologue, an opening that Lynch's camera (again) follows inside to find the Man in the Planet (Jack Fisk), his levers kicking off their own sparks, desperately trying to maintain control of his machine before all is lost in the final, white-hot union of Henry and the Lady in the Radiator.

But *Eraserhead* also opens with a similar irrational fantasy of interior design. In fact, its inaugural montage functions less as a cosmic allegory than a kind of lesson in the plastic architecture of cinema and its difference from the hellish built environment in which Henry lives. The dazzling sequence ends abruptly with the contrast between the mysterious, textured insides that are assembled and traversed in the prologue and the monumental, impassive urban architecture in which Henry first finds himself in the city. The contrast seems to stage, in inverted fashion, the tension between the supposedly fixed frame of the photographic view and the mobile experience of body within architectural space: for Lynch, it is the camera's frame that is volatized, and against the interiorizing movements of the prologue, the static menace of Henry's built environment that rigidly circumscribes his movement becomes all the more apparent. The mystery of the Man in the Planet, his hand on some monstrously powerful lever that seems to join in machinic assemblage a host of discrete insides and outsides with no rational connection, is thus also the aesthetic wonder of *Eraserhead*'s baby. The magical plumbing over which both the Man and baby-maker preside is cinema as interior design.

In the film's prologue and concluding apocalypse, the Man in the Planet sits before a broken window. As a design feature, the window has, at least since the seventeenth century, framed the ideology of bourgeois humanism. A limpid glass membrane between the inside and the outside, the window buttressed a middle-class denial of the public world, offering both protection against the trauma of public life and ways of folding it inside, domesticating it. The window also abetted the humanist fantasy of unmediated representation—of the optical veracity of a world set in front of, framed for, the presiding viewer. This dream culminated, or collapsed, in the modernist glass utopias of the early twentieth century and their foundational myths of transparency: "transparency of the self to nature, of the self to the other, of all selves to society, and all this represented, if not constructed . . . by a universal transparency of building materials, spatial penetration, and the ubiquitous flow of light, air, and physical movement."[17]

And yet this rationalist myth was always haunted by a counter-Enlightenment tradition of visual opacity—of windows marred by dust and dirt, panes ruptured by the terror of political life, or uncannily darkened by non-knowledge and anxiety. The Man in the Planet's cracked windows frame *Eraserhead*'s consistent deployment of windows that fail as humanist technologies of transparency, unmediated representation, and sheltered privacy. Henry's first glimpse of Mary, which is also ours, finds her face pressed nervously against the grimy glass of her parents' home—besides her face, only darkness is visible. The relentless opacity of the windows Henry passes on the street is echoed in the lonely window of his apartment, whose view onto a brick wall becomes one of *Eraserhead*'s running visual jokes. While its panes are intact, the window is doubly broken—it fails to frame a dematerialized view, finding brick where light and air should pass, and it proves threateningly porous to Henry. Later in the film, it passes from its usual state of excessive, even comic, opacity to reveal a murky view of some vicious beating on the street outside. When asked about the main influence of *Eraserhead*'s anxious interior design, Lynch's standard reply is "Philadelphia." Living with his wife and daughter in an impoverished South Philly neighborhood, Lynch has often described his urban life as the experience of a vulnerable interiority that, in fact, psychologizes urban architecture: "There was racial tension and just . . . violence and fear. I said to someone, all that separated me from the outside world was this brick wall . . . But that brick wall was like paper."[18]

Yet the film itself refuses to establish a conservative version of privacy against the depredations of the inner life. Instead, *Eraserhead* offers Lynch's first, antihumanist formulation of the bourgeois domestic sphere as virtual. The electrical storm that follows Henry's infanticide is itself a kind of virtual window. As a series of insides and outsides are magically traversed by air, electricity, and light, the dark room of Henry's apartment returns the window to its etymological roots—wind and eye, a visual opening, an aperture—for the passage of air and light. And yet both Henry and Lynch's viewer experience this opening not as a frame onto a painterly view but as an exposure to the entrance of blinding, stroboscopic light that disrupts the security of our controlled view, plunging us into intermittent darkness. The light entering through this kind of window dispossesses the human being, exposing it to an alterity within itself. What's more, this kind of violent overexposure happens in a dark room that is explicitly photographic. In other words, *Eraserhead* offers us Lynch's first fully mediated living room—this domestic interior, like Henry's own, is primordially displaced from itself, its artificial light linked up to a strange circuitry of rhythms, currents, and forces that keeps home life always uncanny. Henry's apartment room is an avant-garde interior—a domestic laboratory that refuses to settle finally into culturally legible patterns and habits. Its experiment is to keep the scenes, bodies, and behaviors that constitute proper domestic life always estranged from themselves.

Inhuman Windows: *The Elephant Man*

The Elephant Man's large budget, high production values, and esteemed cast of British actors would seem to mark a significant departure from the low-budget design of *Eraserhead*. The famous nineteenth-century case of John Merrick (John Hurt), circus freak turned medical curiosity turned proper Victorian gentleman, offers Lynch a fitting window to historicize bourgeois humanism and its inhuman, monstrous, or grotesque limits. In *The Elephant Man*, this fantasy and its impossible outside are given precise architectural and cinematic forms and inserted into a relentlessly spectacular society. Merrick's anguished plea to be recognized as "a human being, a man" rather than an animal plays out visually and narratively as a search for normal bourgeois interiority that, Lynch makes clear, is both a kind of proper human feeling and a style of home decor alike contaminated by performance.

After playing his part as an unspeaking prop in Dr. Frederick Treves's (Anthony Hopkins) medical lecture, where his mental state is described as complete idiocy, Merrick returns to his other life of exploitation in Bytes's (Freddie Jones) freak show, where he is brutally beaten. Merrick is then rescued by Treves and, for a time, hidden in the isolation ward in the attic of the London State Hospital. This room is surely an improvement over the windowless Victorian dungeon that was his home as Bytes's property, but the nature of its own isolation is evident in the room's absence of decor and privacy. It possesses a fireplace with a bare mantel and a tiny window cut crudely out of the ceiling. And it has already been intruded upon, first by the unsuspecting nurse delivering Merrick's food, whose shocked first glimpse of Merrick's face doubles Lynch's spectators' first, unmediated view of the elephant man, and then by the night porter, who threatens another form of spectacularization under the guise of being sociable. As in *Eraserhead*, so in *The Elephant Man*, mise-en-scène stages the problem of the vulnerable human interior. As Merrick sits silently on his bed, the head nurse explains to Treves the terms of Merrick's status as a social creature: "It's like talking to a brick wall." Convinced that Merrick has something to say, Treves explains that to help him, he has to understand what he's feeling and thinking: "We have to show them that you're not a wall, do you understand? I want you to talk to me."

Merrick's apparent inhumanity is figured through his wall-like opacity or idiocy, echoed by Lynch's framing. The two shot corners a frightened Merrick at frame left, an aggressive Treves at frame right, and in between them an expanse of bare wall, punctuated only by the tiny window—the promise of Merrick's opening to speech and feeling, to the transparency of human sociability. Lynch cuts to a close-up of Merrick's disfigured, grotesquely textured face, the editing rephrasing the question of Merrick's "thingly" obscurity or human transparency in a specifically cinematic register. The close-up is cinema's most storied window onto human interiority—an inside accessed in the face's promise of legible human character. Lynch's more overtly sentimental features— *The Elephant Man* and *The Straight Story*—are highly skilled manipulations of the affective work of the close-up and other melodramatic conventions.[19] Yet technologies of sentimentalism in Lynch's work are consistently undermined by the affective uncertainty of the grotesque. Lynch's windows, as *Eraserhead* makes clear, are forever clouded by the obscurity or density of matter, just as the window's membrane of protection from the public world is ever threatening to morph into a proscenium framing a more uncanny otherness within the self.

Ensconced in the isolation ward, Merrick's speech acts turn him from wall to window. His recitations of biblical verse at first seem merely rote animal parroting but are later proven to be spontaneous expressions of a noble soul moved by the products of human culture. They set him on the path toward the acquisition and cultivation of a better, more fully human interior. Its rituals have to be learned, of course, which is why Merrick, just after receiving his new room with a view on the ground floor of the hospital, is so emotionally overcome by his visit to Treves's house. There, he meets the good doctor's lovely wife (Hannah Gordon), a vision of beauty that sends him into a burst of tears. Having composed himself, he is treated to a proper spot of tea in the Treveses' overstuffed living room. We now know that Merrick is quite sensitive to Victorian life's finer things—artful language and beautiful women—so we are not surprised when Merrick apologizes for his sentiment and then promptly asks after the Treveses' decor: "I like the way you've arranged the pictures on your mantelpiece," he notes. "Is that how they do it in most houses?" The question provokes an exchange of photographs: the Treveses take from their mantel images of their children and parents to show Merrick, and Merrick reciprocates the social gesture, showing them in turn a small image of his dead mother. Merrick's sincerity leads Jane Treves to burst into tears—another sentimental effusion sparked not so much by the pathos of Merrick's impossible desire for his mother's accepting gaze as by her own shame at having removed her children from the home—presumably so as not to be too shocked by Merrick's appearance. If Merrick's fit of weeping follows from his fear of having spectactularized himself, Mrs. Treves falls to pieces for having played her role in a disingenuous sham of home life. As in *Eraserhead*, photographic absences—here the faces of beloved others who can no longer see or cannot be allowed to see—trouble the security of the bourgeois family and its architecture.

Nevertheless, Merrick's many acts of nest-feathering within his new, windowed room are clearly attempts to become more at home— "normal"—in the Victorian domestic order. Home decoration becomes its own kind of mimetic performance. Before Merrick is welcomed into his new room, his well-meaning caregiver bans mirrors from the room to keep Merrick from seeing himself as he was seen by a cruel public world—a grotesque thing, a freak. This kind of external, dehumanizing gaze, troped by the mirror, is juxtaposed with Merrick's own act of careful, humanizing design—his methodical construction of a tiny replica of St. Philips Church. Importantly, Merrick builds this church while seated in front of another, putatively humanizing structure—the window. The window is first shown to look directly onto a brick wall, returning to *Eraserhead*'s running visual joke. But this opaque view is reframed from Merrick's seat and now looks upward, over the wall topped in iron spikes, and toward the majestic spires of St. Philips in the distance. Merrick's church-building is an obvious metaphor for the kind of humanistic, interiorized seeing that would emerge in the nineteenth century under the rubric of the Romantic imagination, another reaction formation to industrial modernity. Notice how quickly Merrick has made this new turn inward: only recently given his own room, he's already fleeing its creature comforts for the immaterial rewards of the mind's eye. The scene also frames Merrick's act of imaginative design as a virtual solution to a mimetic problem: mournfully, he turns his gaze from his artwork in progress to a picture hanging on his wall across the room. The charcoal sketch portrays a girl lying peacefully in bed under a window—her own massive head of hair perhaps a nod to Jack Nance's gravity-defying 'do in Lynch's first feature, but surely an ironic echo of Merrick's monstrous macrocephaly. If the church requires an act of imagination—of seeing inside, and representing, a complete building that remains physically obscured to Merrick—it is one that responds to certain, painfully felt, limits of representation. Merrick may become schooled in bourgeois social rituals, his room nested with its stuff, but he will never fully imitate the act represented in that picture. His physical deformity destroys his wish to sleep like normal people—the price of this kind of simulation is certain death.

And so Merrick, trying so hard to be a good bourgeois, will decorate his room with photographs, a dutiful portrait of Queen Victoria above his hearth, and other gentlemanly clutter. Celebrated as a public curiosity in newspapers that Lynch's editing shows to be read by London swells and working stiffs alike, Merrick begins to enfold the public world into his room. The more Merrick's interior plays host to society, the more his room becomes stuffed with the compensatory trappings of bourgeois privacy. In a particularly striking piece of editing, Lynch cuts from Merrick's nurses, reading aloud the details of a gossip paper, to the inside of Merrick's room. The nurse reads aloud: "Owing to a disfigurement of the most extreme nature, Mr. Merrick has never been properly presented to London society, but knowing that wherever Mrs. Kendal goes others inevitably follow, the question arises, will London society present itself to him?" On the word *others*, we cut to a slow tracking movement across Merrick's mantel, now littered with photos of his guests, the frozen gazes of others in his home. Merrick, once a guest in a similar scene, now plays the host, in front of his own glowing hearth, pouring tea for his guests, who have just given him a silver-handled walking cane. An apt pupil, he has stolen the Treveses' decorating tricks, and in the process he seems to have accommodated himself to the inhuman limits of his society's forms of hospitality.

Merrick, his room inside the hospital, is always both host and guest. The limits of bourgeois hospitality, Lynch makes clear, are echoed in the hospital's own rules of caregiving. The debate over whether Merrick's room should be vacated "for more deserving cases" hinges on utilitarian protocols of care. The hospital's sacred duty is to aid the sick—namely, those who can be cured. Since Merrick's case is incurable, his room should be given to another. The debate among the hospital's governing committee is promptly overruled by the visit of Alexandra, Princess of Wales (Helen Ryan). She reads a letter from Queen Victoria commending the board for providing Merrick with "a safe and tranquil harbor, a home." But the princess's rhetoric of charity may very well just be good public relations; the queen reads the papers, too, and thus has an investment in maintaining the appearance of the state's infinite compassion now that Merrick has become a celebrity. Lynch's more cynical reading here is evident in a visual pun. Merrick's acquisition of a stable interior in the London hospital is symbolized by the gift of another fine thing—an exquisite gentleman's dressing case. This nested interior is the case Merrick deserves, having been deemed a "deserving case." Care is contaminated by giving. In the next scene, this case fuels one of Merrick's most extravagant acts of bourgeois performance. Dabbing himself with perfume from one of the case's bottles, holding his new silver cane in one hand and a cigarette holder theatrically in the other, Merrick announces to his photo of the celebrated actress, Mrs. Madge Kendal: "I'm John Merrick, very pleased to meet you" (fig. 5). His fantasy of Victorian dandyhood is interrupted by the night porter's abrupt entry into the room. Another show is about to begin.

Merrick's room has always been subject to ritualistic spectacularization from desiring spectators on both sides of the class divide. Sonny Jim, the night porter, will now "carnivalize" Merrick's interior with yet another retinue of paying viewers. Spectacular culture is, of course, omnipresent in *The Elephant Man*: in its repeated performances of

Figure 5. The performance of bourgeois propriety |

bourgeois humanity and its rituals (tea, hosting, gift giving, psalm reading, exchanging photographs, and sentimentality itself) and in its various
theatrical cultures (the freak show, the traveling circus, Shakespeare,
photography, and the Victorian melodrama). For Lynch, nineteenth-
century sociability is primarily spectacular. Merrick's trajectory of bourgeois humanization (from inhuman freak to interiorized human seer)
founders on the inevitability of spectacle, of being always subject to
curious views. Merrick moves from Bytes's freak show (stage), to the
hospital (room), back to Bytes's circus in France (stage), and then back
again to the hospital (room), and yet every seemingly final room is always
a stage, every window looking out becomes a proscenium for the self's
own spectacle. While wealth is divided unevenly in the Victorian world
of *The Elephant Man*, classes are joined in *curiositas*—the lustful wish
to see secrets hidden on the inside of things.

The obsession with seeing, and talking about, the most unseen and
obscene dimensions of private life was one of the signatures of Victorian
England's disciplinary society—its myriad ways of talking about secret
life so as to better control, order, and classify the social world, separating "the normal" from the deviant or monstrous. And these disciplinary
protocols were evident not just in modes of spectacular culture like
circuses and freak shows, or new visual technologies like photography,
but also, as Michel Foucault argued famously, in the new administrative
institutions of the state: schools, prisons, clinics, and hospitals. In fact,
Merrick's change of room from the isolation ward in the attic to his more
vulnerable interior on the ground floor is less an act of humane charity

than a disciplinary technique of visibility. As Mr. Carr Gomm (Sir John Gielgud), the kindly director of the hospital, explains, "A hospital is no place for secrecy, Treves."

Put more bluntly, *The Elephant Man*'s interior design is inevitably *pornographic*. The following scene confirms the architectural terms of this spectacular culture, hell-bent on obscene insides. Merrick, seated at night at his window and building his church, is interrupted by Sonny Jim, tapping at the window outside. At night the windowpane's transparency thickens into a dense, textural surface. Merrick is doubly spectacularized—both by Sonny, who leers through the pane menacingly, and by the mirrored reflection of his own face and the tower of his church, all of which seem to occupy the same flat plane of the brick walls and iron outside. As in *Eraserhead*, this kind of irrational visual opacity is matched by another stunning montage of Lynchian "bad plumbing." A terrified Merrick murmurs "nighttime," and we fade to black. As we fade in, a low sonic hum swells as the camera moves alongside the top of Merrick's textured head and pushes into the darkened eye-hole of his cloth mask. Fade to a tracking shot along a line of moist, sweaty pipes bolted to the ceiling of the bowels of some building as the audio track shifts to the sound of the muffled billows of an unseen machine. The camera tracks backward out of a door, its movement superimposed with the image of a woman in the throes of an open-mouthed, slow-motion cry. The blurred scream, one of the film's several visual echoes of Francis Bacon, will recur in Lynch's later work. Here we know it to belong to Merrick's pregnant mother, whose trampling by wild circus elephants, revisited in the film's opening montage, caused her untimely death and Merrick's disfigurement in Lynch's version of Merrick's tragedy. We cut to a shot of a hole ripped in a brick wall and then to another shot of three men carrying a mirror toward the camera in which Merrick's face becomes visible. The close-up of Merrick's eye, cinema's own technological window onto the soul, is itself rendered opaque—superimposed with the mouth and then the eye of an elephant. We cut to a time-lapse shot of clouds outside, and the sequence ends abruptly with a cut to the interior of the Treveses' home.

The sequence replays, in more specifically nineteenth-century terms, the infrastructure of the violated interior. The montage bridges and deterritorializes disturbed insides, beginning with Merrick's nightmare, but ending with Treves's own fitful sleep. The rational doctor is awakened to the fact of his own irrational kinship with Mr. Bytes. Like Merrick faced with the mirror, Treves is disturbed by a surprising foreignness in himself: "I'm beginning to believe that Mr. Bytes and I are very much alike . . . It seems I've made Mr. Merrick a curiosity all over again." This nightmare of uncanny dispossession, shared by Merrick and Treves, is also the story of industrial modernity's own haunting by the very kinds of monsters that have always frustrated its taxonomies and schemes of order—hybrids of nature and culture, animal and machine, human and inhuman. Notice how the sound of wild elephants dissolves into the clanking of machines and shots of bare-torsoed men laboring over clanking wheels and levers throwing off steam. In an earlier scene in which Treves ministers to the victim of a grotesque industrial accident, Lynch has shown how modern machinery produces its own monstrous calamities of the flesh. Like mad elephants, machines, Treves observes, are "indomitable things . . . You can't reason with them." The shared unreason of organic nature and machinic culture is clearly the obscene outside of Merrick's humanity, haunted by both its thingly, inhuman exterior and its status as mechanical second nature.

Lynch tends to understand broken windows dialectically: they belie the transparent self of the Enlightenment, but they also serve as media for mysterious correspondences between human and inhuman orders. This is one way to consider the conclusion of *The Elephant Man*. The sequence follows Merrick's final trip to the theater, which would crown the achievement of his humanity and his social normalization by changing the terms of his relationship to spectacle. In his opera box high above the stage, Merrick is a fully humanized, empowered seer who looks through opera glasses at a magnificent Victorian spectacle that seems to unfold just for him. Mrs. Kendal clarifies this when she emerges at the end of the performance to dedicate it to Merrick, and when Merrick stands in his box to accept the crowd's applause, he is, in reverse angle, looked at yet again. This time, presumably, the spectacularization is benevolent; Merrick is finally enjoying himself in public. We fade to Merrick's room, after the performance, where an excited Merrick relives moments of the performance, and Treves promises to take him there again. When Treves leaves, Merrick takes his seat by the window. With a gentle breeze rustling the window curtains, Merrick signs his name to the completed simulacrum of St. Philips, and Lynch's camera, in close-up, traces the magnificent arches, windows, and spires of Merrick's own making before Merrick stands, gazes twice at the image of the sleeping girl across the room, and lies down in his bed, ending his life. The camera pans slowly across the photographs of Mrs. Kendal and Merrick's mother at his bedside, lifts over his church, and holds at the open window. We fade to a starry sky, in which first the voice and then the face of Merrick's mother appears against an eclipsed sun. The mother's stilled, photographic face is magically, cinematically reanimated, pronouncing that "Nothing will die."

The ending's transcendent gesture is a cinematic solution to the architectural problem of the broken window—here the historical failures of the category of the human. Merrick's humanity, within Victorian architectural protocols of care and curiosity, is impossible. His last human act is not the completion of a successful work of the imagination but a failed performance. Rather than stabilize Merrick's humanity, Lynch's window opens a gap between the "John Merrick" who signs the built church, and thus confirms the human as *homo faber*, and "John Merrick" as a botched performance of bourgeois humanity and its deadly nineteenth-century limits. The window fails as a technology of human interior but succeeds in opening webs of relationships with a network of fantastic, inhuman outsides—solar eclipses, or the stagey implosion of a cloud of smoke, or dead mothers made cinematically alive. Transcendence, the promise of immortality, is the ideological compensation for the cruel materialism and determinism of Victorian life, and its medium is cinema, a virtual window.

Sexy Tchotchke: *Blue Velvet*

The dream of total design that Lynch first fulfilled with *Eraserhead* during its four-year-long production on back lots of the American Film Institute, and that collapsed so spectacularly in the big-budget debacle of *Dune* (1984), would be realized again in the astonishing degree of creative control he exercised over *Blue Velvet*. For better or worse, *Blue Velvet* persists as Lynch's masterpiece. It is also the film in which Lynch's idiosyncratic style of interior design becomes typical, hardening into a glossy adjective: after *Blue Velvet*, certain kinds of rooms, verging on self-parody, will inevitably be described as "Lynchian." Their quirky collections of objects, textures, and details of decor will be read as recurring, directorial obsessions. One can't *not* be fascinated by *Blue Velvet*'s details. As Pauline Kael noted in her approving review of the film, the style is so theatrical, so flagrant, that "you feel as if you're seeing every detail of the architecture, the layout of homes and apartments, the furnishings and potted plants, the women's dresses. It's so hyperfamiliar it's scary . . . The style might be described as hallucinatory clinical realism."[20]

The intense debates sparked by *Blue Velvet* over the last few decades—debates dominated by the question of Lynch's postmodernism and, relatedly, the nature of his overt interest in gender, sexuality, and erotic desire—hinge on the politics of room tone. How exactly should we interpret the ambivalent atmospheres of *Blue Velvet*'s well-built environments? How to feel about their surfaces and psychological depths? Consider one influential answer, Fredric Jameson's landmark reading, "Nostalgia for the Present." Jameson's interpretation dwells on the design of *Blue Velvet*'s most conspicuous interior: Dorothy Vallens's (Isabella Rossellini) room at the Deep River Apartments. This is, of course, the room where young Jeffrey Beaumont's (Kyle MacLachlan) drama of sexual maturation unfolds so theatrically over the course of the film, but Jameson is particularly interested in Lynch's final staging of this space. Jeffrey's curiosity as an amateur detective having merged with his taste for perversion, and brought him deep "in the middle of [the] mystery" of *Blue Velvet*'s shaggy-dog criminal plot, Jeffrey returns inexplicably to Dorothy's apartment. He finds there a deathly tableau ringed about the floor of the singer's living room: Detective Gordon, or "The Yellow Man" as Jeffrey has dubbed him, stands, dead but uncannily erect, positioned between a smashed television set, encased in wood, and another relic of the fifties—a floor lamp with a black lacquered bell shade. The Yellow Man's frozen body is turned toward Dorothy's once-kidnapped and now-quite-dead husband, Don. Dead Don is seated in a chair—his brains splattered on Dorothy's Formica kitchen counter behind him, his severed ear visible, and a scrap of Dorothy's blue velvet robe protruding from his open mouth.

For Jameson, this monstrous interior is nothing less than Lynch's conservative parable of the "end of the sixties" itself: "What *Blue Velvet* gives us to understand about the sixties . . . is that despite the grotesque and horrendous tableaux of maimed bodies, this kind of evil is more *distasteful* than it is fearful, more *disgusting* than threatening: here, evil has finally become an image, and the simulated replay of the fifties has generalized itself into a whole simulacrum in its own right."[21] This room's stagey collection of inert bodies and outmoded furniture contains the threatening political energies and affects of the '6os by converting them to a static image bereft of historicity. In the process, "the end of theories of transgression," the politics of the 1960s are aestheticized in their conversion to furniture—distasteful, even disgusting, but nothing to really worry about. A wax museum of transgression-cum-kitsch, Vallens's apartment, for Jameson, is of a piece with the gothic shelter of small-town Lumberton itself, "lovingly preserved in its details like a simulacrum or Disneyland under glass somewhere."[22]

The political aesthetics of Lynch's interiors come up rather short for Jameson. But isn't that kitsch doing its job? Kitsch always poses the problem of aesthetic inadequacy, of art falling short of its capacity for powerful, "transgressive" sensations in a cool, postmodern world of flat affect. It is a quintessentially modern problem, connected to the post-Romantic fall of aesthetic experience from transcendence to immanence—now the product of tangible, finite works of art. But also, in the form of camp, it encodes a more transgressive historical relationship between aesthetic and erotic object choices, recalling a mid-century queer sensibility that would became a crucial aspect of the radical political energies of the 1960s. *Blue Velvet*'s kitschy mise-en-scène is the primary terrain of the film's aestheticization, its irony, and its investigation of the false boundaries—aesthetic and sexual—between "normal" and "perverse" taste. This, in part, makes it one of Lynch's most Hitchcockian films, continuing Hitch's aestheticist associations between artifice itself and "human sexuality that is deemed incipiently perverse."[23] Kitsch is the sign, in the domain of taste, of *Blue Velvet*'s denaturalizing of heterosexual domesticity, of the home's campy becoming plastic. Its final false robin is as queer as Hitchcock's antisocial avian attacks. In this way the persistence of the 1950s in the 1980s of *Blue Velvet* can be understood less as nostalgia for an earlier, simpler time of American cultural and family life than as a knowing micro-history of the mid-century psychologizing of interior design and its reformulation of the seemingly boundless "nature" of bourgeois taste and bourgeois sexuality.

Some of Lynch's favorite architects and designers, like Charles and Ray Eames and the émigré Viennese architect Richard Neutra, participated actively in the mid-century's broader transformation of modernist architectural and design principles. Postwar architecture and design in the United States saw the modernist formal orthodoxies of functionalism and rational efficiency give way to a new interest in domestic pleasure. If a certain dominant strand of modernist architecture of the 1920s and 1930s fetishized the pure, universal space of an abstract void, mid-century designers rethought domestic spaces as dynamic environments. The "affective mise-en-scènes" of domesticity, in Silvia Lavin's terms, were "traversed, constrained, polluted, agitated, modified by a whole range of forces."[24] Central to this shift was the popularization and domestication of psychoanalysis in the Unites States in the postwar period, where, in the work of Neutra and others, it developed a new relationship to architectural practice. Now competing with interior designers like the Eameses, catering to an exploding middle class, the modern architect was himself rethought of as a kind of haute bourgeois *collector*. The postwar shockwaves that followed from modern architecture's new attention to the habits of middle-class consumption and taste were also felt at the normally elitist CIAM (Congrès Internationaux d'Architecture Moderne). In the immediate postwar years, the CIAM hosted intense debates about whether and how postwar architecture might expand its vocabulary of forms to make room for the "common man," so that "peoples' emotional needs can find expression in the design of their environment."[25] As Yoke-Sum Wong explains, the CIAM meetings of 1946 and 1949 were haunted by Clement Greenberg's seminal essay, "The Avant-Garde and Kitsch"; at the heart of the matter, in other words, was the conflict between a new "postwar egalitarian sentiment" about modern design and the "fear of architecture sliding downward into ordinariness and ultimately kitsch."[26]

Like young Jeffrey himself, *Blue Velvet*'s interiors undergo a sort of trial by kitsch, but without sacrificing affective complexity to cheap sensation in the process. Greenberg's famous, modernist indictment of kitsch decries its "self-evident meanings," its tendency to "pre-digest art for the spectator and spares him of effort, provid[ing] him with a short cut to the pleasure of art that detours what is necessarily difficult in genuine art." Kitsch, for Greenberg, is plastic—"synthetic" art that provides "vicarious experience for the insensitive with far greater immediacy" than real art.[27] Kitsch is all happiness and sensation with no work. And yet in Lynch's case, rather than waning or burning out, room tone increases in intensity and complication in the presence of pseudo-art—no easy trick, but one mastered by Lynch. In fact, avant-garde sensation (shock, disgust, horror, unease) and bourgeois sentimentalism become inextricably tied in *Blue Velvet*'s exploration of their shared hedonism and obscured complicity in matters of taste and fantasy.

As a moment in the history of modern design, Lynch's "fifties" names a broader transition through which modernist architecture scraps avant-garde austerity for bourgeois pleasure. As the mid-century home is warmed up, turned into a dynamic environment, and made newly moody through a widespread middle-class taste for Eames chairs and Freud alike, it merges fitfully with the enveloping coziness of middle-brow culture, sentimentality, and bourgeois contentment. This historical fact helps make sense of Lynch's otherwise curious response to the question of what kinds of modern architecture most impress him: "I like Bauhaus," Lynch answers, "that kind of pure, formal thing. I like grey rooms that have nothing in them except a couple of pieces of furniture that are just right for a person to sit there. And then, when the person sits there, you really see the contrast, and then the room looks very good and the person looks very interesting. Architecture is *really* the most fantastic thing."[28] Why, one might ask, would the creator of some of cinema's moodier, more irrational films single out for praise this school of modernist rationalism if he didn't somehow understand avant-garde minimalism and kitschy maximalism as always dialectically bound? This, then, is the dilemma of sensibility raised by *Blue Velvet*'s interior design and its minimal ornamentation: what happens to the powerful sensations and uncanny feelings of modern interiors when psychoanalysis itself goes mainstream and becomes its own form of kitsch?

The film's narrative arc is most often described as a too-familiar masculine coming-of-age story, one that courts banality and cliché at every turn and yet manages to produce something both strange and familiar. Jeffrey Beaumont's arc of maturation begins with the traumatic collapse of his father, the victim of some unaccountable seizure while watering the family lawn, which brings young Jeffrey home from college to mind the family hardware store. It passes through the delirious narrative middle of Jeffrey's awakening to the threatening mysteries of adult sexuality. And it ends with Jeffrey's return to the safety and mundane comforts of the family nest. The patriarchal circuit is thus restored once Jeffrey chooses love (for the blonde, sweet Sandy Williams [Laura Dern]) over sexual passion (for the exotic, melancholy Dorothy Vallens) and kills Frank Booth (Dennis Hopper), the film's bad daddy and the human incarnation of whatever form of evil is understood to seethe between the polished surfaces of Lumberton. It is, in short, a psychoanalyst's dream text.

Lynch's interior design in *Blue Velvet* suggests that the drama of innocence and experience in the film is more properly an eroticized aesthetics and that Jeffrey's quest is also a story about bourgeois taste and its monstrous limits in bad object choices. Two examples of Lynch's clever mise-en-scène underscore the point. During Jeffrey's initial sexual encounter with Dorothy after his acts of closeted voyeurism, she asks him, "Do you like me? Do you like the way I feel?" Yes on both counts. At her invitation to sensation, he touches her breast and feels her hardening nipple, but when she begs him to hit her, Jeffrey has, at least for now, reached a limit to his erotic preferences. Later, in a nightmare, Jeffrey replays scenes from his bad night in Dorothy's closet. Lynch's montage stages Jeffrey's anguish as a sequence of grotesque faces and open mouths: a distended, step-printed howl of terror; a slow-motion image of Frank's snarl; and a return to the close-up of Dorothy's inverted face, her closed eyes darkened with blue eye shadow, her ruby red lips begging to be hit. Erotic transgression is figured through voracious maws, opening to take anything in. Upon waking, Jeffrey lifts his arm to the wall above his bed, and Lynch's camera follows it to a strange object above— another grotesque mouth. All bared, animalistic teeth, it hangs on a string, casting an ominous shadow and providing a (perhaps too obvious) visual metaphor for Jeffrey's dream of animal passion. It is expressionist kitsch and a savvy reference to the queer plastic idiom of Francis Bacon, whose mid-century paintings consistently turned recycled images into new arenas of sensation, dehumanizing its subjects by reducing their faces to grim messes of teeth. We cut to the Beaumont hardware store, where Jeffrey calls Sandy. In the middle of the conversation, Lynch cuts away to a large man, a lumberjack presumably, given his archetypal red plaid shirt, buying an enormous axe from Double Ed. The unmotivated insert is unsettling and recalls Fritz Lang's defamiliarization of hardware store tools (axes, knives, hammers) in *Fury* (1937), another noir domestic about small-town America's lurking penchant for irrational violence. There is no accounting for the stuff that everyday folks consume, and who knows, really, what kinky fantasies it might serve?

In a later, rhyming scene, Lynch subtly reworks and modifies the relations between a similar cluster of textures, objects, and images, drawing and crossing the bounds of taste in the process. Now, after Jeffrey has acceded to Dorothy's masochistic wish, and has himself also been violently beaten and symbolically raped by Frank, Jeffrey again mentally replays in his bedroom another long night of the soul. Here, Lynch frames Jeffrey in a medium shot, the toothy totem dangling just behind his head, a visual stain reminding him of the preceding night's sexual chaos. Jeffrey's flashback echoes the earlier montage and includes a rhyming close-up of Dorothy's face: her open mouth, struck by Jeffrey, reveals a chipped front tooth. Jeffrey's sexual violence is intercut with a shot of little Donny's (her kidnapped son) cone-shaped propeller hat, and the contrast between experience and innocence causes Jeffrey to double over in sobbing. As before, Jeffrey again calls Sandy to explain what's happened. Sandy's white bedroom is accented with soft pinks and cornflower blues, and her white telephone is contrasted with Jeffrey's black one. But this chromatic dualism collapses, because Sandy is now wearing a red plaid skirt that seems cut from the same cloth as the axe-buying woodsman's shirt. And the wood motif, subtly woven through color and texture, continues as Lynch reveals the second piece of wall art in Jeffrey's room, a hung log, spelling "LUMBERTON" in crude bamboo letters, perhaps glued or tacked on as part of a misguided high-school art project. Like Donny, Jeffrey was once impossibly sincere. An electrical cord dangles from this bit of tackiness, and it takes its place in the film's remarkable series of monstrous lamps, from Dorothy's black and red floor light and art nouveau table lamp, to the deco sconces at Ben's place, to Detective Williams's gaudy teak study light. By this light, remember, Jeffrey first explains his curiosity about the severed ear to Detective Williams, and the lawman, in turn, reveals that when he was Jeffrey's age, a similar taste for mystery was "what got me into this business." The stilted, slightly wooden quality of their repartee acknowledges a shared sensibility that could equally apply to the bad lamp behind them. Jeffrey: "Must be great." Detective Williams: "It's horrible too."

A second, minor encounter between sexual transgression and luminous kitsch happens near the end of the film. Jeffrey and Sandy have been accosted by Sandy's jealous boyfriend, Mike, who, with beery courage, threatens Jeffrey on the street in front of Sandy's house. From the corner of the Williamses' front lawn, barely visible at first, a battered, naked, evidently delirious Dorothy emerges. Like the spectator, not yet sure what he is witnessing, Mike stammers a taunt—"Hey, is that your mother, Jeffrey?"—before being overcome by embarrassment and shock. Mike mumbles an apology and leaves as Jeffrey and Sandy usher Dorothy into the house. Dorothy, shivering and nearly catatonic, cries, "He put his disease in me!" and clutches Jeffrey desperately to her nude body. Lynch is at pains to maximize the unbearable trauma of Dorothy's violation of domestic propriety. But he frames Dorothy's anguished embrace of Jeffrey—one that will send Sandy into her own emotional fit of shock, sadness, and disgust—under the sign of bourgeois kitsch. The third occupant of the shot, besides the outed lovers, is yet another ostentatious lamp, another unseemly hybrid of nature and culture: its glass base encloses a stuffed bird that guards its nest and its candy-colored eggs (fig. 6). The lamp's contamination of the scene is all the more obvious because it continues the avian motif established by Sandy's romantic dream of the robins and comments in various ways on the drama of the scene. Like the now-obscene openness of the Williamses'

Figure 6. Lamp life under glass |

living room, the transparent lamp is either an exposed nest or a lovingly preserved fantasy of domestic propriety sustained by kitsch. Alternatively, the lamp's bourgeois banality might be the tacky ground against which the figure of Jeffrey and Dorothy's erotic transgression more shockingly emerges. "My secret lover," Dorothy calls Jeffrey, much to Sandy's shock and disbelief. And she repeats the line "He put his disease in me," which here helps establish another cluster of nested interiors: the fragile comfort of the hetero-bourgeois living room, the nest built inside its happy furniture, and Jeffrey's unnamed disease—a pathology that critics often read as a tacit acknowledgment of AIDS and that sullies all of these insides at once. Like the Lumberton log lamp, the reminder of some earlier moment of Jeffrey's innocence and civic pride, this piece of kitsch stands in for a kind of cozy domestic sentimentality undone by the sensational appearance of Dorothy's body.

Blue Velvet blurs the extremes of middle-class consumption with sexual transgression and tends to describe erotic life (its normalcy or its perversion) as of a piece with Jeffrey's changing patterns of taste—what he "likes" or prefers, what he finds "great" or "horrible," what he deems "curious," "strange," or "interesting." Jeffrey's odyssey into Lumberton's underground in pursuit of more "interesting" experiences begins soon after it is first pitched to Sandy at Arlene's. A vaguely fifties diner and the early incarnation of *Twin Peaks'* Double R, Arlene's allows Lynch to spatialize innocence and familiarity and to establish both the common tastes of his romantic couple and their divergences of sensibility. Over Cokes and pie, Jeffrey proposes his scheme: "There are opportunities in life for gaining knowledge and experience. Sometimes it's necessary to take a risk. Now, I got to thinking: I bet someone could learn a lot by getting into that woman's apartment. You know, sneak in, hide, and observe." Sandy's response—"It sounds like a good daydream, but actually doing it is too weird. It's too dangerous"—describes Jeffrey's plan for what it is: the stuff of bourgeois compensation, which is to say, kitsch. A form of daydream in the realm of objects, as Walter Benjamin once put it, kitsch makes a vague, hallucinatory promise to escape the flat, empty time of everyday life. It is as if Jeffrey was destined to get mixed up with Dorothy once he left home for college and got his ear pierced; his sensibility is predisposed to weirdness and corruption from the get-go. Sandy senses this in the laughable ornamental excesses of his scheme—Jeffrey's secret signals and his ready-to-roll exterminator costume and props and Sandy's absurd supporting role as a Jehovah's Witness.

Later that night, at the Slow Club, the couple takes another step on the path of experience, moving clearly out of Sandy's comfort zone. Jeffrey again performs his budding connoisseurship. He and Sandy raise their beer glasses and toast to "an interesting experience." "Man! I like Heineken," Jeffrey declares and is shocked (or is he?) that this malted sign of continental sophistication has never crossed Sandy's lips. "My dad drinks Bud," she explains. "King of Beers," Jeffrey nods, understandingly. We have yet to meet Frank Booth, the film's most infamous beer lover, but can it be a coincidence that the same monster of sensibility who prefers Pabst Blue Ribbon, one trashy extreme of consumption, is also the film's consummate sexual fetishist? Frank's later anxious cry—"I'll fuck anything that moves!"—however inaccurate, gets at the democracy of experience that joins the polymorphous perversions of sexual and aesthetic taste in *Blue Velvet*'s dream world. It is in the sheer vagueness of what might become "interesting" that all the danger lies—in this, bourgeois kitsch and avant-garde kinkiness find their shared hedonism.

In *Blue Velvet*'s dreamy topography of middle-class life, two interiors call out for special attention by virtue of their careful design and their centrality to Jeffrey's coming-of-age-process: the Deep River Apartments and Ben's place, or "Pussy Heaven." An early sequence makes evident the way these spatial "outsides" to small-town domesticity declare their status as desired and feared. Forbidden and thus impossibly attractive, they are folded into the bourgeois interior as kitsch. Jeffrey descends ominously from his upstairs bedroom to take the nocturnal walk around the neighborhood in which he first meets Sandy. He pauses at the foot of the stairs, where his mother and aunt Barbara are plopped in front of the glowing TV. When Jeffrey finally leaves the house, Lynch pans slowly to the television screen, revealing what looks like a black-and-white film noir. On television a man's feet are shown slowly mounting a set of stairs in some moment of heightened suspense and danger. The shot is a visual gag—an obvious echo of Jeffrey's recent descent and its own cinematic coding. But it also situates the famously troubled affects of film noir within the domain of fully domesticated middle-class pleasure—the tchotchke effect. Before showing us the full television screen, the pan reveals assorted knick-knacks resting on top of the TV—we can make out a photograph and a miniature Christmas tree set atop the white lace antimacassar. And the screen's chiaroscuro contrast itself echoes the objects on the table next to Mrs. Beaumont—a white table lamp, its base some hieratic Asian head, abuts a black Sambo figurine, a truly horrific bourgeois curio and the inanimate double of the hardware store's Double Ed minstrel duo (who, by the way, also wear cute red jackets). The sequence aligns the threat of "Lincoln" (where Aunt Barbara fears Jeffrey might go), the pleasure of televised film noir, and the comfort of the racist curio on the same dreamy terrain. All are compensatory outsides of white, bourgeois domesticity, the anxious others of its fantasy structure. In *Blue Velvet*'s map of the middle-class "neighborhood," the strangeness and strangers on its limits are clearly marked, and uncannily proximate. As Sandy notes of the Deep River Apartments, "It's really close by, which is why it's so creepy."

By the time we actually get inside Dorothy's apartment at Deep River, this interior has been overdetermined as the zone of middle-class fantasy. Once inside, Deep River immediately recalls Henry's apartment building in *Eraserhead*; the erratic electricity responsible for that apartment's malfunctioning elevator is now fully on the fritz, and Jeffrey, disguised as "the bug-man," will have to ascend by the stairs like the noir character his aunt has just seen on TV. It is a stagey approach to a theatrical room—one that seems to be entered only by people wearing some kind of costume or another, and one situated in a dense virtual network of correspondences to an array of cinematic rooms, past and present, Lynchian and otherwise. The drama is enhanced by the room's ostensive, frontal presentation—Lynch tends to shoot it as a tableau, taking in the open expanse of the living room with new, telescopic wide-angle lenses.[29] And this spacious feeling is especially acute when presented from the perspective of Jeffrey's voyeurism in the closet. From this place of hiding, Frank and Dorothy's sadomasochistic rituals play out for Jeffrey as scenes at once obviously primal and specifically cinematic.

Dorothy's apartment room is a space of sexual experience and knowingness, but it also poses the problem of knowingness on the level of Lynch's own aesthetic reflexivity. It is an arty, stylized room and a controlled collection built to cater to visual pleasure. Its architecture is ironic. When Lynch talks about his favorite films, many, like Wilder's *Sunset Blvd.* (1950) or Fellini's *8½* (1963), possess a particular intensity of mise-en-scène whose hermetic, canny design doubles back on the experience of cinematic fantasy itself. The mysteries of cinema and theater are also cued by the thick, blood-red folds of the curtains that seal Dorothy's window from the light of the outside. A recurring Lynchian design fetish, these curtains echo the deep blue ones adorning the Slow Club stage, reminding us of the proscenium of fantasy buried in *Eraserhead*'s radiator. Curtains, for Lynch, frame the ritual of cinema itself, the revelatory, fetishistic dimensions of cinematic pleasure that constitute cinephilia: "It's magical—I don't know why—to go into a theater and have the lights go down. It's very quiet, and then the curtains start to open, maybe they're red, and you go into a world."[30]

But as *Blue Velvet* seems to acknowledge, here and on the noir reruns viewed on the Beaumonts' TV, the otherworldly aspects of cinephilic pleasure, its gestures toward another, excessive dimension *beyond* the image, are the lure of an elsewhere to everyday bourgeois life. It is worth remembering that the thick, pleated material that often drapes the stages of fantasy in Lynch's work and joins the mysteries of cinema and Oedipality was also a particular design feature of the mid-century suburban home. The changed ratio of window to wall that was typical of mid-century interiors built a kind of ostentation into the domestic spaces of postwar suburbia and apartment life alike, framing the subjects of its interior as objects for consumption. In this way, the home window became "a display window; it dissolves the self into the material world, collects and proliferates desires."[31] Lynch's ironic point about Jeffrey's closeted voyeurism is that the perverse strands of pleasure on display at Deep River are less the absolute other of bourgeois domesticity than the uncanny double of middle-class taste.

A virtual space, Dorothy's room is also the plastic space of a formalist experiment—an examination of relations between depth and surface, texture and pattern, geometry and ornamentation that, for Lynch, goes under the loose design rubric of art deco. We tend to think of deco as an aesthetic of black-and-white elegance, which we owe to the rich cinematic appropriations of deco style in the Hollywood of the 1930s. But the style was also marked by a variety of bold colors—apple greens, putatively "exotic" jades—and rich textures that Lynch also stages in Dorothy's Deep River apartment, whose design details conjure the decadent space of mid-century modernity. Deco motifs are everywhere—in its streamlined, modular pink couch, bisected by the hallway leading from the living room to the bedrooms and bathrooms in the rear of the apartment; in the black, purely decorative parabolic moldings between the ends of the couch and the mauve wall; in the chinoiserie of the folding black screen, set up at the end of one couch, which picks up the strands of deco orientalism to further exoticize Dorothy Vallens; in its curvilinear wall extending from the doorway to the main living room; in the range of synthetic materials in the room—the Bakelite knobs prominent on the blond, open radio adjacent to the couch, the linoleum geometry of its black-and-white kitchen floor, the black Formica kitchen countertop, opening to the interior; and in the apple-green containers holding the twin snake plants near the entryway. The snake plant, which thrives in interiors with little if any light, strikes a balance between organicism and simple geometry that helped make it a staple of twentieth-century interior design.

Of course, the room's most fascinating, unstable artifact is Dorothy Vallens herself, not so much a woman as a piece of deco *plasticity*—a fantastic, malleable assemblage of twentieth-century design elements. Like the deco feminine, Dorothy is associated in *Blue Velvet* with a kind of urban sophistication (deco was described as a "nightclub style"); with the synthetic artifice of Hollywood cinema, whose late 1920s and early 1930s glamour was pervaded with deco sensibilities at "virtually every level of film form"; and thus also with a broader culture of consumption and fantasy and with the vagaries of modern taste.[32] Deco names one important historical apotheosis of modernist aesthetic seriousness as "the Style *Moderne*," a transformation interpreted in various ways. For some of its contemporary critics, deco exemplified the fatal decadence of the avant-garde *in* and *as* mass culture and consumer fantasy. For its champions, deco was a sign of modern taste's "egalitarian potential" and part of the expanded palette of bourgeois consumption.[33] For yet others, writing in tame, homey domestic periodicals like *Good Furniture* magazine or *House and Garden*, deco was fundamentally strange—foreign to American tastes and sensibilities, "exaggerated," "bizarre," "vulgar," and "grotesque." For Lynch, deco seems of interest for precisely the way it allows him to pose—through the character of Dorothy Vallens—these dilemmas of modern consumer sensibilities and the affective ambivalences produced by their design fantasies.

Dorothy is one of *Blue Velvet*'s many forms of femininity as furniture, gender as design. Notice the way that shortly after Jeffrey ducks into the closet, Dorothy arranges her semi-clothed body, for both Jeffrey and the spectator, alongside the low-slung couch. Ostensibly, Dorothy assumes the position to remove a photograph of her husband and son from under the couch. But in the process, she turns into another piece of the room's decor. The lines of her prone body are brought into alignment with the low horizontals of the furniture, her exposed skin echoes the flesh tones of the couch, and the dark, muddy red of her high heels matches its cushions too well.

When Dorothy gets up, she removes, for the first time, her outrageous wig of messy black curls to reveal a short, modern bob. In this change of hairstyles, Lynch stages two modes of coding femininity—the unwieldy, snakelike locks of the art nouveau femme fatale, a sign of her perverse sexuality and decadence, and the graphic, androgynous simplicity of deco's modern women, whose hair was immortalized in the 1920s fashion designs of Erté. Lynch's Dorothy, however, can't be slotted into a stable design category. Oscillating between deco, nouveau, and noir, she is so clotted with design fantasies and so thickly encrusted with the stuff of fetishistic detail that she becomes grotesquely material—a figure of decadence. In her room at the Deep River Apartments, for Jeffrey and for us, Dorothy is a plastic sensation, or, as Pauline Kael put it, "a kitschy seductress."

The design of Dorothy Vallens cues us to read the sadomasochistic rituals that shortly unfold in her living room as a similarly kitschy collection—a polymorphous assemblage of pleasure and desire, with its accompanying fetishes and fantasies. This sequence has been given every conceivable psychoanalytic reading, which probably it has been designed to do. As Dorothy and Frank perform their scenes of sexual perversion, their positions and roles change vertiginously, warping and distorting the normative geometry of the Freudian triangle—Mommy, Daddy, Baby—in irrational combinations. Lynch encourages us to consider Deep River's sexual assemblage in more properly Sadeian terms—less a kind of Oedipal vaudeville than a mode of formal complexity, a sign of sexual sophistication:

> Some people may have this stuff in them, but they live through television or the movies or someone else to satisfy the urge. So it's one step

removed and it's cleaner. They don't get their hands dirty, but they're still *there*. The people watching the soap operas are digging this sick stuff so much, and they understand it—and if they had the chance, they would do the same sick stuff. Sex is such a fascinating thing. It's sorta like you listen to one pop song just so many times, whereas jazz has so many variations. Sex should be like jazz. It can be the same tune, but there are many variations on it. And then when you start getting out there, it can be shocking to learn that something like that could be sexual. It would be kind of, you know, strange.[34]

The Sadeian rituals at the Deep River introduce similar questions of sensibility. What is the difference between real sexual transgression and its mediated experience as consumed by Jeffrey, or Aunt Barbara, or us? What distinguishes the vicarious pleasures served up by middle-class soap opera from the kinds of prosthetic kicks vaporized in Frank Booth's gas mask?

Such is the designed artifice of erotic sensation—both potent and prosthetic and joining transgression and bourgeois comfort in a shared taste for perversion. Ben's place, *Blue Velvet*'s other masterpiece of mid-century kitsch, is similarly sensational. In the initial tableau shot of the living room, Ben (Dean Stockwell) holds court on a Naugahyde couch, surrounded by a klatch of chunky, silent, middle-aged biddies. Lounging around a bamboo tiki-table littered with pill bottles, the women smoke distractedly and peruse their nails, building the room's general vibe of mid-century languor (fig. 7). Like Dorothy, they are elements of a Lynchian design collection and part of the sequence's strong connections between kitschy ornamentation and femininity. The women's passivity and servitude, like their general availability for consumption, suggest that they may well be Pussy Heaven's prostitutes and Ben their pimp. They recall Jean Baudrillard's observation about the erotics of collecting—the way some collections carry "a strong whiff of the harem," positioning the owner as "the sultan of a secret seraglio."[35]

The collection quickly becomes populated with a perverse variety of objects and consumables—the portly working girls, the tacky mid-century furniture, and the more obviously aesthetic arrangements that cross boundaries of culture and media alike. One of these matronly hookers classes up Frank's case of P.B.R. by serving it in Ben's glass mugs, and the film's second toast is proposed, this time by Frank: "Let's drink

Figure 7. Ben's place as design collection |

to fuckin.' Here's to your fuck!" Blurring the erotic rituals of consumption and sex, Frank de-sublimates Jeffrey's own toast to "interesting experiences." Another woman sits next to a life-sized doll sporting a tutu and a grotesque clown mask; on the wall above the uncanny pair is a painting of a female nude, supine and oriented toward her beholder; and the whole feminine triad is framed by a lime-curtained proscenium. Through this stage, Frank, Dorothy, and Jeffrey will momentarily make their own entrance for Ben (and for us). A theater of mediation, the stage's curtain is abutted by another gramophone encased in wood, and on its top rests a 1980s boom box that Frank uses to play a tape of Roy Orbison's "In Dreams" for Ben's lip-synched performance. The aesthetic value of this mise-en-scène at Ben's, typical of camp and cult objects, lies in their accumulation and arrangement.

Kitsch's lesson is to separate the values of novelty from originality, erotic pleasure from authenticity. Kitsch denaturalizes aesthetic sensation. This is also the point of Ben's lip-synching and the heart of the sequence's presentation of cinematic fantasy. The episode hinges on Frank's fetishistic pleasure in the Orbison tune, which seems to stanch some unknown loss, but its tableau staging links the plastic balm of fifties pop to the mechanisms of celluloid illusionism writ large. The frontal staging of the sequence recalls the visual style of early cinema, with its ostensive, flat presentation. Cinema would eventually leave this spatial heritage behind as it moved beyond the autarchy of the tableau toward more complex strategies for delivering the illusion of haptic depth. In fact, the sequence offers a sustained investigation of the formal props of cinematic illusion. Lynch teases us with the relations between the surface of the image—toward which the characters at one point gather in a line, as if about to bow to us, their audience, and seem to examine their own frame—and its unseen depths: the obscene, offscreen space from where Frank and his posse emerge, or the obscure room behind Ben's coffee table where, presumably, Donny is being kept. But he also disassembles, through Ben's improvised microphone, cinema's constitutive play of light and shadow, its synchronized sound-image relations, and its fundamentally uncanny play between stillness and the moving image. Frank, of course, is in the process of being himself synthetically moved by vision and sound. As he watches Ben, he is nearly motionless; only his lips open as he mouths the lyrics. And Ben's theatrical poses seem to freeze into photographic stasis, even as the song continues. "In Dreams" is abruptly interrupted when it no longer performs its soothing function for Frank and when the surface of his own face, frozen in dreamy rapture, twitches and contorts as if disgusted by some deep-seated trauma. The faltering of Frank's fantasy is then doubled on the level of Lynch's image; having stopped the tape, and again in an impotent rage, Frank shouts, "I'll fuck anything that moves!" and then vanishes in a jump cut. Aurally, the cut is punctuated by the pealing of unseen tires as Frank's crew tears off, but visually we see only an unmoving doll/clown on the couch—the uncanny residue of the joyride that is cinema.

When the plastic gloss of fantasy, built up through cliché and repetition, has finally rotted, what spills out is the more unsettling knowledge that, as Michael Moon puts it, "what most of us consider our deepest and strongest desires are not our own, that our dreams and fantasies are only copies, audio- and videotapes, of the desires of others and our utterances of them lip-synching of these circulating, endlessly reproduced and reproducible desires."[36] This problem of the radical unoriginality of desire is taken up in a rhyming, lyrical scene set in the Williamses' basement. As at Ben's place, here time again seems to slow as Jeffrey and Sandy dance to Julee Cruise's "Mysteries of Love" in a sea of teen kitsch, surrounded by a series of interchangeable young couples with seemingly identical hairstyles. The faux-blond patina of the basement's wood paneling echoes the girls' hair and the color of a tacky wooden fish on the wall, joining them all as different forms of processed wood. The homey bourgeois basement is, of course, another exemplary postwar design fantasy, dreamily concealing its other anxious function as a refuge from nuclear fallout.

The latent proximity between the middle-class basement and the underground is clearest in the figure of Ben himself. Stockwell's campy ghoul presides over the film's kitschiest collection, and his sensibility most forcefully joins sophistication and erotic perversion. Lynch codes his monster of taste as gay, and Stockwell's over-the-top performance clarifies the tight relationship between kitsch and camp, historically a subcultural aesthetic of resistance for gay men. In doing so, Lynch, on the one hand, picks up a long-standing cultural association between the arch tastes of gay men and their erotic transgressions—the way the very idea of aesthetic sophistication entails some guilty deviation from "nature." An awed Frank, overcome by Ben's style, calls him "one suave fuck," a line that collapses Ben's erotic and aesthetic sensibilities and contrasts the calm, poised violence that seems to accompany Ben's maturity in matters of taste with Frank's rough and twitchy sadomasochism. Next to Ben, the film's greatest sophisticate and decadent, Frank seems like an impotent child, a lesson in aesthetic and sexual mal-development. On the other hand, Ben is the figure whose camp sensibility is most telling of *Blue Velvet*'s own; it aligns this style with the countercultural aesthetics of sixties underground cinema and with avant-garde filmmakers like Andy Warhol and Kenneth Anger, whose postwar pop aesthetic rethought the terrain of mass culture and liberated kitsch from its modernist, Greenbergian purgatory. Warhol, especially in his Death and Disaster series (1962–1964), proved himself a shrewd analyst of the dialect between the soothing repetitions of mass-produced fantasy and the traumas against which they are founded, and which their glossy images never finally hold at bay. And Anger's *Scorpio Rising* (1963), nearly twenty-five years before Lynch, used Bobbie Vinton's "Blue Velvet" as an ironic counterpoint to the spectacular fetishism of gay biker culture and its hyper-phallic leather and metal props.

Has Lynch seen *Scorpio Rising*? In posing this question, Ben's kitschy sophistication returns us to the question of Lynch's own aesthetic knowingness. The question has long preoccupied critics, many of whom have ascribed to Lynch a naive expressivity, an innocence that surges directly from unconscious wells. Proponents of Lynch's naiveté seem determined to defend Lynch from influential feminist encounters with *Blue Velvet*. In various ways these readings have been forced to confront how the film's stylized interior design extends to the stuff of inner life, riffing on psychoanalytic dynamics and processes willy-nilly. The sheer range of conclusions drawn about Lynch's design in *Blue Velvet* only further underscores the film's tonal complexity. On one level this problem is internal to the very idea of tone, which seems ambiguously located both in aesthetic objects themselves and in viewers' particular emotional responses to them. It is no surprise, then, that the curious tone of *Blue Velvet*'s interiors has spawned various ideological readings, but with fuzzy, inconsistent results. Is the feeling of its fifties furniture the postmodern pathos of political transgression bowdlerized as merely outré decor? Or does its design artifice provide the cold gloss of indifference, hiding a more profound anger toward the feminine and its schlocky ornamentation? Is Lynch a nostalgic postmodern conservative; or a late prophet of modern, Nietzschean rage against women; or, as Laura Mulvey claims, the purveyor of a cutting "camp wit"?[37]

Blue Velvet is a powerful work of art because it raises these questions without ever finally answering them and because it produces such strong feelings from such kitschy material. It is the product of a rather sophisticated designer, who crafts his atmospherics (and his persona) carefully and by subtle gradations of distinction from other artists. Take Lynch's considered response to an interviewer who, reading the campy tone of *Blue Velvet*, compared it to the work of John Waters, an early supporter of Lynch:

> I've met John Waters, liked him, and feel a genuine kinship with his stuff. But there are a lot of differences. His way is making so much fun of those absurd, polyester things. I want to come at them sideways in a drier way, for that certain kind of humor. And also so that you can slip into fear. See, *Ronnie Rocket*, the film I've been trying to make for five years, is very absurd but it can also turn slightly and become very frightening. You can't just be so camp or so blatant. Waters is very up front, sorta like a loud saxophone, and I want to back off into something a little different.[38]

There is no aesthetic naiveté here, only connoisseurship and the knowing cultivation of tone. This refined sensibility *requires* the plastic, the ersatz, and the sentimental, but bends the stuff of consumer pleasure to the point where it becomes something darker, more foreboding and grotesque. In the same interview, Lynch explained how, like a number of avant-gardists before him (and like John Waters himself, despite Lynch's effort at distinction), his aesthetics seek a kind of emotional authenticity not through taste exactly, but through the strong sensation of disgust, the sublime other of taste. If "you back off from the [disgusting] stuff," Lynch explains, "you risk shooting right down into lukewarm junk."[39] In the fantastic collections of *Blue Velvet* and elsewhere, Lynch makes clear that disgust, a kind of aesthetic catastrophe, is the feeling you get when you run out of plastic or have way too much—in other words, when the glossy assemblages of fantasy fail. And *Blue Velvet*, Lynch explains, "is what could happen if you ran out of fantasy."[40]

Blue Velvet ends with a similar undercutting of happy artifice by something more disgusting that belies it. Before we see Dorothy and Donny fantastically reunited and the camera pans to the too-cerulean sky above, an obviously fake robin perches on the sill of the Beaumonts' kitchen window, holding a bug in its mouth. Jeffrey summons Sandy and Aunt Barbara to the window, sensing the fulfillment of Sandy's dream that "there'll be trouble 'til the robins come." Aunt Barbara, shuddering in disgust, exclaims, "I don't see how they could do *that*! I could never eat a bug!" before enjoying a bite of her own lunch, watching the bird with curiosity and fascination. It is a final joke about the fragile limits of consumption in a film that is predicated on the middle-class's healthy appetite for transgression.

Furniture Porn: *Lost Highway*

In 1997, while promoting his new project, *Lost Highway*, Lynch granted his first interview to a design journal, the Swiss publication *form*. Question: "Do you ever dream of furniture?" Answer: "I day-dream of furniture, yes." The stuff of fantasy, furniture is also a long-standing hobby for Lynch and became a minor business venture for him in the 1990s, after the critical and commercial failure of *Twin Peaks: Fire Walk with Me* and during a period when Lynch struggled to get another film off the ground. In the interview, Lynch explains that he had been making furniture ever since art school and sold his first piece at Skank World, a small Beverly Hills shop specializing in mid-century design. In April 1997 several of Lynch's pieces, including the Club Tables featured in the photograph of the interior of the Beverly Johnson House, were displayed at Milan's Salone del Mobile, one of the world's more prestigious furniture exhibitions. Lynch sold the line—including the Steel Block Table, the Floating Beam Table, and the Espresso Table—exclusively through the Swiss design company Casanostra, with the small constructions of wood and steel priced between fifteen hundred and two thousand dollars. On Casanostra's website the last piece is sold with the tag, "Coffee in an asymmetrical world," a deft bit of cross-marketing that reminds us of Special Agent Dale Cooper's love of the bean and Lynch's own company, Asymmetrical Productions, whose first feature coproduction was *Lost Highway*.

Similarly, the October Films press kit for the picture promoted it as the work of a visionary auteur who conceives of film as an inherently intermedial endeavor, combining music and art direction, painting and photography in a symphony of design:

> The design within the house also corresponds to Lynch's overall vision. "I always like to have the people stand out, so the furnishings have got to be as minimal as possible so you can see the people." Lynch adds, "There were many things that had to be built for the story to work," and since Lynch has lately expanded his activities to include the design of furniture, he actually built some pieces for this set himself, most notably the case that contains the Madisons' ominous VCR.[41]

Lost Highway's furniture, it seems, is transparent, opening onto views of Lynch's eccentric genius. The romantic idea of the auteur, developed most famously in the 1950s in the pages of French film magazine *Cahiers du cinéma*, was bound to a related notion of expressive mise-en-scène, of a controlled cinematic decor bearing the traces of a presiding aesthetic personality. Style, for the discerning "Hitchcocko-Hawksiens" at *Cahiers*, would have a soul, humanizing the industrial products of Hollywood's dream factory. And it is hard not to think of Lynch's furniture as a kind of artistic cameo, the equivalent in the realm of objects of the cheeky appearances of his beloved Hitchcock, always popping up in his own films and turning them into ever more reflexive and ironic gizmos in the process. What's more, the furniture—and the domestic drama of Fred (Bill Pullman) and Renee (Patricia Arquette) that occupies roughly the first half of the film's disjointed narrative—is staged in an über-modern home that is Lynch's real property, one of three houses (including Lloyd Wright Jr.'s Beverly Johnson House) owned by the director in the same canyon outside of Hollywood. The feature article on *Lost Highway* in *Rolling Stone*, which put Lynch on the cover with Trent Reznor, Nine Inch Nails' front man and the producer of the film's soundtrack, explains how Lynch remodeled the house inside and out for the film, adding the tiny, narrow slot windows to the exterior and building a "tunnellike hallway" on the inside, into which Fred Madison will repeatedly be made to disappear (fig. 8).[42]

The press kit also insists on the centrality of the home's design to unlocking the film's secrets or producing more of them:

> The house inhabited by Fred and Renee is similarly integral to the film's scheme, combining stylistic elements of yesterday, today and tomorrow, just as the narrative does. In fact, the house's peculiar design could almost serve as a metaphor for the entire film: when seen from the front, there are a few small windows, providing limited opportunities to see inside. But when it is approached from other angles, one realizes that there are many ways to observe the interior.[43]

The Madisons' home, we are assured, is like the broader style of the film's decor, both "blazingly modern and absolutely retro in look and

Figure 8. The badness of modern homes |

feel."[44] Dropping references to expressionism, the surrealism of André Breton, psychoanalysis, and film noir, *Lost Highway*'s marketing announces David Lynch's return to form through his modernity, and his modernity through an unlikely equation between the modern, minimalist house and modernist narrative complexity. Less is more.

Aesthetic modernism is part of the film's status as stylistic pastiche but also part of its real narrative aspirations and claims to aesthetic legitimacy and power. *Lost Highway* poaches the design lessons of high modernist architecture—utopian rationalism and functionalism, chiefly—and ironizes them in the service of modernist narrative in the mode of art cinema, blurring art and pornography, visionary idealism and mass-market materialism. The paradox of *Lost Highway*'s elliptical narrative is that it becomes modernist, anticipating the more experimental narrative structures of *Mulholland Dr.* and *Inland Empire* (2006), as its interior design becomes less modernist—more irrational, secretive, and inhuman. Lynch becomes more like Bergman by defiling the visionary aspirations of a Le Corbusier. In *Lost Highway* transparency and rationalism fail in precisely the location where so many postwar architects imagined the future of the modernist impulse—the happy, newly pleasurable open-plan design of the mid-century domestic interior, whose dream of more permeable boundaries between inside and outside becomes another nightmare. If in *Eraserhead* this collapse of the boundary is signaled in the aesthetic of the grotesque, in *Lost Highway* it transpires as pornography, which enjoys a long, tangled history with modern art's own quest for notoriety and authenticity through the extremes of feeling and consciousness. The film's relentlessly pornographic imagination is part of its own meditation on auteur self-fashioning as furniture. This befits an artist who, on the heels of two commercial flops, has become well acquainted with the vagaries of mass taste and finds himself embroiled in another campaign to sell himself. In the process, the auteur's romantic soul is hollowed out, hardening into a merely functional thing. The Lynchian signature becomes a design icon, a fetishized commodity, an ironic advertisement for its own hidden mysteries whose views are forever deferred: furniture porn.

In *Lost Highway* these ironic objects—furniture, bodies, and the souls of authors—are set loose in a strikingly dehumanized and unsentimental film, one stripped bare of the melodramatic, romantic handling of emotion that characterized Lynch's previous two features, *Fire Walk with Me* and *Wild at Heart*. Instead, Lynch positions his furniture in a dark, highly reflexive meditation on the enigma of personality itself—on the very idea of human interiority or other, obscene secrets on the insides of things. The Madisons' modern home allows Lynch to pose the question of the interior in several ways: through the troubled status of bourgeois domesticity and privacy, here again contaminated by theatricality; through the etiology of Fred's psychological distress, which Lynch again gives harrowing architectural form and here drives the narrative fragmentation; and through the enigma of Renee/Alice, whose mysterious sexuality is asked to speak its truth, in the fashion of pornography.

The fractures in the Madisons' marriage are exacerbated by the mysterious arrival of videotapes of their home from an unknown observer. The views of the house produced by the camera eye move progressively inward over the course of the three taped recordings, despoiling the Madisons' already strained private life and turning the home's vulnerable interior, in familiar Lynchian fashion, into a theater for the self's more obscene dramas. The first tape consists of a flat pan of the home's minimalist façade, aggressively frontal, almost bunkerlike in its defensive posture. The second tape—which prompts the alarmed couple to summon the police—contains footage inside the house, moving from the living room, through the hallway, stopping to hover voyeuristically above Fred and Renee, asleep in their bed. And the third, discovered this time by Fred rather than Renee, returns to the Madisons' bedroom to find Fred, screaming, next to a mutilated corpse we presume to be his wife. As the tapes penetrate the home, the camera's mode of observation becomes increasingly pornographic, modulating from surveillance footage, to Peeping-Tom voyeurism, to a snuff film that has just missed its big little death.

The space-time of the third tape's view is decidedly fuzzy. Narratively speaking, it follows Fred's introduction to the Mystery Man (Robert Blake) at a party at the mansion of Renee's "friend" Andy. Returning home with Renee, who dodges his anxious questions about her relationship with Andy, Fred sees a flash of light inside their house and goes inside to investigate. After declaring that the coast is clear, Fred and Renee enter and prepare for bed. What follows is a bewildering sequence in which Fred and Renee find themselves doubled in mirrors, and Fred loses himself in the darkened recesses of the house. At one point the camera, tracking Fred through a hallway, plunges into complete darkness and then pulls back out of a black space, which seems bounded by the hallway walls. We cut to the same wide-angle view of the living room that has announced the entry of the previous two tapes into the home, with Fred viewed in and from the precise location of Renee earlier. Now, however, as Fred plays the recording that will end in murder, the framing of the Madisons' TV establishes Lynch's trompe l'oeil: what we had taken for an inky hallway tunnel was, in fact, the TV screen. The interiors—both of Fred's fragile, modern psyche and of his vulnerable modern home—are alike despoiled, displaced by uncanny media.

Given all the trouble caused by these videotapes, one can understand the temptations of the wooden VCR case, built by Lynch, which serves as a failed prophylactic. It is the interior's organic defense against technological incursions. Wood, as Jean Baudrillard reminds us, suggests "organic warmth" and became especially desirable for its suggestive atmospheric values during the mid-century's remaking of the domestic interior as an efficient, quasi-cybernetic system of technical calculation and multifunctionality.[45] In an era of plastic, polymorphous substitutes for natural substances, wood is a nostalgic material that embeds time "in its very fibres . . . In short, it is a material that has *being*.[46] Wood, as *Twin Peaks* perhaps makes most evident, is also an obsessive substance in the Lynchian universe. Wood recurs in Lynch's films as cases or nests for media—Henry Spencer's record player in *Eraserhead* or the reassuring cases for fifties' televisions in *Blue Velvet*, whose designs sought to reassure consumers of the hominess of the new media, of its capacity to be folded organically inside a stable, enduring domestic arrangement that, in fact, TV had irrevocably changed.

The Madisons' living room, with its wooden auteurist prosthesis, draws on the romantic soul of wood—its integrity, warmth, and temporal stability—to protect against the violation of domestic intimacy by technology and psychic malaise. The VCR case's compensatory quality is immediately noticeable because of its functional superfluity (fig. 9). There is already a capacious horizontal niche for the VCR carved into the half wall of light wood, which makes the additional wooden sleeve around the VCR an unnecessary design flourish. The case's evident lack of functionality is all the more flagrant within a semitransparent partition

Figure 9. Wood as media prophylaxis |

designed, in mid-century fashion, for multifunctionality: it is at once media console, storage space, and room divider, separating the living room from the stairway behind it. But the console offers scant consolation, because its design elements are echoes or repetitions of the house's exterior: the row of snake plants that fringe the console are also arranged in a line outside the Madisons' front door, stretching across the front of the house. The plants call our attention to other graphic repetitions: the nested horizontals of the wooden media console and VCR case are echoed in the horizontal vents in the house's façade as well as the vertical encasement of the home's narrow windows—fortress-like slits—and the front door's own rectangular shell. In these ways the inside is always an outside; this modern house wears its heart—the living room—on its sleeve. Indeed, the second of the three of the small paintings on the wall behind the Madisons' couch (works by Lynch's now ex-wife and longtime editor, Mary Sweeney) depicts a cluster of female body parts (hands, elbows, buttocks, torsos), anticipating the grisly scene of the murder that will later flash in color into view during Fred's viewing of the third tape, even as it underscores the feminine as Lynch's most valued design element.

In addition to the VCR case, Lynch crafted the hallway table in Fred and Renee Madison's living room. Our first, partial view of the asymmetrical table in *Lost Highway* is also our first glimpse of Renee. Like Renee, the line of the tabletop seems to emerge magically from the wall, but it also directs our gaze, and Fred's, toward his lovely and mysterious wife. The palette of black, mauve, and desaturated red recalls our introduction to Dorothy Vallens, more fleshy furniture in heels, in front of her couch at *Twin Peaks'* Deep River Apartments. In the manner of other famously magical tables, Lynch's is an instrument of fetishism. More recently, the quasi-pornographic assemblages of Dorothy Vallens and Renee/Alice—comprised of plastic high heels, wigs, lacquered nails, and brilliant lips—have been knowingly reactivated in "Fetish," Lynch's collaboration with famed French shoe designer Christian Louboutin, a series of exhibitions in 2007–2008 that cross-marketed two aesthetic signatures: limited-edition Louboutin red-soled stilettos and David Lynch's signed photographs of nude models (parts of them, anyway) in kinky, vaguely menacing atmospheres and wearing trademarked Louboutin heels. Louboutin explained, "As [Lynch's] movies are extremely coded, I also wanted fetishist shoes. Those shoes would indeed follow those codes . . . He saw a sofa, roses, a lamp and a girl."[47]

A similar mise-en-scène codes the unreal emergence of *Lost Highway*'s Renee. Her curious insubstantiality anticipates her uncanny reappearances, first as the Mystery Man in Fred's nightmare, then as Alice in the second portion of the narrative, when Fred has disappeared from his death-row cell, transformed into or fantastically reimagined as Pete (Balthazar Getty). There, she steps in rapturous slow motion out of Mr. Eddy's (Robert Loggia) iconic, tail-finned black Cadillac before a transfixed Pete and to the strains of Lou Reed's hypnotic version of "This Magic Moment." It is not, as Todd McGowan suggests, that there is the Renee of Fred's desire and the Alice of Fred's fantasy (as virile Pete), but only Renee/Alice in polymorphous combinations with other sexual partners, props, and fantastic scenarios. Part of Renee/Alice's mystery, and fetishistic treatment, is assembled from the *combinatoire noir*. The classic film noir attains historical coherence around particular kinds of anonymous, de-individuated places—nightclubs, bars, hotel rooms, bus and train stations—that offered a perverse response to the idyllic fantasies of a stable, organic home or home front so prominent in American cinema of the 1940s.[48] While American films noir were reimagining American domestic insecurity as a kind of uncanny "lounge time," the country's interiors were also being refashioned by modern architects and designers who, responding to a similar unsettling of domestic relations, carved out the so-called contemporary style as a middle ground between interwar modernist austerity and the climate of overabundance of the postwar economic boom.

Like *Blue Velvet*, *Lost Highway*'s furniture returns to the memory of the same moment, now more specifically recalling the "contemporary" vision of mid-century furniture as mobile, lightweight, and flexible, part of a multifunctional, reconfigurable domestic system of substitutions and combinations rather than a fixed suite. Mid-century architecture and design were marked by two broad impulses—the privatization of public space (as in the dream of the car as a mobile home; the drive-in theater as a living room, bedroom, and kitchen; or even the national park system as a suburban neighborhood) and the publicization of the private: "the TV set was placed on wheels, the walls became partitions," and happy domestic life was imagined through the watchwords of mobility and efficiency.[49] Through the pioneering efforts of designers like Charles and Ray Eames (avowed favorites of Lynch), furniture was built using the latest in malleable, mass-producible materials, such as molded plywood, steel-rod frames, synthetic foam cushions, and fiberglass, and often packaged and sold as fragments of easily transportable, knock-down kits. "The Eames idea of design," Beatriz Colomina explains, "turns on the continuous arrangement and rearrangement of a limited kit of parts. Almost everything they produced can be rearranged; no layout is ever fixed."[50] The texture of Lynch's worlds, as Michel Chion has brilliantly demonstrated, is built from an equally rearrangeable suite, whose combinatory principles Lynch has explored directly in his visual art.[51]

The uncanny interior of the Madisons' living room contains two icons of mid-century furniture. One is the Diamond Chair, designed by Italian-born artist and designer Harry Bertoia. Part of a line that Bertoia developed in 1952 for the Knoll company, the Diamond Chair epitomized the airy, lightweight turn in postwar furniture. The chair's elegant frame, a carefully molded grid of welded steel rods, was produced either nude, with a seat pad, or fully upholstered in a wide palette of solid, bold colors: yellows, reds, blues, greens. Bertoia, who also, like Lynch, is a sculptor of sound, conceived his chair as a marvel of transparency and fluidity. But in the Madisons' living room, the Bertoia chair, with its muted brown upholstery and invisible signature, the wire frame, is rendered fleshy and opaque and finds an apt seat next to one of the room's tiny windows. At the same time, the violations of the Madisons' interior, whose space is nothing if not fluid and permeable, is the uncanny extrapolation of Bertoia's dream of airy furniture.

The room's other flagrant icon is the Madisons' long black living room table, the Elliptical Table designed by Charles and Ray Eames in 1951 for the Herman Miller furniture company, Knoll's rival. Also known as the "surfboard table," the Elliptical Table has a long top built of layered birch plywood and black laminate that hovers only ten inches off the ground on its two-part wire base—its lowness an attempt to approximate the elegance of Japanese-style seating. In a conspicuously low angle, Lynch's camera approaches the abandoned table and the ringing black phone that rests on it as Fred, anxious about Renee's whereabouts, calls home from the phone booth at the Luna Club. The push toward the Elliptical Table encodes Renee's vexing distance from Fred. More subtly, its bent metal base, and its arrangement next to Bertoia's Diamond Chair, contains another hidden enigma—now of authorship and authenticity of design. For as the wire base suggests, the Eameses had also been pioneering bent metal construction techniques, and the similarity of their Wire Mesh Chairs (1951) to Bertoia's Diamond Chairs became a serious bone of contention between Herman Miller and Knoll. Herman Miller disputed in a lawsuit the origin of the bent-wire technique, which, starting in 1955 was patented under the Eameses name and could be used by Knoll only under license. Has Lynch cannily secreted this micro-history of disputed authorship into the Madison living room to underscore Fred's futile possessiveness, or to continue the theme of submerged domestic antagonism, or to further worry the idea of an aesthetic signature?

More likely, *Lost Highway* has found a few ideas in the patented ellipse of the table, a shape but also a principle of narrative organization for this highly elliptical film, as well as a familiar graphic motif of Francis Bacon, whose paintings are replete with elliptical internal framing structures. Art historians have posited a series of inspirations for Bacon's use of the elliptical enclosures of activity, from racecourses to roulette tables, operating theaters, and pre-cinematic optical devices like the zoopraxiscope. Bacon's ellipses often frame bedrooms as atavistic, dehumanizing arenas of sex and violence like that which seems to eventually encircle Fred and Renee in the culminating murder of the film's first segment and then to more fully envelop the narrative's second part, in which Renee/Alice becomes part of a labile circuit of pornographic scenarios. In this sense, Renee/Alice incarnates the mystery of character as furniture, as an element in endlessly recombinant, and overtly pornographic, design scenarios, linked up in increasingly bizarre assemblages as the film progresses. There is Renee–asymmetrical table–black lamp–limpid glass. There is Alice–Cadillac–Lou Reed–platinum wig; there is Renee's lips–black mouthpiece of phone. There is Alice–porno Alice–unseen man–Andy–Pete–shiny gun. There is Renee–Dick Laurent–Renee in a porn orgy with two women and two men, one of whom, incidentally, is Marilyn Manson.

The Elliptical Table asks us to consider the film's narrative as a similar "ensemble." I have in mind Baudrillard's particular use of the term in 1968 to describe the modern transformation of the bourgeois interior away from space as a naturalized arrangement of an "organic" patriarchal order and toward "atmosphere," in which the objects of home decor become abstract objects of mental manipulation, systematizing a limitless range of subjective and cultural associations.[52] In the mid-century's turn toward multifunctional modern living space, gone were soulful, anthropomorphic domestic objects, things that served a moral purpose by mirroring the immanence of the bourgeois family and the permanence of traditional emotional bonds. Instead, domestic objects were increasingly valued less as objects of appropriation or intimacy than as instruments of information, objects of a code in an "unrestricted combinatorial system."[53] Man, "the 'interior designer,' is . . . an active engineer of atmosphere . . . Everything has to intercommunicate, everything has to be functional—no more secrets, no more mysteries, everything is organized, therefore everything is clear . . . modern man, the cybernetician, [is] a mental hypochondriac, as someone obsessed with the perfect circulation of messages."[54] The gambit of *Lost Highway*'s uncertain narrative is to bend this utopian mid-century dream of an atmosphere as information—as clean, cool, abstract communication—toward the work of pornography, which is, in its own crass way, also a kind of information science, presuming to visualize sexuality's unseen truths.[55]

The pornographic imagination, especially in its Sadeian variants, operates by rather similar functional imperatives of exchange and interchangeability. Persons are things, bodies so much sexual furniture endlessly rearranged. One of the two silly cops tasked to follow Pete after his baffling emergence in Fred Madison's cell observes that Pete "gets more pussy than a toilet seat," a crude joke, but also a meta-pornographic one about the film's own conversions between sex and furniture. What pornography produces, then, is not sexual knowledge or "truth"—the perception of the essence or interior of things—but rather *information*, comparisons or displays of value judged publicly, in the theaters of its repetitive action that tend to proliferate over the course of *Lost Highway*.[56] In other words, the relentless exteriority of pornography is exemplary of a turn against metaphysical notions of depth, essence, and identity and toward the power of physical environments to produce value and meaning. What makes pornography pornographic is neither the experience nor its represented content at all, but its public, social arenas of visibility, which give the visible texture.

Lost Highway's visual style packages its sexual ensembles through contrasts that invite its spectator to compare sexual action and its atmospheric values. Sex is arranged by temperature ("cold" Renee vs. "hot" Alice); by color (not just of the fetishized wigs, nails, and heels of Renee/Alice, but also the watery blue of the poolside orgy, the muted black of the Madison bedroom, the intense scarlet of Mr. Eddy's parlor, the bright orange of Pete's horrified glimpse of Renee/Alice in a hotel room); by physical and social location (the flat, frustrated bedroom sex of Renee and Fred against the better, but predictable, car sex of Pete and his girlfriend, Sheila, or the passionate, forbidden sex of Pete and Alice, *in front of* a car; by number (any of these substitutable couplings against the more exaggerated orgies of the final third of the film); and by the various levels of mediation from "actual sex" introduced by time and technology (the evident present of Fred and Renee's conjugal sex, against the ornamental excesses of Alice's recollected sex with Mr. Eddy, against the filmed sex of Alice in couplings or larger assemblages).

"Experiences aren't pornographic," Susan Sontag famously insisted; only "structures of imagination are," public contexts of judging pornographic utterance.[57] *Lost Highway* manipulates these contexts deftly, as in the remarkable sequence in which Alice explains to Pete how she came to know Mr. Eddy and work in his porn business. The flashback shows an initially frightened Alice entering Mr. Eddy's mansion and baroque living room. Mr. Eddy, seated by a roaring fire, motions for Alice to strip naked, which she does, slowly and to the accompaniment of Marilyn Manson's cover of "I Put a Spell on You," which theatrically swells in volume as Alice disrobes and finally strides confidently across the floor to a position between Mr. Eddy's legs. The room is crowded with ornate furniture and leering men, and its collection of objects are theatrical props for pornographic fantasy, which Alice's account recreates for Pete and Lynch's camera recreates for his viewer.

Perhaps most striking about the scene, so evidently outrageous and choreographed, is the way the room's baroque decor comments on the scene's own kitschy excesses. Visually, the room would seem to be as hot and cluttered as the Madisons' living room is cold and spare. And yet, much as we've seen in *Blue Velvet*, the film doesn't so much oppose the modernist scarcity of the Madisons' home to the obscene extremes of Mr. Eddy's pleasure palace. Instead, it invites us to see them as two sides of the same pornographic machine of visibility, which produces loads of information and plenty of mystery but no inner meaning. The objects of the Madisons' modernist home are theatrical by virtue of their very minimalism; offering themselves to curious public inspection and interpretation, they can be made to mean almost anything. The obscene stuff of Mr. Eddy's living room, on the other hand, is theatrically self-evident, caricatured, and designed to set the pornographic imagination to work on its most familiar, banal scenarios. Both kinds of rooms explain nothing.

The mystery of character in *Lost Highway* is produced through similarly vexing assemblages. The switchboard at the heart of its experimental narrative, halfway through, ditches Fred for the younger, more sexually proficient Pete, and dumps the redheaded Renee for the platinum porn star Alice. As portions of *Lost Highway*'s elliptical narrative intercommunicate and fold back on itself, the film's characters merge and morph into each other, occupying the positions of other characters, taking their sexual partners as their own, and even assuming the positions of characters from other Lynch films. When Pete returns to his modest suburban home in the valley, his seat in the yard—and its iconography of white picket fences, dogs and garden hoses, and toys—conjures the domestic bliss of Jeffrey Beaumont, having muddled through his own trauma. And later, when Pete climbs the stairs of Alice's "friend" Andy's house, he finds himself in a hotel hallway, passing a door that bears the same numbers (26) as Henry Spencer's apartment in *Eraserhead*.

The promiscuous communication of its design elements, spilling into other films, has produced several recurring critical explanations, as well as the obvious comparisons to Luis Buñuel's two Conchitas in *That Obscure Object of Desire* (1977) and Hitchcock's Madeleine/Judy in *Vertigo* (1958). Perhaps motivated by Lynch's failed attempts to make a film of Franz Kafka's *The Metamorphosis*, early reviewers described the obscure events of the film's pivotal prison sequence, following Fred's apparent murder of Renee, as either a literal, perhaps supernatural, transformation into Pete Dayton. Or they read it as the first full segue into the second of two ontologically discrete, parallel worlds, between which we continue to oscillate throughout the film, whose final utterance ("Dick Laurent is dead"), because it is also its first, returns us, in Möbius-strip fashion, to the narrative's beginning. Others, more attuned to the species of psychological trauma at the heart of the narrative, understand Pete and Alice as Fred's hallucinations or fantasies. But these accounts, like the reading of the film's narrative as a "Möbius strip," a Kafkaesque transformation, or an attempt to approximate a psychological fracture in the form of a "psychogenic fugue," are all prepackaged by the film's canny promotional discourse, as is the centrality of the Madisons' home, which informs my own interpretation. This does not invalidate such readings so much as it suggests how *Lost Highway* is a kind of furniture kit, a readymade critical object designed to produce contexts in which its mysterious surfaces and ever inscrutable, prosthetic insides can be judged. This, too, is furniture porn.

Like pornography and furniture, *Lost Highway* seems to court stupidity, reveling in its thingly resistance to meaning-making operations. Its narrative impossibilities are marshaled against the general, metaphysicalizing tendency of art cinema's own mode of narration, which packs itself with complexity and ambiguity and, from that visual evidence, invites its viewers to reverse-engineer the signature of the auteur. *Lost Highway*, by contrast, tends to offer its unsettled interiors—the Madisons' modern house, for example—as machines for making views, chiefly, of Renee/Alice. The point is best made in the stunning sequence in which Pete, having now bought into Alice's noir plot to rob her pornographer friend

Andy and escape with his money, breaks into Andy's tacky mansion from the rear and walks into its high-ceilinged living room to find a large pornographic image of Alice projected on the inner wall. The face of Alice's sexual partner is obscured, but his movement behind her pushes her face, contorted in pleasure, rhythmically toward the camera and toward the flat surface of the image that she always is. Lynch exaggerates the enigmatic truth of her sexuality by displaying the image silently, stripping it of the aural track that would authenticate her pleasure and playing over it the blaring, non-diegetic song "Rammstein," by the German black-metal group of the same name. Andy, upstairs being preoccupied by Alice, descends, and Pete brains him with a vase. But when Alice comes down to approve of Pete's job, Andy comes to and charges Pete, who flips him overhead. Pete lands with a sickening squish on the sharp edge of the living room's semitransparent glass table. Death by furniture.

The sequence invites us to think of Alice's projected image and Andy's projected body as built of the same substance—the grotesque stupidity of the body. There will shortly be more views of Alice and more splittings of character and narrative, but Alice, as she later tells Pete directly, will never be had. Similarly, Lynch gives a first view of Andy/ table from above, then another, more ghastly one from below, but Pete, aligned with the first of these looks, can't seem to fathom what he sees, and all the more so because Alice is herself glacial, totally unmoved. The sequence recalls Sontag's argument about the deadpan tone shared by slapstick and pornography, both functionalist genres that depend upon external, behaviorist approaches to character. Sontag's claim is that pornography, like comedy, requires a "self-cancelling" emotional climate, a kind of affective minimalism, to better maximize sexual arousal. What is most "Lynchian" about this scene, then, is not the furniture itself but the constellation of uncertain affects produced by the thingly conjunction of flesh and furniture, oscillating between shock, horror, disgust, and comedy. Barry Gifford, the novelist and noir aficionado who cowrote with Lynch the screenplay of *Lost Highway*, characterized the director as "a pornographic fabulist, but a real, effective one."[58] He was referring to *Blue Velvet*, but the sentiment applies equally well to *Lost Highway*, which seeks authenticity on the level of affect, felt on the surface of the body as yet another effect of the well-built thing.

The Art of Being Moved

In 1991 the editors of *Parkett*, the prestigious Swiss journal of contemporary art, solicited responses to the query "(Why) Is David Lynch Important?" The inquiry's parenthetical qualification hedged the journal's bets on a filmmaker who, whatever his aesthetic merits, had become an indisputable cultural phenomenon. The previous year was arguably Lynch's annus mirabilis: his innovative TV series, *Twin Peaks*, became a massive success during its first season, nominated for fourteen Emmys; his fifth feature film, *Wild at Heart*, won the Palme d'Or at the Cannes Film Festival; and in October 1990 he landed on the cover of *Time* magazine as the "Czar of Bizarre."

The fascinating answers to the inquiry gravitate toward the problem of affect in Lynch's work and to the famously unstable emotional tone of his films. The work seems "hot" and "cold," moving and artificial at once. It blurs affective intensity with detachment and impersonality. So much depends upon the question of irony, which is always a political problem. In raising the specter of rhetorical insincerity, irony appeals to shared values and morals: it summons a ground of convention that can either stabilize ironic statements as such or be repudiated by the more radical forms of ironic suspension or negation that came to be synonymous with high postmodernism but that, for Lynch, were equally apparent in the films of Alfred Hitchcock, whose romantic irony powerfully shaped Lynch's own stylized vision.[59] In this vein, some of *Parkett's* respondents echoed the Jamesonian belief that Lynch's weak affect spells the eclipse of historicity, the sacrifice of politics, and the banalization of truly transgressive aesthetics on the altar of ironic style, style bereft of commitment or a horizon of moral value. At the same moment that Lynch's early 1990s media ubiquity announced, for some, the triumph of homogenized American pseudo-culture at the end of Hollywood's "high-concept" decade, his sensibility had also hardened into an adjective for the primary uncanniness, the *pseudo*-ness, of pseudo-culture itself. The "Lynchian" became a twin symptom of cultural banality and banality's self-overcoming—the capacity of iconic American quotidiana to be defamiliarized by irony and affective ambivalence.

The late David Foster Wallace, who wrote novels in the long, postmodern shadow of Thomas Pynchon, offered in *Premiere* magazine in

1996 a characteristically prolix anatomy of Lynch's aesthetic import in the guise of a profile of the director on the set of *Lost Highway*. In it, Wallace defined the "Lynchian" as "a particular kind of irony where the very macabre and the very mundane combine in such a way as to reveal the former's perpetual containment in the latter."[60] The ambit of the Lynchian and its particular "tone," Wallace insisted, pervaded contemporary American film, especially the sensibility of rising "independent" directors like the Coen brothers, Jim Jarmusch, Carl Franklin, Todd Haynes, and Quentin Tarantino, as well as the art cinema of Atom Egoyan, Arnaud Desplechin, and Guy Maddin. And yet, strikingly, the essay ends by finding Lynch exemplary of "contemporary artistic heroism," a "weird hybrid blend of classical Expressionist and contemporary postmodernist" in "this age when ironic self-consciousness is the one and only universally recognized badge of sophistication."[61]

Wallace's effort to redeem Lynch's irony by finding in it something more sincere is typical of critical studies of Lynch, which have been forced to reckon with the power of cliché in the work's affective force. The Lynchian cliché has been alternately decried as a threat to the larger realms of subconscious energy in his work (Nochimson), or celebrated as the redemptive encrustation of fantasy, which underscores the fundamental incoherence of the symbolic order (McGowan).[62] McGowan links affect to the psychic power of phantasmatic clichés as such—the way they continue to move us in spite of their illusory fullness. And yet McGowan's smart Lacanian reading, like Žižek's, tends to discuss affect in Lynch's work only as an incarnation of lost, pre-symbolic enjoyment or as the site of a confrontation with the impossible traumas of the Real.

Lynch's films are more affectively ambiguous than even his best critics have accounted for. To keep affect ambiguous or indeterminate is one way of generating affective intensity, but it is also a way to maintain the enigma of personality, to assert claims to aesthetic authenticity and distinction, and to estrange or refuse the politics of feeling attached to any number of cinematic genres, techniques, and narrative forms. These gambits on behalf of ambiguity have been historically associated with various forms of modernism in the arts—modes of aesthetic innovation, from painterly impressionism to postwar European art cinema, whose claims to novelty often hinged on a dissatisfaction with the stultifying over-coding of feeling and its bourgeois instrumentalization. Modernists often endorsed the nondiscursive and non-epistemic dimensions of aesthetic experience—art's capacity to mobilize affects that are neither culturally preformed nor wedded to the business of getting things done. Lynchian affect, at its most ambiguous, is modernist in this rather specific sense. His famous tonal ambiguity is best described as "affective" rather than "emotional," because it privileges the less structured, less cognitively interpretable dimensions of felt life—the subtle disorientations and defamiliarizations of feeling that frustrate cognitivist approaches to "emotion" proper.

Such approaches, which have fueled a growing subfield of film theory, understand emotions and emotional states (anger, fear) as basically *instrumental* cognitive processes that take objects (about which we are angry and fearful) and require beliefs about those objects (that we have been wronged or are in harm's way). Through emotions, we sort information and appraise actions; they are reason's way of orienting our moral and ethical life. If emotions are conceived of as ways of organizing perception and shaping action in everyday life, then the genre codes of narrative fiction films are highly structured ways of organizing spectator's beliefs; they stack the deck with what Noël Carroll calls "criteria of appropriateness" that allow us to slot cinematic objects into categories ("harmfulness") that license any given emotion (fear, say).[63] This is genre's way of being emotionally manipulative, moralizing.

Lynch is no more a genre director than he is a moralist. Yet much of his best work depends upon the very obviousness and recognizability of genre and its affective protocols only to surpass or estrange them, or to turn their banality into a kind of possibility—aesthetic freedom on the level of affect. Genre and morality alike are social forms whose hectoring emotional templates undergo a trial of deformation in Lynch's films. The boundary-violating move, affect's trespass against taxonomies and classifications, itself is not new, but rather the quintessentially modern gesture of the past two centuries. Lynch is, we might say, an archivist of modern affect. His cinema takes up the privileged emotional forms of aesthetic modernity writ large: the lyric, trauma, melancholy, melodrama; the sentimental and the grotesque; the sublime and the uncanny. His films subject this archive of feeling to a series of crossings, morphings, and delirious assemblages that constitute the complex affective environments of his work and make him a constructivist—but one freed of dogmatism.[64]

In the wake of davidlynch.com and *Inland Empire*, where the reme-diated terrain of the digital now helps us to see Lynch for the multimedia experimenter he has always been, we can begin to notice how so many of Lynch's films take as their abiding concern not just the false paradox of mediated feeling (is there any other kind?) but also the particular pres-sures of specific media environments on the very operations or circuits of feeling. In his most affectively complex films, *Wild at Heart*, *Twin Peaks: Fire Walk with Me*, and *Mulholland Dr.*, the layering of media environments—so central to producing the vague sense of "pastness" in these films and their unstable temporality—shape the forms of affect and experience modeled in the films. Lynch's attentiveness to media environments and their protocols, we might say, is his way of being historical. And, conversely, his devotion to the "art of being moved" is how David Lynch does media history.

Radio-Affectivity: *Wild at Heart*

Wild at Heart, Lynch's follow-up feature to *Blue Velvet*, is a film that makes people anxious. Though it won the Palme d'Or at the 1990 Cannes Film Festival (the jury was headed by Bernardo Bertolucci), it was decried as "abject" in the pages of *Libération* a few years later by none other than Jean-Luc Godard and alternatively derided and celebrated as a symptomatic work of postmodern aesthetic politics. Its gestures to the 1950s rang nostalgic and hollow, as removed from the historicity of the past as they were detached from the film's own present. Several years after the film's release, Chris Rodley, asking Lynch about the adverse re-actions to the film's violence (during one test screening the audience left the theater angrily, en masse), noted that the film seemed "to have been very much in tune with a climate in Los Angeles" that was to explode shortly after the film's release.[65] Rodley's question hopes to reinsert *Wild at Heart* into time and history through anxiety—a diffuse, explosive LA zeitgeist, tuned in by a Lynchian antenna. Lynch's answer insists on the film's ambiguous temporal horizon and its uncertain historical object:

> Well, when I first read *Wild at Heart* it was well before the riots, and they didn't follow immediately after the film. But there was craziness in the air and people were picking up on it. It's as if the mind is a top: it starts to spin faster and faster and then, if it starts to wobble, it can go

wildly out of control. Everybody feels it. It happens in traffic—people lose their temper. And you can't even relax at home: the television is sending out more stuff, and it's just mounting and mounting. It's like you're riding in a 747; you have no control if something goes wrong.[66]

What is *Wild at Heart* anxious about? "Stuff"? "It"? In other words, nothing specifically, and possibly everything. This is the predicament, precisely vague, of anxious people—people who experience their affects "in the air." And anxiety, Lynch knows, has a special temporality. Like fear, anxiety is what Ernst Bloch calls an "expectation emotion," oriented toward an unknown, anticipated future, aiming "less at some specific object as the fetish of [one's] desire than at the configuration of the world in general, or (what amounts to the same thing) as the future disposition of the self."[67] Unlike fear, though, which depends on the specificity of a feared object, anxiety has "nothing" certain as its object, generated instead by an indefinite something. If *Wild at Heart* provokes anxious responses in its viewers, it also takes anxiety—and the drifts of vaguely airborne feeling—as an abiding affective and *temporal* problem for its main characters. The flighty passions of its heroes, Sailor (Nicolas Cage) and Lula (Laura Dern), are combustible and anxiously situated in time.

Michel Chion has described *Wild at Heart* as both the director's most "directly emotional film" and a key part of Lynch's search for a "non-psychological cinema."[68] And it takes up nonpsychological feeling through the problem of anxious affect. The film is largely about the condition of affects "on the air": free-floating anxiety, atmospheric tension, smoldering passion—and their latent combustibility. And *Wild at Heart* thinks of anxious affect through the media protocols of radio—in particular the transmissibility of radios. The radio's airspace promises the film's protagonists, Sailor and Lula, an ethereal elsewhere, a balm for the contingency of the road, but it also links their restless passions to an expansive world whose largeness and otherness consistently infiltrates their intimacy and turns them into its moody, volatile receivers. There's a hollowness to Lula and Sailor, but Lynch sees it less as a sign of weak affect than as a spacey prerequisite for affective intensity, the channeling of stronger feelings. An airy vessel, the body sounds nothing so much as human contingency.

The film owes its memory of the postwar youth culture of the 1950s, in part, to the source novel of Barry Gifford, a talented American novelist and screenwriter whose excessive and often comic prose style is influenced by the picaresque romanticism of the Beats and, like much of Kerouac's fiction, is populated by quirky outsiders. Gifford's eccentric characters proved irresistible to Lynch, who was alerted to Gifford's work by producer and director Monty Montgomery, a friend of Lynch's who had bought the rights to Gifford's then-unpublished novel with hopes to direct an adaptation, with Lynch as producer. At the time, Lynch was working on a script of a 1940s detective novel for Propaganda Films. Gifford, for his part, had just finished his run as the editor of Black Lizard Books (1984–1989). Under Gifford's aegis, Black Lizard republished the crime fiction of Jim Thompson, Charles Willeford, Charles Williams, and David Goodis, much of which had gone out of print in the United States, and played no minor role in the resurgence of Thompson's popularity and a spate of neo-noir adaptations. Lynch was moved by Gifford's unpublished manuscript "Wild at Heart: The Story of Sailor and Lula" and decided to direct the adaptation himself, drafting the screenplay in just one week. Gifford had no direct role in the script (though much of Gifford's dialogue is preserved intact) but would later collaborate with Lynch on the script for his HBO television special, *Hotel Room*, and would cowrite with Lynch the screenplay for *Lost Highway*. Gifford has said that Lynch made the darker aspects of his novel perverse and the violence more extreme. But he also made the novel's sad ending happy, which begins to suggest the affective ambiguity of Lynch's picture.

Lynch's radio-active approach to narrative and character becomes apparent in those moments of repose that follow Lula's sex scenes with Sailor, when she becomes receptive to memories that unfold into stories of her troubled sexual past and quirky reflections on the present. The first of these talky sequences, which retain the vocal acuity of the source novel (Gifford explained its origins as the channeling of speech), opens with a shot of Sailor lying on their Cape Fear hotel bed, his feet aloft, balancing an antique radio.[69] It transmits a muted jazz tune, and Sailor holds its red cord gently between his legs. Sailor's delicate handling of the umbilical relic seems to comport with the song that calms his body. With Lula in the hotel, Sailor's mood has shifted. His quiescence before the radio now seems a far cry from the lethal, frenetic violence of the film's notorious opening sequence. There, the moody volatility of his character erupted into a killing scored to the speed metal of Powermad's "Slaughterhouse," its blaring chords Mickey-Moused to the image of Sailor's brutal movements, ironically drowning out the softer strains of Glenn Miller's "In the Mood" that introduce the scene. Now Lynch cuts from the becalmed Sailor, reframing the bedroom to accommodate Lula, who praises Sailor's sexual performance. As she dresses, Lula recalls Marietta's (Diane Ladd) early warnings against sex, and Sailor remembers Lula's admission that she was raped by her uncle Pooch at thirteen. The sexual memory produces the film's first flashback—to the immediate aftermath of the rape, to Lula's intense sobbing and Marietta's angry discovery. The flashback begins the sequence's editing pattern in which the couple's moods and movement are subject to battling transmissions—here, the noise of Lula's sexual past, or story of Uncle Pooch's death, or the uncanny offscreen cackle of the material voice, and the postcoital quiet of bodies harmonized by the radio, the film's non-anxious ideal of an emotional and embodied attunement to the world. The sequence ends, aptly enough, with the couple's kiss—like the romantic tenderness it stands for—presided over by the radio, still balanced by Sailor, now lowered by his feet to his hands into a threesome with the lovers, its jazz swelling in an audio close-up (fig. 10).

The sequence establishes the radio's utopian airspace within a broader sphere of compensatory gestures and movements. Shortly, the couple's sexual bliss will be coded visually with a lovely shot of the two

Figure 10. Sailor, Lula, and the radio:
affective receivers

lovers illuminated by the soft glow of an antique jukebox. "Be-Bop-a-Lula," which has accompanied the passionate sex that climaxes in the time-space of the jukebox, swells in its presence and seems to source the non-diegetic music in a site of ineffable tenderness. As Sailor takes Lula's hand and places it on his heart, we are returned to the couple's bedroom, where Lula makes a wish that they stay in love forever, for their future to be "simple and nice." Sailor confesses his past misdeeds; he wants to start doing good things for good reasons, but he knows that "there's more than a few bad ideas runnin' around loose out there." The very badness and looseness of these ideas is confirmed in several disjointed edited scenes that contaminate, in sound and image, the peace of the lovers' bed and are framed by two old media players—the jukebox and the radio.

The first infiltration comes with a blaring sound cut and a smash cut to a distraught Marietta looking in a mirror, smearing bright-red lipstick around her face. We return to the couple's bed, and Lula tells a story with "a lesson about bad ideas," the tale of her paranoid and deranged cousin Jingle Dell, played brilliantly by Crispin Glover. Dell's embedded story is a mini-masterpiece of the grotesque—bizarre, funny, and loaded with excessive visual and narrative detail. Dell is himself a bad receiver, a conduit controlled by black-rubber-gloved-wearing aliens on earth, who have conspired to ruin the idea of Christmas. What Lynch's montage shows us of Dell's response is a series of obsessive and compensatory gestures—his year-round celebration of Christmas, his lunch-making, his anxious attempt to box a menacing black "alien" glove in a perimeter of tape measures, his fearful movements on the sidewalk outside his home.

But what is Dell's "lesson," exactly, since he disappears so quickly from Lula's story and from the film? As signs of his mental distress, his compulsive gestures are perverse exaggerations of Sailor's and Lula's own states of emotional intermittence. They betray a similar desire to be at home in the world's noisy menace. "Too bad he couldn't visit that old Wizard of Oz and get some good advice," Sailor muses on poor Jingle. "Too bad we all can't, baby," Lula agrees. The references to the classic MGM musical summon its central fantasy of mastery and knowledge and its basic themes of airborne displacement and homecoming. They also remind us of the eventual fragility of the Wizard's voice—not all-powerful, but thrown by audiovisual smoke and mirrors. Sailor and Lula have no sooner wished for the Wizard's mastery than we get another abrupt sound cut, now to the angry snarl of feral dogs on some grainy television, fighting over carrion. In Johnny Farragut's hotel room, the sonic badness piles up in another loose, intermedial circuit—from the animal aggression on TV, to its goofy human mimicry by the barking Johnny, to Johnny's jingling phone.

The voice on the other end of the line is, of course, Marietta's, but we first see only her lipstick-stained hand next to a pink, heart-shaped jewelry box on her vanity top (a nice touch: the grotesque unfolds, as it often does in Lynch's films, in close proximity to the excessive sweetness of sentimental kitsch). Eventually, Marietta swivels in her chair into a shocking close-up—the extremity of her painted-red face is matched on the soundtrack by a crescendo of noisy horns. Coming unglued, she confesses to Johnny that she has done something "real bad" and begs him to meet her in person. The conversation ends, and Marietta, moaning and heaving, pukes in her toilet. We return to Johnny's hotel room and get another close-up of the television—now vultures pick at the carcass of a zebra, and we cut from this gross stuff directly back to Marietta at the toilet. She stops vomiting and slumps to the floor laughing as the camera tilts down and holds on her black, curled-tip witch's shoes. Thus Lynch produces a mediated circuitry of disgust and abjection, as if the phone lines, the TV airwaves, and the annals of cinematic history have crossed wires or have somehow conspired in the same bad network.

This bad air would be cleared in the next shot and its radio-dream. It opens with a close-up of the Bakelite AM radio resting on the windowsill of a roadside gas station and pulls back slowly to reveal an old, African American man seated in a metal chair, nodding his head as he observes Lula and snapping his finger to the beat of "Smoke Rings," a melancholy swing tune from the 1930s by Glen Gray and the Casa Loma Orchestra. As Lynch cuts between performer and spectator, Lula and the old man exchange gestures, pointing at each other silently and blowing kisses. It is an astonishingly nostalgic sequence. The radio music and the black old-timer (who just doesn't seem quite *all there*) together conjure a space of temporal suspension, on the air, as it were, and signed with an ethereal pantomime. Lula now inhabits it with the movements of her micro-performance.

The respite is brief. We dissolve from the man still snapping his fingers to a point-of-view shot through the windshield of Lula and Sailor's car, and the soundtrack cuts to their car radio, the voice of an announcer on a call-in show: "Come on in, San Antonio, what's on your almost-perfect mind this evening?" The line confirms the frenetic radio-activity of mind and affect in the film, both prone to bad reception, both courting disaster. The caller has had heart trouble, triple-bypass surgery, and this doesn't suit Lula's driving mood. As she turns the dial, she is subjected to a mounting catalog of sonic trauma. "Holy shit, it's night of the living fucking dead! I can't take much more of this radio!" she screams. Lula pulls over, jumps out of the car, and wakes Sailor to demand that he find her some music. Lynch's perverse sound gag continues as Sailor turns the dial to the sounds of "sexual assault," "mutilation," and "rape" before finally reaching a station playing the couple's favorite heavy metal group. Cage screams, "Powermad!" and flips out of the car to join Lula.

The sequence's restless knob-turning operates as a metaphor for the episodic narrative structure of the film as a whole. While the film's oft-remarked image-sound discontinuities—its flashback structures, its abrupt editing patterns, its recurring explosions of sound—were dismissed by its less-favorable critics as a banal shock tactic and part of the degraded "video-clip" aesthetics of MTV, they could also be thought of as various ways of coding the film's basic narrative and affective condition—intermittent transmission, interrupted broadcast, the film-heart as a restless receiver. Like the troubled minds, energetic bodies, and wandering affects of its heroes, *Wild at Heart* is built like a radio that just can't seem to stay on one channel for very long.

When Lula turns the radio's dial in search of a sound that moves her, sound is made to cut abruptly into and out of communicability, much in the manner of the film's own ostentatious sound editing. Chion has noted how *Wild at Heart*'s sound cuts are used with "special emotional force throughout the section of short, alternating scenes" that follow Sailor's parole violation and his vow to take Lula to California.[70] Notice Lynch's parallel editing between the couple on the road and the scene in which Marietta asks her ex-lover Marcello Santos to kill Sailor. Marietta's request quickly snowballs out of control, like talk tends to do in this film: the threat of the maternal voice is redistributed through Santos's telephone call, which sets into motion a bizarre criminal network (Mr. Reindeer, the disabled contract killer Juana, her henchman Reggie, and Perdita Durango). These eccentrics materialize out of the sonic ether and are tracked in a complex editing pattern of brief scenes that link them to the movements of their targets, Sailor and Johnny Farragut. The dense, baroque network of character is the film's own bad airspace, the unnerving, manic clutter of its channels. Like Lula, the more Lynch turns the dial, the more bad shit he tunes in, and the more he travels the airwaves for something more soothing.

What calms Lula, strangely, is Powermad's machinic song "Slaughterhouse." In one of the film's loveliest shots, the camera cranes up as the song pounds, and Sailor and Lula dance in a frenzy, kicking up the desert dust made luminous by a gorgeous sun sinking in the open expanse of the landscape. As the crane reaches its zenith on the setting fireball, we hear an audio dissolve from "Slaughterhouse," whose sonic force has now escaped the diegetic confines of the car radio into the Dolby "superfield," to Richard Strauss's romantic "Im Abendrot." The sequence is perhaps the film's crescendo of romantic intensity, and its romanticism is expansive, moving from the frenetic gestures of bodies to their stilled expenditure in medium close, where they mouth their love for each other, from the cold aggression of speed metal to classical, cosmic tenderness.

Lynch sets Lula and Sailor's passion on another frequency. Here, passion's excess would seek to escape talk and discourse altogether, unfolding in a space of sensuous intensity. As the extremities of sound, feeling, and gesture are here brought into alignment with the radiance of the sunset, we are reminded of Lula's prophecy of solar apocalypse. Is the intensity of the romantic couple, whose emotional vitality causes the rest of the world to fall away, the outside of the world's traumatic texture, a defense against the deadly radioactivity of the sun? Or is it just another version of the same self-consuming heat and energy? The Powermad song "Slaughterhouse" is both an escape from radio's traumatic airspace and one of its most unsettling channels. This is the basic paradox of the film's obsessive interest in combustion, of energy's explosive movement toward exhaustion, when it goes up in deadly flames.

Two of the film's most famously intense and emotionally unstable scenes play precisely with the notion of the human body as an airy vessel. On the road at night, Sailor and Lula come across the wreckage of a violent car accident and observe the last seconds in the life of a bloodied, distraught survivor (Sherilyn Fenn). The scene's power lies primarily in its astonished witnessing of the event of death, and Lynch's rare use of a handheld camera gives the scene a sense of uncertainty that befits its confusions of "thingliness" and animation. If the scene is tragic, its pathos comes from the gap between Sailor and Lula's shocked awareness of what they see and the girl's ignorance of her mortality, a kind of innocence before death that is picked up in the high, sweet, and sad piano notes that now preside over Badalamenti's mournful score. But there's also a cruel irony in the way Fenn's traumatized girl assumes a place in the film's series of "almost-perfect minds" that collapse into the stupidity and primal chaos of the body, from Bob Ray Lemon's dashed brains to Bobby Peru's accidental self-decapitation with a shotgun. Her absent-minded movements and gestures, her ways of stumbling on in the face of traumatic contingency, are forms of compensation not unlike Sailor's and Lula's own airy gestures. On the road, the couple encounters their own fragility. This more basic trauma is no sooner acknowledged than it is again wished away by radio: the sound mix blurs the sad piano notes with Lula's sobs, and both vanish in the return of Chris Isaak's "Wicked Game" as Sailor and Lula leave the scene of the accident into the night.

The second is the notorious "Say 'Fuck Me'" scene between Lula and Bobby Peru (Willem Dafoe). The scene also casts Bobby's violation of Lula as a specifically airy form of bodily possession—of being seized by passion, and in a way that reminds us of passion's etymological roots in a kind of passivity, the visitation of the soul by demons of affect. Part of what is so disturbing about the scene is the way Lynch's staging, like Bobby, exploits Lula's vulnerability. She lies on her hotel bed wearing only a lace negligee and red high heels, and she suffers from morning sickness, her untimely pregnancy (à la *Eraserhead*) a reliably Lynchian way of coding the self's violated intimacy. Bobby is the film's best example of the chaos of the body, most evident in his grotesquely bad teeth, but more powerfully in the nasty shit that comes out of his mouth—the materiality of the human voice at its most base, his breath fouling the air. Bobby's bad words point to the chaotic tropism of sound and language in the film.

In Bobby, sound is body, and body is sound. His voice does nothing but return the airy, unseen, and invisible to the realm of the embodied. He discerns the smell of Lula's offscreen puke and names it and her unseen bodily state. And his aggressive words are all forms of hollowing Lula out. Critics have often described Bobby's violation of Lula as a kind of sonic rape, but it is only possible because the scene has been constructed to collapse the boundary between sound and body, speech and action, saying "Fuck me" and actually fucking. The film as a whole insists on this kind of excitable speech—the combustible boundary between saying and doing and its pornographic tendencies. Recall the provocations of Bob Ray Lemon's initial vulgar words, which send Sailor into a deadly frenzy; or Lula's inability to tell Sailor of her pregnancy out loud and thus make it real by saying it; or Sailor and Lula's own randy sex talk. Sailor's cock, Lula coos, is so sweet she swears she hears it talking to her, and Sailor's absurd stories of his past sexual misadventures are pornographic forms of arousal for Lula, getting her "hotter 'n Georgia asphalt," just as they are self-reflective bits of meta-pornography loaded with fetishistic details of image and language.

As Lula comes under the spell of Bobby's voice, so Lynch implicates his viewers, yet again made to feel dirty and disgusted for looking and hearing, with a series of tight close-ups—most tellingly, of Bobby and Lula's nearly touching open lips, his bad air spilling into her, hatching feelings she would never recognize as properly hers (fig. 11). It is a

Figure 11. Passion at the limit of volition |

menacing scene not because he finally gets her to say "Fuck me" by threatening to "tear her fucking heart out"—though this is scary as hell—but because, through the insinuations and contagious repetitions of his voice, she actually *becomes* sexually aroused, making the same extended gesture with her hand that Lynch has used to authenticate her climax during her previous sex scenes with Sailor. Lula's passion operates at the limit of volition: Bobby Peru rips out Lula's radio-heart through a transmission of the most grotesque sort, estranging her from herself in a way that will not be remedied by the anguished clicking of her ruby-red heels.

By showing passion's undoing in a kind of senseless automatism, these sequences also underscore an uncanny involuntariness at the core of human behavior that fuels *Wild at Heart*'s bizarre, comic sensibility, comedy that is central to the basic affective intermittence of the film's characters and form of address. Take just one of the film's throwaway gags: At the bar of a New Orleans jazz club, Sailor and Lula are approached by a dancing old man (Lynch regular Freddie Jones). He looks at Lula, smiles, and then turns his gaze to Sailor. They look back and nod. Sailor looks directly, silently at the man. In the reverse shot, the man nods back at the couple yet again, his smile becoming a bit frantic; then he returns his gaze to the band. "Yeah!" he chirps, digging the music. But his distorted voice, like the scene's awkward timing, is off, sped up into a cartoonish quack. "Pigeons spread diseases, and mess up the place!" he chirps, and leaves. This bit is typical of Lynchian comedy and its special relationship to duration. These minor gags work by a distention or studied refusal of comic timing and pace that is evident in gags that drag on too long, or in the explosive affect of a joke that detonates too soon, before the listener is ready for the punch line. At the bar, Sailor and Lula wait for Jones's eccentric dancer to say something, and when he finally does, his voice is nearly unrecognizable, its pitch—too fast and too high—is inhuman, its message of avian contagion yet another form of airborne foulness in the film.

Comedy depends upon a temporal horizon of expectation—of the management of pauses, silences, and hesitations—that can, and in Lynch, usually does, turn into anxiety as the pleasurable tension of anticipation extends into a climate of apprehension or fear, or is instantly deflated into a void of incongruity, nonsense, or absurdity. Lynch's comedy tends to privilege incongruity at the level of the speed or timing of human behavior, contrasting and modulating characters through the varying speeds and slowness of their bodies and gestures, movements and voices. In fact, part of the humor of this exchange is how, unlike Lynch's viewer, Sailor and Lula are so unfazed by the appearance of this twitchy paranoid and his gnomic utterance. Faced with this weirdo, Sailor and Lula persist in their own quirky behavioral orbits, prone to their own lurchings into different rhythms and moods—another sign of their hearts' basic radio-activity. Tempting as it is to contrast a youthful vitality of their movement to the mechanical motion of the older, moribund eccentrics, Lynch steadfastly refuses this distinction in *Wild at Heart*. This may be the point of the gag's opening-match dissolve between Sailor's machinic wind-up of Lula in bed and her own slow turning of the mermaid toy in the bar: the lovers, like the inhuman dancer they will soon encounter, are haunted by involuntariness and mechanism, and comically so. Laughter, Henri Bergson famously observed in his influential 1900 treatise on comedy, *Le Rire*, often comes from the "momentary transformation of a person into a thing." For this reason, the repetition in comic behavior, which Bergson describes as form of "absentmindedness," produces not just pleasure but uncanniness.[71]

Lynch's comedy of human character in *Wild at Heart* returns often to just this insight—the basic absurdity of a human person acting like a person, and not the stupid thing it really is. So much of what strikes us as humorous in Sailor and Lula's behavior stems from their own abrupt shifts in behavioral speeds, the slow burns and combustible eruptions of their affects and moods, which makes their characters as fundamentally quirky, involuntary, and inhuman as the film's parade of evil eccentrics. Sailor is mercurial, surely, but his modes of characterological discontinuity—his grotesque beating of Bob Ray Lemon, or his speedy turn from violence to tenderness at the Hurricane—are also impossible, belying the normal speeds and rhythms of human bodies and affects. They voice a person as a hollow, thingly bundle of machinic movements and explosions of energy, a picture of the self confirmed in Sailor's fetishistic gestures, defending against while affirming his basic insufficiency. Through his Elvis impersonations and his snakeskin jacket (Nicolas Cage's property but also an afterimage of Brando's own in Sidney Lumet's *The Fugitive Kind*), Sailor confirms his basic secondariness by proclaiming his uniqueness—loudly, stylishly, and repeatedly. Another form of living death, the jacket makes Sailor a walking cliché and inserts him into a comic temporality of repetition.

This comic work is most direct in the film's cruel black humor, perhaps the single most aesthetically influential aspect of *Wild at Heart*, and one with a decisive impact on the stylized violence of American independent filmmakers of the 1990s, especially Quentin Tarantino, the Coen brothers, and Jim Jarmusch. *Wild at Heart*'s grisly botched hold-up sequence with Bobby Peru and Sailor is emblematic of this mode. Is Lynch sick? It is not just that we see Bobby accidently blow his head off, or that we hear Sailor's dumb comment on the gross spectacle ("Oh, for Christ sakes!"). It is that Lynch sets the death fully in the key of an absurd, extended slapstick gag by cutting to the interior of the feed store, whose two employees writhe on the floor in their own blood. One man has lost his hand in the shootout and searches for it as the two scramble together on the floor; the other assures him that "they sew them things back on. Works good as new!" "Gotta be here somewhere," quips the handless man, and we cut outside again for the punch line: a dog leaving, severed hand in mouth, around the corner of the store. Toto, we're not in Kansas anymore.

Lynch's violence here is objectionable for many viewers because the human body is reduced to a plastic, unreal prop in a crude joke and a cheap thrill. Shock, so the argument goes, is part of Lynch's cold, cynical manipulation of spectatorial affect. Death, for Lynch, is unreal, the body an inorganic assemblage, affect impossible—like the laughable cry for lipstick by Fenn's traumatized accident victim, or the feed store employee's unbelievable praise for surgical magic. But the hold-up gag's inescapable ironic distance, its framing as spectacle, is also essential to the operation of black humor (*l'humour noir*)—a modern aesthetic sensibility first codified in 1941 by the French surrealist André Breton. The "mortal enemy of sentimentality," black humor, for Breton, turns the traumas and contingencies of the material world into sources of subversive enjoyment.

Similarly, Lynchian black humor depends upon a kind of ironic self-mockery of human propriety. It acknowledges the human's carnal absurdity or impotence, our inability to simultaneously *be* bodies— animal-like, unthinking—and *have* them, as reflective beings.[72] Lynchian absurdity encourages us to laugh at the way comic inauthenticity, rooted in the flesh, that spells the end of Bobby Peru, is the same fate as the handless feed store clerk, and ultimately the same as Lula and Sailor. Poor bastards, all. Lynch's black humor is thus fully in keeping with *Wild at Heart*'s picture of human personality and feeling as stupid and in time; it is most human not in pure air but in mortal forms of temporal indecision and uncertainty. This is anxious airspace, *Wild at Heart*'s dominant affective key.

Anxiety like this only becomes more apparent the more strongly it is wished away or disavowed by fetishes and other airy gestures. The film's comic conclusion, its final happy joinder to one of Lynch's major changes to Gifford's book, casts this wish, and this fetish, under the sign—and "power"—of Elvis, one of the late twentieth century's greatest undead objects. The ending has often been described as phantasmatic, explicitly screened through the gaze of Pace Fortune, a Lynchian innocent and thus another version of a nostalgic banishment of Oedipal distress. But Lynch has been careful to show Pace's gaze as vulnerable to the same road-bound trauma as Lula and Sailor. His cuteness, like Sailor's and Lula's, like the film's, is a form of vulnerable happiness built on anxiety and powerlessness. Driving to meet Sailor, Lula and her son come across *yet another* car accident, *yet another* head-wound victim. The gag casts the final comic union—and Sailor's Elvis impersonation—as itself compensatory, a repetition that manages the unending, absurd trauma of mortal contingency.

The "Love Me Tender" performance is the film's final, romantic wish for its couple to be sonically at home in the world's chaos, and it comes, fittingly, in the utopian wish of the musical: supra-diegetic orchestration. Sailor, through Nicolas Cage's own voice, is channeling "the power E had," but, as in his first Elvis impersonation at the Hurricane, the power is discontinuous, coming too quickly and too forcefully. We'll know that Sailor *really* loves Lula when he sings "Love Me Tender" to her just as we'll know that Lula *really* has been undone by passion when she says "fuck me" to Bobby Peru. Both lyric performances underscore affect as the stuff of volatile transmission across channeling vessels. The wild world falls away as the film's radio dial turns up the volume on Elvis, but this power is the façade of a more basic powerlessness. With Sailor's absurd, broken nose, Lynch asks us to remember that Sailor, like all of

Wild at Heart's vessels, is a comically damaged container. His last lyric is as cute as it is anxious.

Melodrama's Crypt: *Twin Peaks: Fire Walk with Me*

Consider two Lynchian long takes. The first is from *Twin Peaks* (episode 15), shot in the Palmer family living room. A slow pan, which begins from a painting of a Montana mountain scene, crosses the mantel, cluttered with kitsch and photographs of the dead Laura, to reveal the wounded Palmer family—Leland (Ray Wise), Sarah (Grace Zabriskie), and cousin Maddy (Sheryl Lee). Reconstituted in a hysterical semblance of normalcy, the family seems barricaded by a surfeit of objects extending toward the conspicuously empty couch in the foreground of the shot. In the fashion of postwar melodrama, the anxious mise-en-scène announces the failure of domestic happiness: Laura's absence. Maddy will shortly announce to her aunt and uncle her own departure. She has decided to return home to Missoula; she misses "having a life of [her] own," a line that acknowledges her prosthetic function for the grieving Palmers, who are rattled by the imminent loss of another girl. The camera movement, which has paused during Maddy's announcement, resumes behind, and then around, the corner of a monstrous wooden record player spinning Louis Armstrong's "What a Wonderful World" (fig. 12). Armstrong's famously compensatory song—an impossible wish

Figure 12. The medial life of the Palmer family

to be outside the violent realities of race in 1968 America—is finally sourced with brutal irony: sound finds its home in a domestic tableau that replays the lost, happy home compulsively. Before this episode is over, Leland, possessed by the demonic entity BOB, will murder Maddy in the presence of this same record player.

The second take is Lynch's contribution to *Lumière and Company* (1995), an omnibus film made to commemorate the centennial of the invention of cinema and comprised of a series of one-minute films, made by a roster of forty international auteurs with the original Lumière cameras. All films were shot with the following restrictions: only three takes allowed, only natural light, no synched sound, no stopping of the cameras. Lynch's film, "Premonition Following an Evil Deed," consists of six scenes, presented in a nonchronological temporal loop. Three police officers discover a female body on the ground in an open field; the screen is doused in black. A mother, from inside her living room, looks anxiously to frame right; the screen goes dark. A beautiful woman is drawn away from a couch, where she has been lying with another girl, and approaches the camera; the image is engulfed in a flash of white light and smoke. As the smoke clears, the camera pans along a series of men with bulbous, alien faces. The men surround a naked woman enclosed in a tank filled with water and administer shocks to her with metal poles. The pan ends in front of a paper screen, which explodes in flames that part like curtains to reveal the same bourgeois living room. The woman and her husband, now visible next to her, rise from their seats as a police officer enters and removes his hat. End of film.

The rebus of suggestive situations, which begins in death and the mysteries of absence, reduces melodrama to its gestural essence. The structure of melodramatic repetition is built into the elliptical editing, which cycles back to the living room, ready for more bad news. But it is also played out on the audio track that begins in a machinic clanking and is later mixed with the redundant scratching of a needle on a record player that has run out of grooves and is picking up nothing but noise.

These shots suggest that Lynchian melodrama is not just a durable emotional template but also a seemingly undying one, with its surfeit of bad homes and girls in trouble and its penchant for a grandiosity of gesture and passion. However much Lynch estranges or ironizes melodrama, particularly the family melodrama of the postwar bourgeois home, he remains devoted to it as a basic category of modern experience. Domestic experience, these shots remind us, is famously warped and fissured, shot through with contingency and replayed in various modes of medial reanimation in Lynch's work. Melodramatic tableaux are disturbed by unnatural changes in speed, time, and movement, and by uncanny transfers between forms of media. This is not a refusal of melodramatic form but rather an extrapolation of its fundamental excesses, which beggar, by exaggerating, the stable spatiotemporal texture of the real. Melodramatic experience, as Thomas Elsaesser once put it, is fundamentally nonpsychological, its dramatis personae figure "less as autonomous individuals than to transmit the action and link the various locales within a total constellation."[73] Melodramatic characters, too, are radio-active: not plausible, psychologically motivated individuals so much as receivers and transmitters in a mediated network of affect and action. The melodramatic environment is tailor-made to host the kinds of affective transmissions that pulse through, and de-realize, the character vessels of Lynch's films.

Laura Palmer—passive, suffering, already victimized—is one kind of a melodramatic myth, and *Twin Peaks,* both the series and the fictional town, is Lynch's most enduring melodramatic network, a famously quirky environment of character. The television series, created by Lynch and Mark Frost, openly declared its melodramatic heart. The plots of its first, eight-episode season unfolded in front of televisions *within* the diegesis playing the mawkish soap opera *Invitation to Love,* whose conventions were doubled, ironized, and reworked in *Twin Peaks'* unfolding mysteries. In fact, the series' oft-remarked references to films like Otto Preminger's *Laura* or Hitchcock's *Vertigo* are perhaps less interesting as forms of postmodern pastiche than as canny acknowledgments of *Twin Peaks'* melodramatic common denominator—a mode crossing genre and media and linking televised soaps, the postwar film noir, the police procedural, the suspense thriller, and the family melodrama.

If the mid-century psychologizing of modernist interior design is, for Lynch, one of the more anxious environments of cold war plastics, the postwar family melodrama of Douglas Sirk, Vincente Minnelli, Elia Kazan, and Nicholas Ray, is another. Like mid-century architecture, melodramatic affect is warmed up through the postwar mainstreaming of Freudian models of the psyche—only now these models find expression through the plastic dynamism of mise-en-scène that codes, in grand style, the forms of condensation and displacement that are the basic operations of Freudian dreamwork. Lynch's *Fire Walk with Me* is a similar machine of affective redistribution—it re-constellates, by estranging, the emotional energies of the iconic American middle-class family.

As a matter of form, this estrangement is basically modernist. Here, it is worth recalling that the critical recuperation of the once-debased category of melodrama in academic film studies in the 1960s and 1970s happened chiefly by asserting its "modernism"—specifically, a Brechtian anti-illusionism, which then held a new prestige for neo-Marxist critics. Thus could melodramatic excess, through the name of Douglas Sirk, be cast as a kind of modernist irony and films like *Written on the Wind* (1956), *All That Heaven Allows* (1955), or *Imitation of Life* (1959) championed for their deployment of a "boomerang image"—their aggressive staging of bourgeois fantasies that double back on the audience, revealing the social contradictions masked by fantasy and the costs of middle-class wish fulfillment.[74] As modernist melodrama, *Fire Walk with Me* has undeniably ironic dimensions, but it also depends on melodrama's long-standing capacity to respond—through affect—to larger crises in social value, signification, and significance. Emerging as a modern, bourgeois response to the post-Enlightenment loss of the sacred, melodrama ministered to this disturbing absence of traditional systems of ethics and truth. It did so through what Peter Brooks has called "the moral occult," a "domain of operative spiritual values which is both indicated within and masked by the surface of reality."[75] Melodramatic calls for moral certitude, its Manichean polarities, and its demands for a transparency of character and affect, are thus ways of ministering anxiously to a vexing uncertainty. The specificity of melodrama, then, would lie in the sincerity of a desire to "force into an aesthetic presence, desires for identity, value, and fullness of signification beyond the powers of language to signify."[76]

Lynch takes melodrama's compensatory dynamic between negativity and presence, absence of value and emotional extremity, as *Fire Walk with Me*'s abiding problematic and basic affective engine. The modernism of his melodrama lies not in its Brechtian irony but in its affective ambiguity—the way the wish for melodramatic certitude is displayed only to be undercut by the withdrawing of emotions from the scene of direct, unmediated representation, or by enfolding them thickly into medial networks. The animating temporality of *Fire Walk with Me* is melodramatic—founded on a desire to return to a prior state of innocence before loss and the tearful realization of being always "too late." This mournful temporal structure is written into Lynch's concept for the film as a cinematic prequel. Having just signed a four-film contract with the French production company Ciby 2000, one that offered him artistic freedom in exchange for reduced budgets, Lynch proposed a *Twin Peaks* film set during the final days before Laura's murder, catering to the curiosity of *Twin Peak*'s rabid fans who had, to recall another *Laura*, fallen in love with a corpse. As Chion has observed, there was something "generous" about Lynch's desire in *Fire Walk with Me* to move Laura from fantasy to flesh, this wish to say "this character existed and suffered—take an interest in this woman."[77] Lynch has described the film as an exercise in necromancy, a raising of the dead: "At the end of the series, I felt kind of sad. I couldn't get myself to leave the world of *Twin Peaks*. I was in love with the character of Laura Palmer and her contradictions, radiant on the surface, dying inside. I wanted to see her live, move, and talk."[78]

By this time, of course, *Twin Peaks*, cross-marking sensation, was itself a post-secular, multimedia myth, and Laura had already undergone various forms of reanimation. The smash success of the first season had spawned a series of media artifacts and spin-offs, including *The Secret Diary of Laura Palmer* (1990), written by Lynch's daughter, Jennifer; *The Autobiography of Special Agent Dale Cooper: My Life, My Tapes* (1990), written by cocreator Frost; *Twin Peaks: An Access Guide to the Town* (1991), a compendium of character bios, town maps, and cherry pie recipes penned by Lynch, Frost, and Richard Saul Wurman; an audiocassette compilation of Cooper's tapes to his unseen secretary, Diane; and a series of soundtrack albums seeking to launch the career of Julee Cruise. A few weeks after the debut of the series, vigilant fans created the online discussion group alt.tv.twinpeaks, whose obsessive desire to crack the codes of the increasingly baroque series has since become a case study in media ethnography and the modes of "collective intelligence" of early convergence culture.[79] In the relatively early days of the VCR, *Twin Peaks* had become the most-videotaped show on network television, with 830,000 recordings per week. In seeking to reverse time, to return to the life and suffering of Laura Palmer before her virtual lives in the pervasive *Twin Peaks* media network, Lynch is already too late. And this mournful film acknowledges the emptiness at the heart of this quest for reanimation, which fuels the melodramatic emotional extremity of the film and makes it so powerful and so sad.

Fire Walk with Me's opening credits are set against a melancholic background of blue, white, and black shapes that play slowly across the screen. Flowing abstraction will turn out to be flickering static—television's way, in the absence of the specific information provided by a signal, of being electrically present and semiotically absent at once. As the credits end, Lynch pulls back to reveal the screen of a television set in a darkened room. Abruptly, the set is smashed with an axe. We hear a woman's scream, and the screen is plunged into blackness. The play between abstraction, static, and signal is at the heart of the film's exploration of melodramatic affect, always receding from transparency to the condition of mediated noise. *Fire Walk with Me* thus announces the gambit of its thirty-minute "Prologue": minimize explanations, maximize ambiguity, and estrange *Twin Peaks* from itself, a forest of baffling signs and densely encoded gestures.

Lynch cuts from the darkened room to a long shot of a body, wrapped in plastic, floating down a river edged by pines. A conspicuous caption at the bottom of the frame identifies the body, "Teresa Banks"—in other words, not "Laura Palmer," who famously washed up in a similar shroud in the pilot episode of the series. The audience has been promised a homecoming to Twin Peaks and to Laura, its homecoming queen. But evidently we are not there quite yet, a point Lynch makes repeatedly in the prologue. Emblems of the iconographic series have been made visible but are slightly deformed by iteration. Lynch now cuts to a medium close of FBI chief Gordon Cole (David Lynch) in profile, against the background of a lake whose shoreline runs horizontally through a densely packed forest, much like that surrounding Banks's floating bier. The graphic match domesticates "the natural" scene as wallpaper, folding the piney familiarity of Twin Peaks into Cole's Philadelphia office but defamiliarizing it as bureaucratic kitsch. With the characteristic earpiece of the nearly deaf Cole dangling from his right ear, Cole/Lynch summons a new character, Agent Chet Desmond, before turning to present himself directly to the camera—one object of interior design among others in an iconic Lynchian tableau. The static camera holds for an extra beat, and we hear a familiar sound mix on the audio track: thunder, Badalamenti's jazzy ride cymbal, and a low menacing hum that bridges the cut to the next shot.

It is another sign, iconic and ostensive. It begs reading yet remains inscrutable: a canary-yellow school bus, stilled inexplicably in an expanse of grassy meadow and surrounded by "Fibbies" in beige trench coats. One lawman has his pistol drawn, presumably pointed at the bus driver, who is being frisked by another agent against the side of the vehicle and under the windows of panicked children. We hear the children's screams and the click of the handcuffs that Special Agent Desmond (Chris Isaak) clamps on a pair of teenage girls outside the rear of the bus. We see a sign on back of the bus that reads "School Bus," in that tautological way of school buses, and another sign on the emergency exit below it: "Unlawful to Pass When Red Lights Flash." We cut to a shot of Desmond's unmarked car, a red light flashing on top, as the phone inside rings. It's Cole.

With the call, Lynch begins another installment of a running sound gag, based on the miscues stemming from Cole's faulty hearing, familiar to fans of the television series. Cole's message to Desmond, which sets into motion the prologue's investigation plot, is quickly re-encrypted, bent back from a signal toward the film's inaugural static, as Cole promises a surprise at the Portland airport. Before he does, though, the camera returns us to the side of the school bus, where the distraught children, screaming and banging at the closed windows, watch their driver get patted down at gunpoint. More noise. We never learn anything more about the school bus, the terrified children, or the arrest of the two young girls. Instead, the gag anticipates the entropic semiotic drift of the prologue as a whole, its proliferation of teasing signs.

Gordon's "surprise" is Lil (Kimberly Ann Cole), whom Desmond is introduced to in the next sequence at the airport, where he meets Cole and Agent Sam Stanley (Kiefer Sutherland). Lynch delivers his introduction of Stanley to Desmond in a near rhyme, folksy and false. We cut to a surprising, inexplicable shot of a woman in a bright red dress, with matching wig and high heels, standing next to the propeller of a canary-yellow airplane (fig. 13). "Her name is Lil," Cole explains, and Lil runs toward the agents, stops, and makes a curious grimace. A light

Figure 13.
Lil's gestures as acts
of encryption

blue fake rose is pinned to her dress. Holding the exaggerated squint, she opens and closes her left hand and twirls around as Cole explains, "She's my mother's sister's girl," raising his right arm so that his hand blocks his face. Chet murmurs, "Federal," Cole nods, and Lil twirls and flashes her hand gesture again. Cole wishes the agents good luck together, telling Sam that Chet "has his own M.O." Then he elaborates: "Modus Operandi." Cole explains to Stanley what is unnecessary, readily understood, but leaves encoded the scene's sequence of bizarre gestures. "Modus Operandi," "School Bus," the caption "Teresa Banks"—all announce semiotic certainty in much more ambiguous environments.

The gestures are all the more curious for the way Lynch's mise-en-scène reassembles the audiovisual texture of Agent Desmond's introduction. The yellow plane and Lil's red dress pick up the colors of the school bus and the flashing red light on Agent Desmond's car. Lil could also be said to spin in place rather like this light, her hand gestures flashing signals legible only to the agents. Or like Cole's unexplained handwork, these could be audiovisual puns, different versions of giving the "glad hand," as Desmond is instructed to greet Sam. The point is not to stabilize a reading of these gestures, though Desmond will shortly attempt to do just that, but to notice how Lil allows Lynch to set Laura's story in the register of melodrama. In pantomime, melodrama seeks to bypass the ambiguities, insufficiencies, and misprisions of being in language altogether for truths spoken by corporeal gesture. The moral order of the melodramatic universe hinges on the emotional legibility of personality, coded transparently in gesture and revealed to its readers/spectators.

In the cinematic melodrama of Lynch's childhood, mise-en-scène *itself* becomes gestural, objects and decor over-coded with emotional resonance. Indeed, the domestic melodramas of the 1940s and 1950s replayed in *Twin Peaks* (the series and the film) are, Thomas Elsaesser explains, perhaps the most "highly elaborated and complex mode of cinematic signification that the American cinema has ever produced . . . because everything, as Douglas Sirk said, happens 'inside.'"[80] In this sense, the Lil episode is a kind of object lesson in the workings of Lynch's melodramatic imagination. In her "surprise," for Desmond and for us, the general hysteria of the prologue is sublimated into vivid color and mute gesture, and the film's world, with Laura as its enigmatic center, is established as a vexing code to be cracked. Lynch's strategy, and it is a basically modernist one, is to refuse melodramatic transparency, to withdraw affect from forms of unmediated representation and legibility, to confuse signs of emotional and moral clarity.

Instability is produced through the narrative device of the fold—the way the prologue proceeds by folding inside its own mediated network of significance and progressively deforming and re-encrypting it. Opening with static and the smashed television, the prologue—as critics have long noted—everywhere distorts the familiar iconography of the *Twin Peaks* series by positioning its singular icons against a series of types they both resemble and differ from: Banks as not Laura, Agent Desmond as not Agent Cooper, Haps Diner as not the Double R, Sheriff Cable as not Sheriff Truman, Carl Rodd's rank cup of "good morning America" as not the ever–"damn fine coffee" of Cooper's connoisseurship, and so forth. As the prologue ends and Agent Cooper arrives to proclaim his bafflement at Cole's own disappearance, *Twin Peaks'* famous credit sequence begins— remediated as film. The effect is uncanny, an uncanniness that requires the prior existence of the famously rabid fan culture of *Twin Peaks*, whose expectations, hopes, and fantasies have, from the beginning, deformed the inner aesthetic patterns of *Fire Walk with Me* because those patterns have been so clearly fashioned with this media community in mind. This is true of all prequels, but in *Twin Peaks* the fact of the always already botched homecoming—the inner only as an effect of a prior medial circuit through the outer—is especially important for its temporal quest to reanimate

Laura Palmer, and pangs of loss are felt when the basic nostalgia behind this melodramatic return to origins fails.

The film's emotional energy is basically melodramatic, centripetal, and finally entropic, but in a way that is acutely attuned to its own mediated encryption. Lynch seems attracted to melodrama as a complex ecosystem of emotional kinetics—a container or assemblage of affective energies and forces subject to the pressures, often oppressive, of a menacing outside. What is perhaps most original about the melodramatic imagination of *Twin Peaks* is its warping or rewiring of this relationship between environment and character, by opening its closed world to more bewildering circuits. In the process, affect, rather than individualizing suffering, withdraws from the space of unmediated representation.

The wiring of the film's environment is especially complicated in the Philadelphia FBI offices. There, the iconic Cooper shortly finds himself radically displaced in time and space by the office's surveillance cameras, and he witnesses the baffling return of long-lost FBI agent Philip Jeffries (David Bowie), disgorged from an elevator like a man who fell to earth. In a famously disorienting gag—one that Lynch will later rework in *Lost Highway*'s impossible surveillance tapes and the self-observing circuits of *Inland Empire*'s Lost Girls—Cooper tests and retests the technological limits of the FBI hallway surveillance camera, and Lynch prepares us for the office space's folding into a much stranger environment. We see Cooper in the hallway, looking up at the surveillance camera, and we see Jeffries emerge quickly behind him in the hallway. But when Cooper ducks into the surveillance room to observe the hall, he sees not emptiness, but the uncanny image of himself, with Jeffries approaching behind him, that we ourselves have just seen. The "live" surveillance feed has been looped, or warped, and time-space begins to bend as Cooper's past finds itself somehow folded into or reanimated within an impossible present. As a somewhat delirious Jeffries begins to talk, his image dissolves into the televisual static, overlapping with a small figure in red, donning a phallic papier-mâché mask. As we cut in and out of static, the time-space of the FBI office and the sounds of Jeffries's confused narrative are intercut with the otherworldly room above the convenience store. One of the words emitted from the grotesque depths of some televised mouth is, unsurprisingly, "Electricity," since we are in the midst of a Lynchian electrical storm, an environment of intersecting worlds whose circuits are impossibly wired in a network of telephone lines and high-pitched vibrations into which Jeffries simply vanishes. The FBI office, Deer Meadow, the space above the convenience store, the Red Room—all are somehow mysteriously linked together in this mediated environment of surveillance cameras, phone lines, and static-filled television sets.

What does Lynch's electrical environment mean for melodramatic affect? There is no single home for feeling—no domestic green world, no bulwark against the cruelty and menace of the melodramatic environment. Rather, there are too many opportunities for the outside to become an inside, in the fashion of a fold. Everything is "gothicizable." This doesn't defuse the melodramatic imagination so much as spark it into motion. The more insides fail, and the more sentiment is displaced from home into that broader, impossible circuit of plastic insides that seem to constitute "media" for Lynch, the more fervently *Fire Walk with Me* longs for home. The melodramatic desire for a transparency of feeling and morality—as revealed in a tableau or a hyper-legible gesture—yields to forms of explicitly pictorial confusion. Sentimentality becomes obscene, invisible; all we *can* see is loss.

These dynamics are especially evident in *Fire Walk with Me*'s approach to Laura and to the character of her suffering and psychological distress. The prequel concept would explain her suffering through the visible—to "see her live, move, and talk." But Lynch consistently frustrates the melodramatic convention that feminine virtue demands visibility, ocular proof of personality's truth. Instead we get a teasing variety of hyper-visible scenes of suffering and passion that explain little about Laura. She is for the film's spectators what Lil is for the agents—overburdened with meaning and yet, as Todd McGowan puts it, "a void rather than a coherent personality."[81]

The early sequences with Laura bend the generic inconstancy of feeling into a more radical remotion of affect in time and space. During a sexual rendezvous with her boyfriend James (James Marshall), shot mostly in tight close-up, Laura mocks James's cloying sentimentality. She just asks for a kiss and tells James to "quit trying to hold on so tight. I'm gone, long gone, like a turkey in the corn." Like *Lost Highway*'s Alice, Laura is a fantasy object, never to be had. Feelings of loss are quickly bent toward absurdity when sweet James, ever sincere but not the brightest bulb, mutters, "You're not a turkey. A turkey's one of the dumbest birds on earth." The line is banal, corny, and threatens to deflate the scene. But bathos blurs indiscernibly into pathos as Laura, still in tight close-up, looks up and, with lip quavering and eyes brimming with tears, responds: "Gobble . . . Gobble, gobble." Is this a dumb scene? Absolutely. It is dumb in the way Laura's "gobble, gobble" marks an incapacity in language—the speechless suffering often associated with animals and melodramatic gestures. It is as dumb as a doornail, or a pane of glass, those kinds of stubborn materiality with which Laura is often associated in her resistance to interpretive acts or intimacy. And it is dumb in its tendency toward senselessness or failures of understanding even of what is closest to us.

The connection between Laura's affective inscrutability and her spatial indeterminacy is confirmed in a later scene in the Palmers' living room, where Lynch's extreme high-angle shot removes Laura's feelings from us by making her a hyper-visible abstraction, as curiously remote from this as she was previously in tight close-up. Laura and Donna each lie on a separate couch, their faces lifted up to the ceiling, their gazes dreamily elsewhere. The tableau of teenage sentimentality begins innocently enough: two girls arguing about which boy Laura should see, James or Bobby. But Laura parodies Donna's mawkishness by repeating, and hollowing out, her ways of praising him. As the girls are pinned to the living room couches by the camera, Donna, in her saccharine reverie, floats the question: "Do you think that if you were falling in space, you would slow down for a while, or go faster and faster?" Laura's reply links feeling to falling, affect to speed, time, and movement in space: "Faster and faster. For a long time you wouldn't feel anything. Then you'd burst into fire forever." The incredible entropy of this fall—its irrevocable movement toward dissipation—exaggerates the standard melodramatic material of the "fallen woman" seduction plots. But in *Fire Walk with Me* there can be no hope of sympathetic redress or divine intercession, because the fall has already ended in death. Laura senses the post-sacral bind precisely: "And the angels couldn't help you, because they've all gone away."

Yes, and no. There *are* angels in this film, a minor network of them that presides over Laura's dawning realization of the identity of her father/BOB as her seducer and victimizer. But they tend to emerge and recede from the same confusing matrix of emotional mediation that obscures access to Laura's suffering. The Tremonds/Chalfonts are kinds of angels. The duo of elderly grandmother and blond grandson were introduced in *Twin Peaks* as clients of the Meals on Wheels program for which Laura volunteers. Recipients of Laura's generosity, they appear in the prequel outside of the Double R, where, intercut with static, they present Laura with a framed picture of an open door that becomes a visual threshold for Laura's awareness of her father's actions. The picture returns that night, now assuming architectural and subjective properties that would stabilize—but actually derail—this domestic melodrama, whose latent hysteria has begun to crack the surface. Recalling the manic mood swings of James Mason's mad patriarch in Nicholas Ray's *Bigger Than Life* (1956), Leland veers between patriarchal tyranny, erotic jealousy, and paternal love during a painfully uncomfortable family meal. His outburst leaves Laura sobbing in her room. She raises her eyes to a picture of a winged angel feeding several cherubic children at the dinner table. Reminded of the Tremonds' gift, she has—it seems—hung it on the wall next to the kitschy cherubs and goes to sleep. Now, though, the picture, having assumed its place on Laura's wall as an emotionally freighted object of domestic melodrama, is gothicized as Lynch cuts from a close-up of the picture to a shot of its represented content, the darkened hallway and the opened door. There, Mrs. Chalmont beckons Laura and the camera through the door and into a room where her grandson snaps his fingers, and we dissolve to the Red Room.

In it, the Man From Another Place reveals himself to Agent Cooper as the source of the vibrating sound coursing through the telephone wires and displays Teresa Banks's missing ring. Cooper, looking directly at the camera, warns Laura not to take the ring. Laura wakes up to find a dead girl in bed next to her, who offers her own warning. The uncanny appearance of the speaking corpse is reminiscent of Buñuel's animated Oedipal ghosts in *The Discreet Charm of the Bourgeoisie* (1972), as is the sequence's nested-dream structure. For Laura isn't yet fully awake, and the pictorial confusion hasn't stopped. As Laura rises and opens the door to her room, she looks back at the picture on the wall and sees not an empty threshold but the impossible view of the back of her own head, her body blocking the door. Observing herself observing herself, Laura's melodramatic distress has been folded in the same mediated network of surveillance that had earlier looped back on Agent Cooper's gaze. The picture is less a key to the truth of Laura's pathos than a prop for epistemological uncertainty and cognitive befuddlement that follow a spatial path: from melodrama's hysterical interior, to the repressions of the gothic hallway, to the ontological zigzags of Lynch's Red Room. If the gothic epistemology of the depths is one version of the melodramatic moral occult—the post-sacred substitute of "realm of inner imperatives and demons" for the wholly other—another is the Red Room, inscrutable home of all the post-sacral passions of the Lynchian cosmos.

Leland/BOB will be summoned to the Red Room after murdering Laura and Ronette Pulaski (Phoebe Augustine) in the abandoned train car. The murder sequence, like the cabin-in-the-woods orgy that precedes it, bends melodramatic pathos to its extremes in a kind of sadomasochistic ceremony, a frenzied ritual of hyper-visibility. In the train car, Leland will place a mirror on the floor in which Laura will be made witness to her own anguish. And Lynch's camera itself will stand in for this mirror several times, shooting Laura's terrified face from an extreme low angle (fig. 14). Ronette, her hands bound, her lipstick smeared, begs for salvation in a way that joins vision to a call for melodramatic moral legibility: "Look at me," she begs, before being visited by an angel and then promptly bludgeoned by Leland, "I'm so dirty."

Figure 14. The boomerang image: being witness to melodramatic sadism

This, too, is a kind of boomerang image, doubling back on the problem of the spectator's pleasure in these scenes of suffering. Lynch's parallel editing between the endangered Laura and Ronette, trapped in the train car by Leland, and the arrival of MIKE (like BOB, his former partner in murder, an inhabiting and now-repentant spirit), who has earlier attempted to warn Laura about her father, is quintessentially melodramatic—at once speeding up the action and prolonging the ceremony of killing. Lynch has a pornographer's way of dilating the time of sexual spectacle. A similar expansion of time takes place during the murderous violence itself, as Leland's blows and Laura's bloodied mouth are intercut with a black screen. Because we know how this story will end, we are, like MIKE, too late. Time is expanded and Laura reanimated, but the pleasure in witnessing the reanimation depends on a primary loss, on our always knowing that Laura will die. The killing of Laura Palmer is an exercise in mourning and memorialization, and Lynch scores Leland's violence to Luigi Cherubini's operatic "Requiem in C-Minor." But it is also a work of secular mythmaking, for the murder animates a series of images that spawned the mythic universe of *Twin Peaks* itself: a close-up of Laura's broken-heart necklace, held by Leland; a shot of Leland wrapping Laura (and the camera) in plastic; a shot of Laura's wrapped body being placed in the water.

Is *Fire Walk with Me*'s critique of the latent madness in patriarchal authority blunted by its recourse to the fantastic—the possession of Leland by the demon BOB and the forces of the mysterious Black Lodge, the submission of both to the power of the Man From Another Place? Lynch's mise-en-scène itself blurs the natural and the supernatural, as the river into which Leland has dumped Laura's body is suffused with an unmistakable, velvety redness, and a spotlight finds Leland in the woods. We dissolve to the Red Room, where the Man From Another Place and MIKE demand from Leland/BOB their "garmenbozia," now retranslated by the subtitles into melodramatic terms: "pain and sorrow." In pantomime, BOB makes a broad gesture as if to render the pain from Leland's levitating body and then throws blood on the black-and-white pattern of the zigzagged floor. With the pain and sorrow magically extracted from Leland's body, Lynch prepares the way for Laura and Agent Cooper's final union in the Red Room, where they encounter another hovering angel. In the Red Room the experience of pain is reduced to sensory fragments: we hear of pain, and we see its bodily effects, which give way to Laura's final tears, observed by Cooper and other, more traditional angels. On the face of it, this is textbook catharsis. But what moral order do these too-visible emotions suggest?

Lynchian melodrama depends upon the wish for a better, more satisfying order outside of culture and the absence of that order that spawns the anxious wish for satisfaction in the first place. This, as Steve Neale once pointed out, is part of the paradoxical pleasure in melodramatic tears—the way they mark the loss or non-attainment of a desired object and call for that loss's reparation "in terms which imply that such a demand can be answered, that such reparation be possible."[52] In this sense, the Red Room is melodrama's crypt, preserving eternally our pleasure in the fantasy structure of wishing. The Red Room is both theatrically visible and maddeningly opaque, morphing with every subject that enters it. It is a space of exaggerated gestures that invite and refuse meaning. It is the melodramatic environment's transcendent outside and the inner motherboard for its impossible circuits. Lynch's technique for handling affect is a similar machine of melodramatic translation and re-encryption, oscillating between code and excess, signal and static. In close-up, Laura, crying and smiling through her tears, nods in acknowledgment of an unknown secret. And Lynch encrypts it for eternity in the film's final freeze-frame. As the occult epicenter of Lynchian melodrama, the Red Room operates by its basic law of diminishing returns: the more ostensively emotions give themselves to visibility and audition, the less legible they become.

Moving Impersonality: *Mulholland Dr.*

Cinema is dead. Long live cinema. Sparked by the centenary of the medium's invention, the late 1990s witnessed a series of impassioned critical elegies for the experience of cinema as—in Susan Sontag's terms, "quintessentially modern; distinctively accessible; poetic and mysterious and erotic and moral—all at the same time."[53] For Sontag and others, "this idea of film as, first of all, a poetic object" was variously imperiled by the rise of digital technologies and their challenge to cinema's photographic ontology; by the phenomenological impoverishment of the small screen; and by the broader eclipse of a particular kind of cinephilic film culture associated with the modernism of postwar art cinema—of

Godard, say, or Bergman.[84] Such films, for Sontag, heroically navigated the divide between art and industry, and did so by catering to spectators willing to have their sensoria stretched. And in 1996 such films, and such filmgoers, appeared fated for extinction. Others, more sanguine than Sontag, insisted that cinema had not so much undergone a medial death (since cinema was never any *one* thing) as another stage of transformation in a *new* new-media environment pervaded by screens of all shapes and sizes and complex global networks for the distribution and exhibition of artistically ambitious commercial cinema.

In the late 1990s Lynch was already participating in cinephilic acts of memory and mourning, most obviously with his contribution to *Lumière and Company* and, more subtly, in his astonishing *Mulholland Dr.* This film was never meant to be a film, and nearly wasn't, but it stands today as, among other things, a paean to the experience of cinema. This is ironic, because during the summer of 1999 *Mulholland Dr.* hovered in medial limbo. Its production status was suspended between a failed television pilot and a remarkable meta-cinematic film waiting to come into being. Just over a decade later, in January 2010, *Film Comment* published the results of an international poll of critics, academics, and programmers that asked them to identify the best films and filmmakers of the decade.[85] *Mulholland Dr.* topped the list. Long live David Lynch.

Mulholland Dr. owes its prestige, in part, to its well-timed exploration of the experience of cinema amid millenarian fears of a moribund medium. Part of *Mulholland Dr.*'s self-consciousness extends to its awareness of its own position in a media environment that—in a romantic fit of love at last sight—had returned to the question "What is cinema?" It takes up this question by reference to its own curious, belated being as cinematic object (since this was not inevitable) and through the idiom of art cinema.

The film's final word, for example, is "*Silencio.*" Uttered by a mysterious blue-haired woman at the Fellini-esque Club Silencio, it is a loaded, ambiguous word. Silence will help Lynch raise the question of cinematic ontology, but speaking "*Silencio*" is also Lynch's way of encoding an allegiance to art cinema, to the films of Bergman and Godard in particular. *Mulholland Dr.*'s references to Bergman's *Persona* (1967), a film admired by Lynch, are quite overt, made through both visual style and theme. The tragic romance at *Mulholland Dr.*'s core shares the thematic links

Sontag once drew between *Persona* and Bergman's previous film *The Silence*: "Both films take up the themes of the scandal of the erotic; the polarities of violence and powerlessness, reason and unreason, language and silence, the intelligible and the unintelligible."[86]

But *Mulholland Dr.*'s ending also echoes the last line of Godard's lush CinemaScope tragedy *Contempt/Le mépris* (1963), like *Persona*, a famously self-reflexive work of art cinema. In *Contempt*, "*Silencio*" is spoken through a megaphone by an unseen Godard, the human voice made metallic, hollow, and unnatural. Ironically, it announces the beginning of the ending of the film-within-the-film, Fritz Lang's vexed adaptation of Homer's *The Odyssey*. But here "*Silencio*" also speaks the death of passion. It follows the bitter end of the marriage between screenwriter Paul (Michel Piccolli) and Camille (Brigitte Bardot). Having left Paul for Prokosch (Jack Palance), Lang's vulgar American producer, Camille is killed in a violent car accident that ironizes Ulysses's classical return to Ithaca and to his wife, Penelope, in the nested film. *Mulholland Dr.*'s final "*Silencio*" caps another romantic tragedy: the failure of a love relation between Diane Selwyn (Naomi Watts) and Camilla Rhodes (Laura Elena Harring); the end of Diane's fantastical reconstruction of herself as Betty Elms, who falls magically in love with the mysterious Rita (also Laura Elena Harring; brought to her by the violent car accident that *begins* Lynch's film); and Diane's suicide. More than knowingness or cuteness, speaking "*Silencio*" is *Mulholland Dr.*'s way of thinking the being of cinema and the being of a person in love as somehow analogous to each other, and of reminding us of bygone films that have explored this analogy.

For Lynch, cinematic and romantic passion are marked by a shared *impersonality*, their doubled, disintegrative ethos. The historical horizon of art cinema is of particular relevance here because of the familiar challenges its modernist textuality poses to the kinds of personalities associated with Hollywood cinema—their psychologies, their affects and motivations, their relationships to the structuring of space and time, their status as erotic spectacles, their "aura," and their reification in stardom. As Susan Sontag once explained in her canonical essay "Bergman's *Persona*," to worry overmuch about what exactly is subjective and objective in films like *Persona* (or *Mulholland Dr.*) is to overlook art cinema's dissenting strategy of filmic presentation, which offers an "abstract body of material, a subject" whose "function may be as much its opacity, its multiplicity, as the ease with which it yields itself to being incarnated in a determinate action or plot."[87] Sontag reminds us that the achievement of films like *Persona*, *Contempt*, and other works of modernist art cinema lies in their ways of courting *impersonality*—the way they use abstraction to resist psychological reduction and instead explore "the abyss of the loss of personality."[88] *Mulholland Dr.* is built over a similar void, exploiting the ambiguities of art cinema, setting into motion its most obviously self-referential categories (time, cinema, spectatorship, authorship) and opting for embodied, technical, and material ways of making and unmaking persons from loss and silence.[89] And it does all of this to link the occluded trauma at its center (the end of Diane and Rita's romance) to the kinds of impersonal affects produced by cinema. More successfully than any of Lynch's films, *Mulholland Dr.* argues that such impersonality *just is* cinema and, further, that this is rather like the feeling of being in love: volatile and insurgent, precarious and affectively unstable. Doubled throughout the film, the impersonal experiences of cinema and of romantic passion are alternatively liberating and tragically self-shattering, and *Mulholland Dr.*'s narrative structure is best understood as oscillating between these alternatives.

Part of *Mulholland Dr.*'s impersonal quality is a structural legacy of its production history as a failed television pilot for ABC. In 1998 Lynch and his production partner Tony Krantz, who packaged *Twin Peaks* for the same network, sold *Mulholland Dr.* to executives eager for an "appointment television" hit to compete with NBC's Thursday night lineup of *Friends* and *E.R.* Lynch had sworn off television after ABC canceled *On the Air*, his absurdist period sitcom about 1950s network TV, but Krantz managed to bring Lynch back around to the medium by reminding him of what he liked most about the series format—its capacity for continuous eventfulness. "Tony knew that I never liked having to bend my movie scripts to end halfway through. On a series you can keep having beginnings and middles, and develop a story forever."[90] So Lynch pitched the film's opening car crash sequence and "Rita," its beautiful, amnesiac victim, as an entree into the series' unfolding mysteries. On this basis, ABC put up $4.5 million for a two-hour open pilot, and Disney's Touchstone contributed an additional $2.5 million, with the proviso that Lynch had to shoot extra footage as a "closed ending" that would allow *Mulholland Dr.* to be released as a film in Europe.

Lynch produced the pilot script quickly. ABC's executives loved the pitch, but when they saw Lynch's 125-minute rough cut, their ardor had cooled. The closed ending, which includes material from the finished Club Silencio sequence, was not "closed" at all, but inscrutable and eso-teric. Watts and Harring, Lynch's lead actresses, cast on the basis of head shots, seemed "too old." There was too much smoking. The close-up of dog shit in the interior courtyard of the Havenhurst apartments was excessive. There were too many Lynchian eccentrics—minor characters who appeared only once. And, most distressingly, the pacing was too slow. ABC made a lengthy series of recommendations for shrinking the film to 88 minutes, and Lynch grudgingly made the cuts. Eventually, ABC shelved Lynch's pilot, giving its Thursday night slot to Kevin Wil-liamson's short-lived drama *Wasteland*. In 2001 the *Mulholland Dr.* pilot was bought from ABC by Alain Sarde (producer of *The Straight Story*) for Le Studio Canal Plus, the film subsidiary of the French subscription channel, which has funded a number of American independent films. Sarde's additional funds (somewhere between $2 million and $7 million) paid for seventeen extra days of shooting and allowed Lynch to complete the film in its released length: 147 minutes.

Before it is anything else, the finished *Mulholland Dr.* is a salvage job that mediates between the "paradigmatic" format common in tele-vision serials—where multiple stories are presented in discontinuous, semi-autonomous narrative seeds—and the syntagmatic linearity of many commercial fiction films, which join character, event, and action in the faux organicism of Hollywood continuity editing.[91] The film's narrative form establishes relations between the budding situations that proliferate in its first, nearly two-hour segment—situations retrospec-tively coded as dimensions of Diane Selwyn's complex fantasy life and her identity as chipper ingénue Betty Elms—and the more despairing linearity of the shorter second section. There, the sad realities of Di-ane's doubled failures—career and love relation—emerge forcefully, tragically, as the closing down of possible futures conjured in the film's many delirious arrivals.

Part of the pleasure in experiencing *Mulholland Dr.* is retrospectively rereading the film's first, long segment once it has been recast as Diane's dream or fantasy following her disappearance from the film shortly af-ter the Club Silencio sequence. Details from the second segment can then retroactively account for the events of the first Betty/Rita section: Adam Kesher's (Justin Theroux) serial humiliations and comic disempowerment, for example, are subjectivized as acts of Diane's jealous wish fulfillment. At the same time, this interpretive process, in which the contours of fantasy materialize recursively through the depressing details of Diane's real life, has trouble accounting for the affective force and germinal, situational thickness of other sequences—the scene in the Winkie's diner, for example. As spectators we notice, or remember, the gap between the affective complexity, richness, and ambiguity of these sequences as they unfold in time and their belated transformation into Diane's psychic property, explained (or not) and amplified (or dampened) by the film's final act. There is a qualitative, phenomenological discrepancy between the retrospective coding of the first section—its conversion into narrative information—and the unfolding experience of it, and this is part of the film's meta-cinematic argument. Diane's fall from fantasy into reality is experienced as a personal tragedy. Or better, she suffers personhood *as* tragedy.

The sad facts about what it means for Diane to be *just herself* are sadder in the light of the liberating impersonality and emotional range of the film's first, pre-personal segment. Diane's refashioning of herself as Betty, and of the end of love for Rita as a series of disorienting arrivals, happens on the edge of melancholy, loss, and psychic cruelty. Its product is not just the intoxicating, transient abdication of personhood for her, but also, for Lynch's spectators, an experience of cinema that moves us by virtue of its impersonality. *Mulholland Dr.* achieves this quality by crafting several overlapping environments in which personality vanishes—an environment of movement, travel, and the shifting time of the deictical utterance; a network of vocal technologies; and the scene of performance. What is lost or mourned as the film falls from these impersonal environments into personhood?

The film's credit sequence features traveling characters and moving vehicles and explores the experience of *emergence*, of people arriving in unfamiliar or unstable locations. Like the opening's jitterbugging couples, who emerge like paper cutouts against a flat purple screen, multiply, and fall away into silhouette, personalities in the film's opening segment tend to move without clear causality or agency, their origins and destinations vague. The smiling, happy person of "Betty Elms" materializes for the first time here, overexposed in her beauty-queen dress and crown, her face superimposed over the dancers, first alone, and then surrounded by an older couple. A person is conjured and disappeared as we dissolve first to a subjective camera, hovering above and then plunging into a magenta pillow, and then to a solitary street sign reading "Mulholland Dr." Subjective camera and street sign are both ways of orienting a spectator's here-ness and now-ness (you are here), but both fail to contextualize fully.

This opening drive establishes this narrative segment's interest in the feeling of anxious arrivals in an uncertain and empty "now." In it, the beautiful and yet-unnamed "Rita" survives a car crash and stumbles, as an alluring amnesiac, into Betty's life, fashioning an identity from the cinematic texture of Aunt Ruth's *Gilda* poster ("There never *was* a woman like Gilda!" the tagline reads). This arrival is anxious because of its abstraction from the specificities of time and place (the drive and the line "What are you doing? We don't stop here!" will later be repeated with Diane in "Rita's" place) and because it enacts the very process of moving into personhood. This is a woman in the process of arriving at "Rita" and into Diane's fantasy life, and as she does so, she will be conspicuously placed by another street sign. It reads "Sunset Boulevard," an obvious homage to Billy Wilder's masterpiece but also an echo of the camera's tilt up to the "Lincoln" street sign in *Blue Velvet* and part of the same texture of cinematic fantasy.

Another conspicuous arrival transpires at a Winkie's diner. In *this* place, for *this-ness* is at stake throughout, one man recounts to another a very bad dream. The sequence announces its location forcefully, first with an establishing shot of the Winkie's sign (an echo of the iconic Denny's logo and further specified by location, "Sunset Boulevard") and then in the dialogue. The dreamer begins, "I wanted to come here." "To Winkie's?" the other man asks. "This Winkie's," the dreamer insists. "I had a dream about this place." The conversation is filmed in shot/reverse-shot but eerily defamiliarized by Peter Deming's use of a special jib arm that allows the camera to float up and down behind the men as the dreamer recounts his dream. In it, both men are in *this* restaurant, and both are scared. The dreamer explains his realization that his fear comes from a mysterious man "in back of this place." "He's the one who is doing it," the dreamer continues. "I can see him through the wall. I can see his face." After the dream is recounted, the men exit the diner to look for the man in back, *who actually appears*, confirming the reality of the dreamer's paranoid dream and causing him to collapse. The uncanniness of the scene comes from its floating camera and the way its editing patterns suggest that as the men prepare to leave the diner, they are restaging precisely the man's dream, and thus perhaps are somehow in it.

All of this transpires through a clever play between the ontological instability of the sequence, its deft editing and framing, and its script's use of deixis: *"I* wanted to come *here"*; *"This* Winkie's"; *"this* place." Filled with these kinds of demonstrative pronouns, the sequence generates its affective power from the content-less quality of deixis. Famously shifty as a mode of signification, deixis points to a here and now that moves depending on context. It is as if the language through which the dreamer recounts his dream opens a space just waiting to be filled out by different people. "You're standing *right over there* by that counter," the dreamer notes, and we get an eyeline match of his gaze toward the cash register, the frame devoid of a person. The shot will then be repeated as the men prepare to leave, but now the frame is full, the man filling out the abstract space of the "you" in the dream. The movement-into-presence of the bum behind Winkie's works by a similar logic: the dream announces the paranoid, abstract position of a man "in back of this place" who is "doing it," a man whose face the dreamer hopes never to see outside of a dream but who will nonetheless spring into being.

As Lynch's camera follows the men behind the diner, it maximizes the potential of the frame to activate offscreen space, cinema's own way of gesturing to the invisible behinds or beyonds of the image and of generating anxiety through the conventions of suspense. In fact, the dreamer's manner of recounting the dream in a relentless present tense—"You're in both dreams and you're scared. I get more frightened when I see how scared you are"—is a way of approximating the *performative* quality of deixis: the way its referentiality is contingent on the endlessly shifting *now* of the utterance. The force of this sequence lies in Lynch's exploitation of this open and fluctuating temporality—the past dream, the time of its recounting in the diegetic present, and, most pressingly, the time of the spectators. Ultimately, we fill out the hollowness opened both by the dreamer's shifting pronouns and by Lynch's moving frame, which directs our look to a here and now: "And you're scared." And we're scared. The telling of this scary dream performs fear. Fear is the abstract property of this impersonal "you" and "I" that has also becomes our "we."

As Rita and Betty arrive at the same place, Aunt Ruth's apartment, their lines repeat this quality of deictic instability: each has made a disorienting arrival at an unstable "here" and a tenuous "I." These moments underscore how identities are fashioned from the abstract tissue of an impersonal semiotic network, which Lynch repeatedly associates with the processes of dreaming and fantasy. We know that Betty is in Los Angeles, because as she descends an airport escalator, we follow her awestruck gaze to a sign that reads "Welcome to Los Angeles!" and we will later get an aerial shot of an even more iconic Hollywood sign. And "Rita," of course, finds herself through a glance at the *Gilda* movie poster.

But they also reflect on the specificity of the cinematic sign—both to make kinds of persons and to generate kinds of feelings about them. Deixis has a special relationship to the problem of indexicality—of cinema as a particular kind of sign anchored in its photographic base. Charles Sanders Peirce, for example, defines the indexical sign both as a *trace*—bearing, in the manner of a footprint or a photograph, a material connection to its referent and testifying to anteriority—and as *deixis*, the pointing finger or "this-ness" of language, which Peirce saw as the purest form of indexicality.[92] As Mary Ann Doane has recently noted, we tend to associate the cinematic sign primarily with the trace because of its quality of perceptual, photographic presence, its connection to what Peirce calls iconicity. Deixis, whose pursuit of an impossible presence requires the "mandatory emptiness of the signifier 'this,'" tends to "exhaust itself in the moment of its implementation."[93] And yet however much the cinematic image seems basically replete and fleshed out, Lynch seems determined in the first segment of *Mulholland Dr.* to imagine the pre-personal freedom of cinematic characters who flicker in and out of being in an empty space like *this*. Think of the sheer uncertainty generated around the film's most overt deictic utterance, "This is the girl!" which links this-ness directly to the photograph, the headshot of Camilla Rhodes (Melissa George). Like Rita, Betty, and the man at Winkie's, we are encouraged as spectators to experience arrival into a deictic here and now as exciting and anxious, exhilarating and threatening. The emotional yield of deictical impersonality is a special kind of anxiety, an unstable erotics of anticipation and apprehension.

Another impersonal network is established through *Mulholland Dr.*'s emphasis on communication technologies, especially vocal technologies like the telephone, microphone, and speaker. The telephone is impersonal because, used by men like Mr. Roque (Michael J. Anderson) in the fashion of Fritz Lang's Dr. Mabuse, it bespeaks a modern system of technologized abstraction in which individuals are subordinated to vast grids of powers beyond their control and that seem to speak them. It is a technology of human dispossession—of the voice, of agency, of self-command—that the film's opening segment understands as analogous to with the disintegrative momentum of Betty's passion for Rita. As such, it connects the network of conspiracy joining Mr. Roque to the bumbling hit men, who refer enigmatically to "Ed's famous black book . . . the history of the world in phone numbers." And, for Adam Kesher, it is a reliable medium for the loss of his authorial control over the "Silvia North Story."

If Adam experiences the telephone as a technology of privation, his loss of power and autonomy is consistently played for comedy—perhaps because Diane is refashioning her own loss as something less traumatic. And so Betty, too, will experience telephonic dispossession, but for her telephony is a mode of eroticism. Betty, in fact, emerges in LA at the tail end of one of the film's several attempts to connect space and time through a chain of telephonic messages and signals that begins with a call placed by Mr. Roque in an empty room where a black phone rings next to a glowing red lamp. The phone rings repeatedly but nobody answers it. We cut instead to Betty's arrival at the airport. The sequence's sound editing, which has carefully separated the four spaces linked in the telephonic network by giving each of them a distinctive ring tone, now fails to clearly demarcate space just when we think we are out of the phone circuit. Instead, the mix bridges the reverberation of the last room's ringing black phone into the swelling sonic orchestration of Betty's arrival at the airport. The sound design thus implies that Betty's personality has emerged as an echo within Mr. Roque's abstract system of phone lines. Human presence seems to dissolve over the course of this series of calls, ending in a phone ringing, unanswered, in an empty room, the only trace of personhood the ashtray filled with cigarette butts next to the phone. Against this image, and bridged with it through reverb, Betty Elms is called into being at the airport.

Soon, Betty's incipient romance with Rita will be channeled through the telephone, which serves as a reliable tool for involving her into the budding mystery of Rita's personality. Initially it is associated with reverie and dreamy self-fashioning as Lynch shoots Betty lying on a couch, talking on the phone to her aunt. She tries on a variety of voices and tones, explaining her plan to rehearse her lines by the pool "like a real movie star," while vocally miming movie-star glamour. On the line she is startled to learn that Rita is not her aunt's friend, sparking the erotic process of discovering Rita's identity, which plays out in a series of phone calls. When Rita suddenly remembers the name "Mulholland Drive," Betty suggests that they place an anonymous call to the police to find out if an accident happened there. Telephonic anonymity is likened to cinematic impersonation: "It will be just like in the movies," Betty urges. "We'll pretend to be someone else." But the call is also part of an erotics of incipience, made to produce the beginning of something, "Just to see . . ." The call is placed at a public pay phone outside of the same Winkie's diner from the earlier sequence, and Rita and Betty seem to just stumble upon it by chance: "There's one!"

Again, Lynch insists on Winkie's as a space of abstract hollowness. Betty impersonates on the phone, and the duo enters the restaurant, where, occupying the same booth as the men from before, a waitress whose name tag reads "Diane" triggers Rita's memory: "Diane Selwyn!" The phone calls produce a teasing tension between the disintegrative dynamic of impersonation—the excitement of *moving away from* who one is—and the process of solving the mystery of Rita—the excitement of *discovering* who one is. With its signals moving away and toward personhood, the telephone is a device of erotic delay and deferral.[94] This becomes especially clear when the women return home, find "D. Selwyn" in the phonebook, and, cradling the phone's earpiece between their two huddled heads, make a call together (fig. 15). "It's strange to be calling yourself," Betty remarks, ironically anticipating the tragedy of Club Silencio, which is cast as a crisis of the lyric voice. The voice on the answering machine, Rita notes, is not hers but is somehow familiar. Betty's strategy is to bend this uncanny voice, which here threatens to return her to herself, into a site of erotic possibility and romantic futurity: "Maybe that isn't Diane's voice," she proposes. "Maybe that's her roommate." The call ends not with the return to personhood but

Figure 15. Telephony and the erotics of depersonalization

with the women's repeated "maybes," their possible futures together. Lynch's ironic sound editing compares the sound of these several "maybes" to the overt sexual provocation of the opening "Baby, baby" of Willie Dixon's "Bring It on Home," which introduces the next scene. As we move from the film's first segment to the second, the telephone is abruptly de-eroticized, now confirming personhood. Diane's phone rings to interrupt her anguished masturbation. As the ringing continues, Diane enters to humanize the room with the black phone, red lamp, and ashtray from the earlier telephonic montage (fig. 16). The shot, the call,

Figure 16. The tragedy of being oneself

and the voice all conspire to assign personhood brutally: the room is only her room, not part of any network; the voice on the answering machine is only her voice, not maybe anybody else; and the call is from Camilla Rhodes, whose voice-off summons her to witness the announcement of her marriage to Adam.

As a medium of impersonality and dissemblance, the telephone anticipates *Mulholland Dr.*'s two signature scenes, both devoted to the ontological mysteries of theatrical and cinematic performance: Betty's audition at Paramount and the Club Silencio sequence. Both are impersonal scenes that insist on their artifice and their affective force at once. Together, they dissociate feeling from personality and show affect instead to be the product of personae—elaborate rituals of masking, illusionism, and the manipulation of semblance. The sequences are clinical in their exploration of personality as a material fabrication—built by bodies, speech, sounds, gestures, movements, technologies—that thrills us when it is magically sparked into life, promising the endless self-fashioning of the virtual, and devastates us when our belief in its ontology collapses in a traumatic void. Part of the power of *Mulholland Dr.* is the way it links this emotional oscillation between possession and dispossession, belief and skepticism, as an *effect* of media illusionism felt by Lynch's spectator, to the internal tragedy of Diane's romantic passion and loss.

In "Auditioning Betty," his brilliant, bravura analysis of Betty's theatrical alchemy at Paramount, George Toles has described, in thick theatrical detail, the layered processes of transformation and affective uncertainty witnessed in this scene. First there is the way Betty turns the bad dialogue of a hackneyed, B-movie script into a dangerous, sexually knowing performance and, *within* a space of hollow industry clichés— from her smarmy partner "Woody"; to the lame platitudes of her director, Bob; to the haughty young assistant with chunky dark glasses—just barely managing to condescend to her job. Then, more subtly, there is the way this calculating eruption of sexual power shatters the spectator's image of Betty as the vulnerable naïf, gesturing toward Betty's hidden tragedy. And finally, there is the way the scene collapses diegetic and non-diegetic performances, confusing our sense of Betty's skill as an actress with that of Naomi Watts herself, who, in Toles's estimation, emerges to steal the scene and establish herself as the film's greatest star.[95] For Toles and others, Betty's audition scene offers a lesson in cinematic ontology, the power of "the Big Movie Scene's life," in which belief itself is at stake: "The skeptic in us came into the room laden with a will to expose (once again) the Hollywood charade, thereby disavowing our once-upon-a-time enthrallment to such things. What happens instead is that the skeptic is unwelcomely relieved of his superior, scoffing pose. Perhaps the skeptic is secretly pleased to have it taken away, and to be suddenly at the mercy of a sincerity hatched at the very core of artifice."[96]

Sincerity hatched at the core of artifice. The line perfectly captures Lynch's tendency to understand emotional sincerity as a spatial dynamic, something nested in a plastic environment with an outside and an inside, a periphery and a mysterious center. This dynamic unfolds, theatrically, in the Club Silencio sequence, the affective core of the film, and in the structural segue between its two main narrative segments. It is an emotionally moving scene, and one of Lynch's most systematic meditations on the art of being moved, drawing parallels between two debunkings: Diane is made to confront the fragility of her fantasy persona as "Betty" through a performance of its simultaneous power and self-shattering emptiness, while Lynch's spectator finds the grounds of cinematic illusionism exposed as similarly empty and full.

Everything begins to fall apart just after Betty has proclaimed her love to Rita, and the two make love. The emotional force of their passion, fantastic as it may be, seems to precipitate the more radical unhinging of persons to come as Rita is awakened by an uncanny voice that seems both to come from her and *speak* her, like a ventriloquist's doll: "*Silencio, Silencio. No hay banda.*" The women take a ghostly cab ride, and the drive is unreal and depersonalized, progressively relocated as a subjective movement toward "somewhere" within Betty/Diane that ends inside Club Silencio. And this inside is classically Lynchian theater, not just because of the way the operations of the unconscious are so often accompanied by theatrical mise-en-scène in the director's work, or because of the thick red velvet curtains that adorn the stage, or the way the first shot inside begins by floating on the painted vaults of the ceiling, recalling the opening of *Wild at Heart*. This inside is more powerfully Lynchian because as the women take their seats in the audience, they are addressed by a devilish emcee who baldly announces the foundational principle of Lynch's art: "*No hay banda.* There is no band . . . And yet

we hear a band." Sensation and involvement, wonderment and enthrallment—all the emotional ranges and expressive powers of cinema, all
of these are material effects on the bodies of spectators produced by a
skilled illusionist.

Cinematic pleasure—the desire for cinema—has long been considered to hinge on precisely such "splittings of belief": between the
"perceptual wealth" of image and sound and the awareness of illusion,
between the pleasure of being carried away by moving pictures and the
appreciation of their technique, between the illusory presence of the object on screen and its actual double absence.[97] This cinematic regime of
belief's most famous affective prototype, in the words of Christian Metz,
is the fetish—a prop that puts presence in the place of absence, testifying
to a vexing lack while disavowing it at once. And the job of Club Silencio's
fiendish emcee is to summon a series of such fetishes as aural objects, the
sound effects of musical instruments. With Rita and Betty we hear the
various qualities and textures of trombones and trumpets materialized
by the spectacle in a sequence that insists both upon sound's power to
spatialize and embody images—to give them a tactile presence—and
upon its airy insubstantiality. It is another big scene about the ontology
of *audition*. Finally, the emcee's gestures summon the natural sounds
of thunder, and light flashes in the auditorium, imitating lightning, as
Betty begins to convulse in her seat. It is as if Betty's vibrating body is
made to enact the basic principle of sonic materiality—objects make
sounds when they are touched, and sound, touching bodies, produces
vibrations. Here, though, the agent for affect's transmission is as magical,
unaccountable, and unreal as the emcee's abrupt disappearance from
the stage in a cloud of smoke.

We know this is false, and the machine of artifice has been defamiliarized again, and yet we persist in our belief. So, too, does Betty cling to her
fantasy as yet another airy vessel, now a human one, is introduced: "La
Llorona de Los Angeles, Rebekah Del Rio." Del Rio's song, a plaintive,
Spanish-language cover of Roy Orbison's 1962 pop classic "Crying," is
not just a moving performance of the end of love but also a specifically
lyric one. Lynch's films are strewn with embedded performances like
this, and they are often explained as part of Lynch's postmodern recy-
cling machine. But, more powerfully, they allow Lynch to take up an
emotional problem long associated with lyric *media*.

A nonnarrative poetic mode privileging intense, solitary experience, lyric is the ur-genre of the expressive voice. Lyric lifts romantic feeling from a subjective inside and exteriorizes it. For this reason, lyric offers a way of understanding the voice as a metaphysical medium with the power to personify. Lyric seeks to call being into presence, to apostrophize, and, in turning toward absence, to animate or reanimate the silence of the world. Otherness is thereby called into an intimacy with the self. Part of the lesson drawn by the romantic lyric's legion of deconstructive critics is the very fragility of this process of lyric personation—its way of naturalizing or auto-affecting the voice, producing, in Paul de Man's terms, the "image of the subject's presence to itself as a spatial enclosure, room, tomb, or crypt in which the voice echoes as if in a cave."[98] These rhetorical acts of personation and romantic intimacy—and the interiors they hollow out for themselves through media—have a way of collapsing into death and trauma.

"La Llorona de Los Angeles" is thus a lyric vessel. Her song is an apostrophe to a love object, Camilla/Rita, whom Diane has not quite given up for lost. Orbison's "Crying" is a melancholic elegy for love, like so many romantic lyrics, and Lynch's approach to Del Rio's act rethinks the moving image as another lyric medium. He does so by joining Del Rio's vocal performance to the shared anthropomorphism of the close-up, cinema's own way of authenticating the freighted emotional depths on the other side of an enlarged, sublime surface. As Del Rio sings, Lynch's close-ups seem to capture the reality and unreality of her passion at once (fig. 17). Her heavily made-up face is airbrushed with tears, and, more unsettlingly, after moving Diane and Betty to weep, she simply collapses onto the floor, her voice continuing but now bereft of body, which falls away like some spent automaton.

By linking cinema and lyric, Lynch meditates on their shared, imponderable materiality. Lyric is a strange, primordial substance. It is, of course, ephemeral, constituted by language, bodies of air. As matter it is as unaccountable as the atmospheric phenomena that spark Betty's convulsions and allow the emcee to vanish into nothingness. And for this reason, as Daniel Tiffany argues, lyric "has a crucial position in the genealogy of the so-called disembodied images of the modern technical media."[99] Like the unnatural vitality of the moving image, lyric wishes to cross the border between the material and the immaterial, the animate

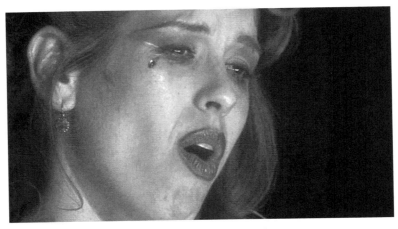

Figure 17. Lyric vessels and the being of cinema |

and the inanimate. For Tiffany, following Paul de Man, the shared sub-stance of lyric and animated pictures is their "irrealization" of objects, the way things "under the spell of lyric oscillate between the literal and the immaterial, the real and the unreal."[100] Tiffany's stunning intellectual history of lyric materiality argues provocatively that this anxious oscilla-tion—this lyric indeterminacy—has been linked, since the seventeenth century, to the uncanny materiality of the lyric automaton, and since the beginning of the twentieth century, to cinema's own uncanny relation-ship to the real.

At Club Silencio the lyric succeeds and then fails at its cinematic magic, anticipating the tragic dissolution of Betty's personality. Lyric is Diane's best, last-ditch effort to summon the fiction of Betty/Rita's lasting intimacy or reciprocal address. As such, it works as a hinge between the liberating cinematic impersonality that Lynch associates with the open *now* of deixis, or the budding eros of the telephone, or the plastic trans-formations of the performing body, and the brutal facts of being Diane.

What, Lynch asks, is the relationship between La Llorona's lyric body and cinema's reality effect? When figures of the chanteuse ap-pear, for example, in French cinema of the 1930s, their world-weariness serves to anchor the films' sociological claims to realism, bespeaking a nostalgia for outmoded forms of working-class performance and community like the music hall. Del Rio is a different kind of singer entirely. Her nostalgia is for a lost object—the this-ness of "Rita," the this-ness of the cinematic image—that the film at once mourns and celebrates as an empty space—"This is the girl!"—to be filled by techniques and technologies of personation. As "The Crier of Los Angeles," Del Rio mourns not the loss of a person but, rather, the end of the experience of impersonality, which is the end of eros, which is the end of what is, for Lynch, most moving about cinema in the first place—its ways of traveling away from the self.

Organism

This, in part, is why David Lynch has often been described as a kind of late surrealist. Like the historical surrealists of the interwar period, he values what André Breton famously described as cinema's "power to disorient," its status as an arena for the experience of otherness and the unknown. Surrealism, so its practitioners always insisted, is not an aesthetic or a collection of particular works, but a practice, a process—and the experience of cinema is a vital site of surrealist activity. Depending on whom you ask, of course, Lynch's filmmaking is either essential to the living legacy of surrealism or yet another weak iteration of a once-transgressive avant-garde practice. It is wise to be wary of aligning Lynch too strongly with the surrealists or their ethico-political agenda. True, his films are oneiric, unsettling, and filled with eruptions of the bizarre and uncanny into the staid texture of the quotidian, and, like the surrealists, he understands popular culture as the horizon of mass fantasy, the reservoir of collective affect. Yet he does not seek any revolutionary de-sublimation of everyday life, nor are his investments in dreams or the unconscious wedded to any explicit political program. One way to make sense of Lynch as a surrealist, however, is to take seriously his understanding of vital media—a necessarily paradoxical phrase that, for both Lynch and the surrealists before him, joins an understanding of media to a basic insight about the strange life of organisms.

As an activity, surrealism pursued what Breton famously described as "a supreme point" at which the contradictions that organize quotidian experience—dream and reality, most famously, but also, nature and artifice, object and image, life and death—dissolve or are brought into a relationship so disjunctive as to fulfill Arthur Rimbaud's exhortation to "change life." The old new media of the early twentieth century, especially photography and cinema, became, for the surrealists, ever more eloquent testimonies to a picture of life—and of human being—as primordially estranged from itself, constituted by networks of inhuman forces that exceed it. Art historian Rosalind Krauss, for example, has read surrealist photography as the medial distillation of the surrealist aesthetic tout court—namely, the "experience of reality transformed into representation. Surreality," Krauss concludes, "is nature convulsed into a kind of writing."[101] This convulsion of the natural into the cultural and coded is evident in the surrealist photographic practice of Man Ray and Hans Bellmer (both of whose influence is clear in the most cursory glance at Lynch's recent photographic experiments like the "Distorted Nudes" series and "Fetish"), and in surrealism's broader predilection for marvelous figures of the immanence of death in life—the mannequin, the ruin, the train stilled in the midst of a virgin forest.

In revealing modern experience as written, surrealism's reckoning with modern image technologies was part of a much broader modernist awareness of the old new media as simultaneously extending human perception and undermining confidence in the sovereignty of noble subjectivity. The new media's troubling of human limits, for the surrealists, happened on two levels: first, it revealed the perceptual experience of reality as photographic—that is, potentially citational—and it pointed to the irrational underside of life heretofore unseen by normal human perception but now revealed through the mechanical prosthesis of the camera and extolled in the broader, "revelationist" tradition of classical film theory stretching from Béla Balázs and Jean Epstein to Dziga Vertov, Siegfried Kracauer, and Walter Benjamin.[102]

Media scholars like Laura Mulvey, Robert Ray, and Adam Lowenstein have recently returned to surrealism to grapple with the technological uncanniness of today's new media environment, and they have done so by transposing surrealism's notion of *life as a productive inorganicism*— life's various modes of self-difference or technical self-shattering—to its variety of aesthetic strategies for resisting organic form and human propriety. To pit, as such scholars do, surrealism's fetishistic forms of spectatorship against the organic whole of continuous filmic time, or of a traditional narrative liveliness less sullied by stillness, what they depend upon—but never quite name as such—is surrealism's picture of organic life as always already second nature. This is the strange life of the surrealist organism: to be born and to live, in uncanny hybridity with artifice, technology, and mediation. It is to live life with media as one's original supplement. Indeed, surrealism's attunement to the primordial role of *techne* in organic nature fueled its subversive critique of the powerful ways culture—as second nature—has of masquerading as truth. Culture, for the surrealists, was an artificial, arbitrary—indeed, incoherent—arrangement of norms, rules, and limits on human freedoms that would be ironized in the various forms of ethnographic surrealism stretching from Georges Bataille's pseudo-ethnographic magazine *Documents* and the base materialism of his collaborations with Jacques-André Boiffard to Luis Buñuel's collaboration with Pierre Unik in his great filmic documentary of the heterological, *Land without Bread* (1932).

A similar plasticity of the organism fuels Lynch's unruly picture of biological processes. In Lynch land the strange life of organisms is rarely teleological, causal, or mechanistic but rather contingent, untimely, and non-anthropomorphic in its challenges to purposive human design. Lynch was, of course, initiated into the mysteries of organic process at an early age through his father, a research scientist for the U.S. Department of Agriculture, who, Lynch notes, frequently experimented on tree diseases and insects in the expansive forests of Montana: "So I was exposed to insects, disease, and growth, in an organic sort of world, like a forest, or even a garden. And this sort of thrills me—this earth, and then these plants coming out, and then there's the things crawling on them and the activity in the garden—so many textures, and movements."[103] "Organic" is a word Lynch gravitates toward when discussing his work, but he always gives it a surrealist inflection: to describe processes of contamination between culture and nature, and their mutual dynamization and mutations. The strange movements with which Lynch endows his organisms are also often enabled by the peculiar vitality of media. Lynch's persistent biologizing of media suggests that "the cinematic," for Lynch, has no essential features but is rather a dynamic quality of heterogeneity. Lynch's ideas about cinema as a vital medium approximate D. N. Rodowick's new answer to the old question "What is cinema?" Taking issue with the concept of "medium-specificity," Rodowick has suggested that we conceptualize a medium as *a self-differing condition*,

expressive of the heterogeneous powers of thought and creative impro-
visation that are not dictated by any material substance and indeed can
never be predicted in advance of the expressive event.[104] What Lynch
shares with the surrealists, then, is an understanding of cinema as an
encounter or a disjunctive experiential event, set into motion by the
waywardness of life.

On Moving Pictures: *Six Men Getting Sick*

Lynch made his first motion picture, *Six Men Getting Sick*, as a second-
year student at the Pennsylvania Academy of the Fine Arts. An intermedial experiment that debuted in an exhibition of vanguard painting
and sculpture in Philadelphia, *Six Men* combined a sculpted screen and
a projected 16mm image of animated figures puking their guts out and
looped in fifty-second intervals accompanied by a blaring siren. The
piece won an award, but more importantly, it garnered the attention of
H. Barton ("Bart") Wasserman, who gave Lynch one thousand dollars
to make another short film, *The Alphabet* (1968). On the merits of *The
Alphabet*, Lynch was awarded an American Film Institute (AFI) grant to
help fund his early 16mm masterpiece *The Grandmother* (1970), a film
whose enthusiastic reception at a handful of small film festivals prompted
the AFI to invite Lynch to apply to its Los Angeles film academy. This famously tortured apprenticeship some six years later spawned *Eraserhead*.
Tempted by the cheap clarity of hindsight, or the retrospective teleologies
of artistic development that are so useful to auteurism or a good bildung-
sroman, we might say that Lynch's career as a filmmaker was born with
Six Men's unseemly concoction of projected light and projectile vomiting,
or that Henry Spencer's bad seed was somehow already, ten years earlier,
a glimmer in the eye of a visionary young poet of the grotesque.

Less heroically, we could say that Lynch's career as a filmmaker began
with an attempt to surmount an aesthetic inadequacy—the failure of his
paintings to move and, in perpetual motion, to produce the experience of
a compelling *interior*. Like *Blue Velvet's* famous subterranean push into
the teeming, chaotic nature beneath the Beaumonts' well-kept backyard,
the imagined inside of Lynch's "film paintings" would be penetrated
by the beholder and secured by the interiorizing force of sound itself,
which Lynch often uses to place his viewers "constantly within something."[105] "When I looked at these paintings," Lynch reflected, "I missed

the sound. I was expecting a sound, or maybe the wind, to come out. I wanted the edges to disappear. I wanted to get inside. It was spatial."[106] The fruit of this experiment was Lynch's first cine-organism—and it is a monster whose medial hybridity and figural grotesquerie comment on the messy substance of cinema.

It all begins simply enough, with a sculpted screen consisting of three distended faces, cast from molds of Lynch's own face and arranged as a tableau in the upper-left quadrant of the screen. The film's anti-anthropomorphism announces itself in these three figures, already disfigured, the first apparently asleep, resting his chin on one visible hand, the others, heads only, in cataleptic stasis. In this series of molds, and their black-and-white palette, Lynch offers what remains of the photographic index in this film: three mottled, arrested facial expressions, embalming moments of impression never again to be relived. The faces are deathly in their ecstatic abandon, and it is against this stasis that Lynch measures the excessive graphic mobility of the projected animation, unfolding in its own repetitive temporality.

This self-reflexive first exercise in cinema is a mini-archive of media: sculpture, drawing, light, animation, and x-rays. Cinema, Tom Gunning has recently reminded us, "has never been one thing," despite the well-known attempts of classical film theory to ascertain its medium specificity, but rather always was, and continues to be, a "point of intersection" or "braiding" of diverse aesthetic and technological capacities within a competitive media environment.[107] Gunning makes these claims about cinema's basic heterogeneity to call for a more expansive notion of cinematic realism—less a realism of the photographic index than one that is attentive to cinema as a complex, often illogical, *phenomenological* process of being moved. Because this kind of spectatorial involvement happens through the physiological and emotional effects of cinematic *motion* itself, it need not marginalize the affective power of, say, animation as realisms bound to the photographic index often do. Even unreal, impossible bodies compel perceptual, cognitive, or bodily effects, commanding a perceiver as they unfold in cinematic motion.

This lesson that motion "need not be realistic to have a 'realistic' effect on spectators" is Lynchian to the core. Here, such motion energizes a surrealist *dépaysement*, casting cinema as a basically theatrical frame for an experience that is inexhaustible. The kind of medial heterogeneity or impurity so prominently on display in *Six Men* was, for a contemporary art critic like Michael Fried, the sign of a contemporary war in the 1960s art world between modernism's formal, self-contained medial purity and a degenerate theatricality (epitomized, for Fried, by minimalism). This theatricality bespoke a broader reorientation of art objects away from their respective essences and toward all the embodied details of the beholder's perceptual experience of the object in a *situation* or an environment marked by temporal ongoing-ness and recursivity.[108]

Six Men's theatricality is also announced by its tableau-like arrangement, a recurring formal motif in Lynch's work and another way of declaring the heterogeneity of the cinematic. The tension between the static, aggressive frontality of the molded screen and the violent motility of the thrown, animated image operates as a kind of tableau vivant in reverse. In its pregnant moment of temporal suspension, the tableau vivant not only arrests the flow of dramatic action but also attempts to incarnate the flatness of painting, bending pictorial representation toward a fleshier real. *Six Men*, by contrast, begins with three-dimensional stasis and progresses toward more dynamic, and more graphic, representation. As the film progresses, the figures become flatter but also somehow *more* embodied, more overburdened with organs and organic functions (or maladies). But this is an organicism in the form of irrational networks and assemblages that assert, over and over again, their common being in lines, dots, and dashes (fig. 18). As the film becomes peopled with

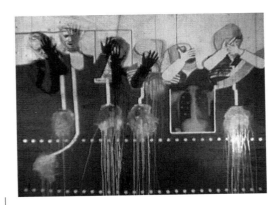

Figure 18. Lynch's first cine-organism

organs, it grows less natural or illusionistic; the more carnal it gets, the less obeisant it is to the rules of bodily life. It is as if the work of the thrown image is to animate the three-dimensional sculpture into a prosthetic life, to make biological processes infinitely plastic by inserting them into a temporal loop that belies the facts of mortality. Never dying, only ever waking to vomit all over again, *Six Men Getting Sick* is a bad organism, humanly impossible.

It is this curious temporality of *Six Men*—the quality of ongoing-ness of the looped film—that is perhaps its most conspicuous formal feature and also perhaps its most self-reflexive. *Six Men* begins with a simulation of the cinematic "leader," counting down from 4 to 1 with each second marked by an aggressive vertical bisection of the frame into black and white. The faux leader pulses in time, time that is at once powerfully embodied and in flagrant disregard of organic law. Its time beats to what Rosalind Krauss has described as "the pulse" of the modernist *informe,* its denial of the disembodied, atemporal field of visual purity privileged in certain strands of modernist aesthetics. But even as *Six Men* insists on an embodied time for its beholder, its own time will not die. The celluloid catches fire, stomachs burst, heads explode, and then the loop begins again with another countdown.

Six Men's use of the leader is particularly knowing, and Lynch himself would later adopt a retro-styled version of the SMPTE (Society of Motion Picture and Television Engineers) Universal Leader as the logo for Asymmetrical Productions, Lynch's independent production company. Leaders, of course, were designed as ways of announcing the beginning of the film and of ensuring a proper start with sound and image in synchronization. The leader, we might say, is the most basic figure of audiovisual "synchresis," Chion's term for the Pavlovian perceptual "join" between audio and visual phenomenon occurring at the same time.[109] By virtue of the organizing function on the film's body, leaders were nicknamed "heads," a pun that may explain why *Six Men* begins both with a head leader and with sculpted heads, appearing simultaneously as the countdown begins—here not in advance of sound but synched with the onset of a siren announcing the film's continuous state of organic emergency. In fact, repeated viewings make clear that the film, and the leader, begins with the count of 5, which barely registers for a fraction of a second before giving way to the second-by-second completion of the countdown.

When critics refer to Lynch's work as "inhuman," they have in mind precisely this refusal of organic finitude, evident, say, in the death-that-is-no-death of *The Elephant Man*'s John Merrick, or *Eraserhead*'s Henry Spencer, or the Möbius-strip temporality that impossibly swaps the bodies of Fred Madison and Pete Dayton in *Lost Highway*. Such inhumanity gets chalked up to Lynch's spiritualist or metaphysical or romantic tendencies—or to his cynicism. Thought a bit differently, though, bad organisms like *Six Men* might be considered less figures of transcendence than as Lynch's way of refusing forms of organic *propriety* in cinema—one that aligns his filmmaking with the avant-garde's transgressions of normative limits.

What kind of unreasonable, "inorganic" affective economy, then, does *Six Men* set into motion? Most obviously, Lynch's bad organicism operates here in the familiar mode of the grotesque, not so much a specific feature of aesthetic objects but a transgressive process or operation inextricably linked to a modern aesthetic sensibility. *Six Men*'s movements toward organic impossibility are precisely the stuff of constant metamorphosis, and they bring the grotesque's familiar boundary violations in line with the metamorphic quality of the work's medial impurity. It is a meta-grotesque work. However, here, that strong sensation of disgust so often produced by the grotesque works not simply as what Kant called the other of taste, refusing identification and introjection; instead, *Six Men* introduces us to Lynch's perverse tendency to marshal disgust as an invitation for his spectator to become sensually involved (**LOOK!**) in the thickening texture of the cinematic image. Pauline Kael sensed just this agonistic quality of Lynch's mode of address when she used as an epigraph to her review of *Blue Velvet* a comment she overheard upon exiting the theater: "Maybe I'm sick, but I want to see that again." Lynch's films consistently solicit a look that seems to implicate their spectators' affects in something obscene or perverse; they entice a libidinous, even pornographic curiosity whose trials will be staged directly in *The Elephant Man*, *Blue Velvet*, and *Lost Highway*. In *Six Men* this Lynchian machine of sensory involvement and disgust never allows its spectators any stable points of identification, so disorganized is its bodily theater of operations. But it still produces a powerfully carnal kind of visual fascination in the image as we are drawn into an experience that seems repulsive, unstable, and compelling repeated viewings.

Like the somatic assemblages to come, *Six Men*'s body is untimely: it begins before it has properly begun, too quickly; and indeed it never really ends but is charged with the character of an ongoing, unstable experience. This experience, the leader suggests, is *cinematic* in a specifically Lynchian sense. The cinematic, *Six Men* announces, inheres not in its photographic base but in its enactment of often impossible organic events: the temporal duration of the work as it happens to a feeling spectator; the vital processes of moved bodies shared by the film's beholder and its vomiting figures; and the teeming graphic freedom of the non-illusionistic image. The perceptual-affective body that *Six Men Getting Sick* wishes for its spectator, and enacts, is primordially excessive, a body otherwise from itself from the jump.

Animated Humans: *The Grandmother*

Mixing live action and cel animation, Lynch's third short film, the thirty-four-minute *The Grandmother*, inaugurates the director's anthrobiological interest in the nature of the domestic environment. It also defines organicism as a mode of aesthetic production—in other words, a dynamic work or ongoing process that removes home life from itself. Here, the fascination with life's movement becomes the stuff of novel aesthetic production and domestic transformation, both within the film's diegesis and as a work of experimental animation. The film's narrative core, once again, is domestic melodrama. An adolescent boy (Richard White), who wears a black suit and white shirt that seem too old for him, is tormented by cruel, animalized parents (Robert Chadwick and Virginia Maitland), who mock their son's repeated bedwetting—a lack of control over the life of his body that seems too young for him. After suffering domestic abuse at the hands of his father (who rubs his face into a flagrant orange stain on his bed) and his mother (whose compensatory attempts to caress the boy grow jittery and violent, pixilated through a stop-frame technique), the boy hears a mysterious whistling sound, which he traces to a large bag of seeds in his family's attic. He finds the singing seed, buries it in a mound of soil piled on a bed, waters it, and thereby grows a giant pod that gives birth to his own loving grandmother (Dorothy McGinnis).

Lynch proposed a seven-thousand-dollar budget for the film and received five thousand dollars from the AFI. *The Grandmother* was filmed over nine weeks, shot in 16mm, largely in desaturated color, and acted by friends of Lynch. Its rich aural environment—absent any live recording—took Lynch an estimated 567 hours to produce. This painstaking process marked Lynch's first collaboration with Alan Splet, who served as sound designer for *Eraserhead* and four of Lynch's other films. The film's nightmarish picture of home life owes something to Lynch's reading of Franz Kafka's *The Metamorphosis*, which also understands bourgeois domesticity as a site of unaccountable transformations of nature. After the success of *The Grandmother* earned Lynch admission to the AFI academy, his first, pre-*Eraserhead* script was an explicitly Kafkaesque project titled *Gardenback*, another story of a bad home—here, a parable of adultery figured through the monstrous growth of an insect in the attic (and head) of a married man, which wreaks havoc on his conjugal happiness.

Even in *The Grandmother* the presence of Kafka is evident, not just in its deforming pressures of the Oedipal family, or its way of carving out lines of flight from the domestic—which transpire chiefly in its dazzling cel animation sequences—but also in the strange nature of its home-bodies, less human beings than *creatures*. This is true not just of the boy's parents, who, devoid of human language, bark like dogs and twitch across the frame like the aggressive bourgeois of Norman McLaren's *Neighbors* (1952), but also of the Grandmother, spawned by the boy's productive act of sensory attentiveness (here, to sound, the call of the whistling seed), planting, and caretaking; and the boy himself, birthed through Lynch's cel animation stand. These creatures, as Walter Benjamin once remarked of Kafka's odd beings, all "still live under the spell of the family," and they mark their entrapment and resistance to that life through their theatrical and gestural qualities—the strongest gesture, for Kafka, being shame. For Kafka and Lynch, "man is on stage from the very beginning," but the drama is not a human one. Instead, the movements of these creatures "divest the human gesture of its traditional supports"; they are "far from the continent of man."[110] Such creatures, then, are the receptacle of a primary alienation, a nonpersonal forgetting—and their most "forgotten alien land is their own bodies."[111]

For Benjamin, attending to this basic condition of creaturely alienation, revealed through codes of gestures given meaning only in constantly shifting and experimental contexts, was a way of rescuing Kafka's work from both natural and supernatural readings. The same operation could apply to Lynch's defamiliations of the domestic, beginning with *The Grandmother* and continuing through *Eraserhead, The Elephant Man, Blue Velvet, Twin Peaks: Fire Walk with Me, Lost Highway,* and *Inland Empire*—in all of these films, the bourgeois home morphs into a kind of gestural theater, a shifting and mobile arena of codes, conventions, and habits that frustrate any attempts to reify the nature of the private. So, while *The Grandmother* was heard, for example, by Seattle's Bellevue Film Festival juror Sheldon Renan as a universal human appeal to the need for familial love, one he saw as especially refreshing in the context of his contemporaries' attempts to address the political trauma of Vietnam, one cannot help but wonder how the nature of the home in *The Grandmother* might provide such a balm. There are no humans in it, only creatures. There is no stable home in it, only gestures. And its nature is everywhere subject to unnatural, infinitely plastic assemblages.

Why wouldn't Lynch be drawn to animation? In keeping with his medial self-consciousness, Lynch exploits animation's inherent self-reflexivity. As a contested subset of cinema, animation has returned to contemporary debates about the digital's challenge to the nature of cinema, debates that Lynch engages directly in *Inland Empire,* his first digital feature. But cinema's fascination, from the moment of its late nineteenth-century invention, always depended on its ability to engender life—or lifelike motion—from the mechanical succession of still photograms, a power that Lynch often deploys ironically in films like "Premonition Following an Evil Deed" or *Fire Walk with Me,* which start with corpses whose uncanny reanimation will, in the style of *Sunset Blvd.,* be their subject. And the affective force of film's powers of animation, its production of lifelikeness is, as *Mulholland Dr.* argues, at the heart of cinematic passion.

But we can also place this interest in the traditions of the various historical avant-garde movements that made and celebrated animated film, and of contemporary experimental animators like Czech surrealist Jan Svankmajer or the Quay brothers. Lynch, too, is moved by animation's liberating non-naturalism: its capacity for abstraction, its stylized stretchiness or flatness, and its violations of the human form, which, in *The Grandmother* and elsewhere, are at once forms of cruelty and tools of liberation. In one sequence, for example, the boy finds himself on stage presiding over his parent's execution: his father is beheaded, his mother stretched out of recognizability. In *The Alphabet*, Lynch's first mixture of live action and animation, cartoonish violence to the human form is named as such. In *The Grandmother* Lynch explores more carefully animation's capacity for the illogical, its penchant for space not "geographical but graphic," and for "time not logical but convoluted."[112] Indeed, Lynch's characters are always finding themselves in logics, times, and spaces like this; they are animated, convulsed, or otherwise possessed by energies and affects that seize them and, in seizing them, catch them in a fetishistic dynamic—one that bends them from things to people and back again, and in flagrant disregard for the laws of organic life. So if animation bears witness to the death-in-life of cinematic motion or the upheavals of human passion, it also, in keeping with Lynch's desire for a nonpsychological cinema, poses a challenge to bourgeois psychology and to an anthropomorphic world that is cut to the measure of human being.

If it is not properly human or psychological, what is life like in the world of *The Grandmother*? How does it understand the relationship between media and the strange life of organisms? On the one hand, the film establishes a distinction between the alienated environment and latent menace of the boy's nuclear family, established in the live-action sequences, and the freeing plasticity of the animation sequences, which give us the texture of his fantasy life in keeping with the historical associations between animation and the dreamy insubstantiality of mental operations. Read this way, *The Grandmother* could be seen as the first of Lynch's films to introduce a structural binary between the world of desire and the world of fantasy, which, as Todd McGowan has shown, so powerfully shapes films like *Eraserhead*, *Lost Highway*, and *Mulholland Dr.* On the other hand, the film's relentless stylization of the live-action sequences belies any easy distinctions between its ontology and that of the cel animation sequences and, in fact, seems to insist they are of the same stuff.

Because cel animation consists of stacked layers of celluloid, historically it has had trouble producing the sense of movement into the depth of the image—the kind of naturalistic movement seen as particularly cinematic and one of Lynch's most reliable methods for crafting an interior. Yet *The Grandmother*'s animation sequences make no attempts to simulate movement into depth; rather, they are all tableaus. And

Lynch's live-action mise-en-scène produces a similar depthlessness in the home's all-black rooms, whose minimalist decor seems to float and whose internal divisions—its doors—are only traced out, graphically, by chalk outlines. Further, the live-action scenes, like the animation sequences, are filled with unnatural changes in speed and movement (stop-frame acceleration, freeze-frames, slow motion) and surprising metamorphoses: the Grandmother's germination and birth in the boy's attic is as equally untimely as the opening cel animation sequence.

The film thus joins the boy's work of uncanny generation, which frees him briefly from the domestic tyranny of his biological parents, to the impossible offspring of Lynch's own experiments with cel animation. The Grandmother's pod is like the animated cel: both are forms of vital media, intermediary agencies or channels for unaccountable transformations. The film's own life germinates in its dazzling opening animated sequences, in which the cartoon mother and father, conjured into being in a bizarre system of subterranean tubes, give birth to their live-action counterparts and then their own son. Here, Lynch oscillates between animation and live action, and the goal is not to separate these worlds but to produce odd passages between them, to join them in an unforeseen assemblage: the parents are birthed through a perverse, animated world of telluric tubes, which disgorges them upward, toward the top of the cel frame (fig. 19). They spawn their live-action counterparts, who couple frantically, in accelerated motion, in the fallen leaves of an anonymous

Figure 19. The family assemblage

garden. From this movement, their child, the live-action boy, emerges from the earth and assumes a position between his barking and yipping parents. Now we return to an animated sequence, in which the father hurls his animation child into the sky, and we cut to the live-action boy, now in his "home." He is not naturally there, of course, but thrown.

The world of *The Grandmother* is the product of a machine, but a decidedly nonmechanistic one that takes as its model the material engine of animation. The animation stand, as Thomas Lamarre has recently argued, is a special kind of machinic *ensemble*: "a series of other technical devices and schema that do not in themselves belong together or naturally come together: a rack, a fixed camera, lights to provide sufficient illumination on the layers and through the layers, manual techniques of applying ink and color, abstract techniques of composing images . . . and the industrially produced celluloid sheets and celluloid film in the camera."[113] As a Guattarian "functional ensemble" in which machines and their human makers co-evolve in productive networks "at once technical/material and abstract/immaterial," animation's materiality points to the precisely kind of nondeterministic power that *The Grandmother* associates with both the life of organisms and the life of media.[114] What the animation sequences demonstrate in their networks of production and reproduction, which everywhere defy causality, is a version of life energized by productive delays between cause and effect, gaps between action and reaction—in short, moments of indetermination in which domestic organisms, having fully lost the gestures that make them most human, spawn something new or unforeseen.

Good Machine: *The Straight Story*

Is it perverse to propose a link between *The Grandmother*'s non-naturalistic animated world, with its strong currents of domestic unease, and Lynch's G-rated Disney film, *The Straight Story*, whose natural environment of all-encompassing Iowan goodness pursues something like a folk sublime? Lynch's work encourages such couplings, which are unnatural at first blush. And maybe in their final bloom as well. Both are films about life and death, anima and animation, stillness and life's movements in varying speeds. And they both explore processes of generation and decay, the uncanny prolixity of nature, as well as the constitution of those labile networks of kinship we call family. Yet

The Straight Story, with its narrative simplicity, its non-traumatized normalcy, and its generous sentimentality, has been described as the director's least "Lynchian" film. Following the critical and commercial failure of *Lost Highway*, *The Straight Story* was cheered by many critics as a sign of the director's own artistic maturation: having set aside his childish obsessions with sex, violence, and narrative dysfunction, Lynch had grown up by making a simple, emotionally honest film that could be (and was) a bona fide hit. It did well internationally at the box office and earned an Academy Award nomination for the brilliant performance of its lead actor, Richard Farnsworth. But simplicity and minimalism are not opposed to complexity and excess in Lynch's work; rather, they are species of each other: to cultivate an aesthetics of simplicity is a decidedly sophisticated operation.

Lynch has described *The Straight Story* as another kind of "experiment" in an ongoing machine of creative production. The project came to Lynch through his then-longtime partner and editor Mary Sweeney, who had become fascinated by press accounts of the charming story of Alvin Straight. A nearly blind septuagenarian and resident of Laurens, Iowa, Straight learned that his estranged brother, Henry (renamed Lyle in the film), who lived three hundred miles away in Mount Zion, Wisconsin, was seriously ill. Without a driver's license or financial means, Straight made the trek to his brother's home on a slow-moving lawn mower. Sweeney cowrote the script with John Roach, based on extensive interviews with the Straight family and the various midwesterners Straight encountered on his journey, and asked Lynch to produce the film. Moved by the material, Lynch offered to direct the picture as well, and the film was shot with funding by Alain Sarde's Le Studio Canal Plus before being distributed by Disney in the United States. When asked by Chris Rodley about the seemingly abrupt transition from the darkness and confusion of *Lost Highway*'s Fred Madison to the serene endurance of Farnsworth's hero, Straight, Lynch disavowed the notion of a creative "break," explaining instead, "So now the machine is slightly changed and is looking for something else."[115] Lynch's machine metaphor captures the version of aesthetic activity, and of life itself, in Lynch's work in general. But it is especially suited to *The Straight Story*'s picture of a giant organism that joins life, family, community, environment—an organism imagined on the model of the good machine.

This phrase, "good machine," will be used to describe a John Deere riding lawn mower that Alvin will eventually use to make it to his brother, Lyle (Harry Dean Stanton), bringing the film to an end. As the key intermediary in the film's dynamic environment, the good machine is secondhand, acquired after the breakdown of his first lawn mower, a prehistoric Rehds-brand contraption that overheats on the road during the first day of the trip. The editing patterns of Alvin's initial, comically slow movement through the landscape fashion the dynamic organism of which Alvin and mower, moving together, are a part. One striking shot begins by unhurried tracking along the road, low to the asphalt, craning up alongside Alvin on his mower, and then lifting higher up toward the powdery white clouds in the blue sky overhead. The shot holds on the slow-moving clouds—allowing us to see their shapes shifting in the sunlight—and then tilts back down to Alvin and his machine moving leisurely down the road. The scene lap dissolves to an aerial shot of a combine moving through a cornfield, its own clouds of dust glowing in the autumn light. These dissolves between Alvin's movement and the aerial shots of the combine will structure his entire journey and, in their own refusal of the cut, testify to the organism's quality of ongoing-ness. Lynch described these shots as attempts to give his spectator the impression of "floating inside nature."

The combine is a well-chosen machine: a tool for harvesting grain, it is named, obviously, for its combinatory function—the way it unites in one assemblage three processes (reaping, binding, and threshing). Before its invention, these activities required separate machines. It is thus a versatile visual figure for the combinatory production of Lynch's camera, a machine that observes—and itself becomes a part of—a natural landscape permeated with machines of different ages, sizes, and speeds. Alvin, his mower, the trailer filled with provisions it pulls, the sky above, the field of corn, the harvesting machines—all are part of the same environment, a natural-machinic network.

The combine also articulates the film's vision of a generous community linked by self-supporting machinic movements. As the camera circles the combine, we see that it is in fact moving in tandem with another tractor that collects the grain. Similarly, Alvin's first movements will fold him into the community by the slow force of his passage through it and show him to be sustained by this environment. A family who lives near the road stands and waves as he passes. And although he is nearly blown off the road by a speeding semitruck, when his old mower conks out, other machines emerge on the road to help him. A tour bus filled with retirees stops to offer Alvin a ride. As the bus drives away into the distance, Lynch contrasts its continued movement into the horizon with Alvin's stalled machine in the foreground. But even this machinic stasis quickly becomes movement again as we dissolve to a shot of Alvin, seated on the stilled mower, the entire man-mower contraption now set in motion again because it rests in the back of a Ford pickup.

At this point the journey begins again as Alvin goes to a John Deere dealership to find a vehicle to replace the Rehds, which has not just expired on the road but has been shot to death by Alvin as if it were an animal that, unable to fulfill its natural function, needed to be put out of its misery. The sequence works again to stitch the machines into a more expansive network of benevolence. Tom (Everett McGill) leads Alvin to an old John Deere mower, a still-functioning relic on a lot where it is dwarfed by the latest Deere combines. These monsters of modern agribusiness looked natural enough, and in their proper scale, in the open expanse of the Iowa cornfield but now seem enormous next to the old technology. Tellingly, Alvin asks after its year (1966), and Tom assures him that although it has been used for parts, the parts have always been replaced anew. It has the old transmission, and its "guts are good." "Is it a good machine?" Alvin asks. "It's a good machine," Tom assures him. The charming exchange observes the tendency of farmers—and of many people whose livelihood depends on an intimacy with machines—to animate and humanize their equipment. In the same vein, it establishes a parallel between this old, good John Deere; the machine that is Alvin Straight, its soon-to-be-user; and the mower's prior owners. Alvin explains that you can learn about old machines if you know their past owner, who is, of course, Tom himself. Enough said. There is no haggling over price; Alvin simply explains what he has to pay. There is no need to question the goodness of the machine, since it was run by Tom, whom Alvin knows as well as Tom knows him. While experiencing changes to its body over time, this is a machine that endures and may continue to live beyond its loving chain of human users. Part of the point of Alvin's acquisition of a *second* lawn mower, his beginning *again* of his journey, is to underscore this quality of excessive life in the face of death. This "good machine" encapsulates the fundamental goodness of the organism in the film: the way machines and humans live together in time and sustain each other in an ongoing network of attention, kindness, and generosity. That the machinic organism is interrupted by inevitable stillness, repetition, and death will not stall a more fundamental dynamism that exceeds individual lives. But the mower is also an intermediate agency, a channel, to other living beings: Tom, Lyle, and indeed all of the people Alvin encounters in his journey. In other words, the mower is a vital medium.

The overwhelming goodness of humans and machines in the film also recasts the kinds of "bad" machines, technologies, and networks that are so obsessively on display in other, putatively more Lynchian films. The human body is consistently endowed with machinic properties in Lynch's work, but *The Straight Story* gives them a different affective quality. The film's opening sequence, for example, in which a neighbor hears Alvin's falling body inside his home, echoes Laura's status as falling in space in *Fire Walk with Me* and anticipates Rebekah Del Rio's sudden collapse in Club Silencio, only here Alvin's abrupt immobility is played for laughs. The curiously intermittent vocal patterns of Rose's (Sissy Spacek) voice remind us of Lynch's interest in "unnatural" distortions of the voice, here naturalized as part of her unnamed disability. The astonishingly slow movements and frozen facial expressions of old men are disturbing, even uncanny, in films like *Wild at Heart* and *Mulholland Dr.*, but here, with the codgers who congregate at the hardware store to remark on Alvin's folly, they play as the earned languor of old folks. Lynch includes one nocturnal, low-angle shot of a grain elevator, and we hear a low machinic hum that so often codes the workings of inscrutable machines. Out of context, the shot could surely be menacing, but Lynch cuts from it to Alvin, who, in addressing Rose, also addresses us, reminding us of the film's principle of machinic goodness: "Listen to that old grain elevator. Harvest time. Look up at the sky, Rosie. The sky is sure filled with stars tonight."

Consider, too, how the flickering of electricity, which serves as a consistent figure for strange transfers of psychic energy between humans and machines in so many of Lynch's films, is cast in *The Straight Story* as an inevitable approach of the end of life. Importantly, it is the scene that sparks Alvin's motion in the first place as he and Rose get the phone call alerting them to Lyle's stroke. In a two shot, Alvin and his daughter sit in their darkened living room, watching a lightning storm outside. We see only their faces, which register first the natural beauty of the storm—the shadows of rain on the windowpanes falling on their bodies, the sound of the rain and thunder—and then the sound of the ringing phone. As Rose rises to answer it in the adjacent room, Lynch links the two offscreen environments through their shared aurality: the space of the telephone call, alerting Alvin to his brother's illness, and the space of the storm. As Rose's voice-off informs Alvin of his brother's stroke, lightning flashes and thunder booms. The doubled offscreen spaces, one technological, the other natural, confer the storm's simultaneous quality of inevitability and surprise on the facts of Lyle's mortal, bodily contingency—such is nature. Lightning, an occurrence that both Alvin and Rose claim to love at the beginning of the scene is, of course, its own form of a stroke—a natural electrical disturbance not unlike the failing nervous system of an aging brain. And the broken circuit of Alvin's love for his brother is what his trip seeks to repair.

"Good machine," then, encapsulates the way Lynch's Iowa landscape has not so much eliminated the machinic monsters of his darker films as he has shown them to be folded into the basic texture of midwestern life—its ways of abiding in a landscape of proliferating hybrids of nature-culture. This is especially clear in the film's reworking of Lynch's familiar fascination with the car crash and related contingencies of road-bound motion. In one of the film's truly strange sequences, Alvin's peaceful journey is interrupted by the trauma of accidental death when he witnesses a woman strike and kill a deer with her automobile. The woman is nearly hysterical, explaining to Alvin that she has struck thirteen deer in the past seven days on her daily commute on the road. "And I love deer!" she cries. We cut from this odd scene to Alvin, cooking meat over an open fire. He is sitting in a field surrounded by plastic deer, whom he eyes with some guilt as he prepares his roadkill. The next day, Alvin is back on the road, only now he has mounted the dead deer's antlers on the trailer he's pulling behind his lawn mower (fig. 20). We dissolve from Alvin's bizarre, so-called rolling home—another combine—to more aerial views of combines moving through the Iowa cornfields. We dissolve again to a close-up of a building on fire, which we soon learn is being combated by firefighters as part of a routine training exercise.

Figure 20. Alvin Straight's rolling home |

Again, Lynch's strategy is to present us with a threatening trope—say, the volatile combustibility of fire from *Wild at Heart*—and fold it into another, more expansive context that domesticates it. As Michel Chion has noted, this happens on the level of scale: the hyper-proximity to the fire gives way to a long shot that turns what would otherwise be a traumatic occurrence (precisely the kind that tend to pop up along the road in Lynch's films) into a routine happening. Time, too, is recalibrated as the sudden event expands into an excessively long take of the fireman spraying water on the flames. Natural elements, fire and water, but also stars and storms, seem marked by duration rather than exhaustion.

The curious deer episode underscores Alvin as fundamentally *at home* in the film's teeming natural environment, a comfort here signaled by his calm resourcefulness with the overpopulated animals (another sign of organic life's ongoing-ness in and through death) and his matter-of-fact handling of contingency—animal life cut violently short. One is tempted to link Alvin's deer-eating with his love of lightning storms and stars, all of a piece with what could be read as the film's conservative equation between the life cycles of the natural world and the unchanging cultural values of small-town Iowa that Alvin incarnates: family, locality, religion, and national service. Alvin will even put a fascist spin on this equation, offering to a wayward pregnant teen a parable of strong families as fasces, "a bundle of sticks." We might expect such family values in a Disney film.

But Lynch's picture of the organism is rather different. Its story of nature, culture, and technology is not really that straight, a fact that the deer episode also makes clear in its visual punning and analogies between the deer that becomes a relic as a trailer totem and the antiquated John Deere lawn mower sparked to life, propelling Alvin's journey. Early in the film, after his fall alerts him to his failing health and he waits in his doctor's examination room, we've seen Alvin's fear of the menacing intervention of biotechnology in his life in an anxious POV shot that pans across the range of medical equipment. It is perhaps the single most disturbing image of technology in the film. Yet Alvin's worry is mitigated in part by the fact that he is already a cyborg whose movement through the landscape is technologically propelled. He needs two canes to walk, a prosthetic mechanical "grabber" to gather kindling for his fires on the road, and a "good machine" to repair the broken family circuit at the end of the film. This last union, again facilitated by the stopping of Alvin's machine and the restarting of his motion by another moving vehicle (a tractor gives him a tow), is framed as the coming together of two aging bodies, carrying on with prosthetic supplements: Alvin, with his canes, faces Lyle, with his metal walker. Notice how Lynch transvalues the prosthetic figures of, for example, *Wild at Heart*, where prosthesis codes the depravity of Grace Zabriskie's Juana Durango, or the canes and walkers of the curious old men in a New Orleans hotel, which underwrite Lynch's unsettling form of comic timing.

In *The Straight Story*, Lynch's mise-en-scène insists that Alvin's comfort with nature is also a comfort in a landscape itself dominated by the processes of technological second nature: the plastic deer in the field, the deer ashtrays, a truck in the shape of a giant ear of corn, the processed meats like Alvin's beloved "wieners" and braunschweiger, the industrial hum of the grain elevator at work, and, of course, Iowa's most unnatural, most monstrously prolix product—bioengineered corn. Alvin will later remark on his easy inhabitation of this environment: "Well, ma'am, I served in the trenches in World War Two. Why should I be afraid of an Iowa cornfield?" The point is not that corn is not monstrous, but that it is a monster no longer to be feared in an environment that domesticates trauma so well. (A similar point is scored when Alvin passes a grotto along the road—a species of the grotesque, but devoid of fear and anxiety.)

There *is* trauma in the film, but it is presented as being folded into larger, restorative contexts that make its inevitable returns bearable.

Alvin's homily about family to the runaway teenager is not gospel but a tacit acknowledgment of the fragility of his own home, haunted by loss, absence, and accident. Alvin's wife is dead, he lost seven of his fourteen babies (he describes it, aptly, as a bad yield), and his fraternal bond has been severed. The sequence in which Alvin and the runaway girl forge a temporary bond by roasting hotdogs over a campfire is an homage to a similar scene in the *The Wizard of Oz*, when Professor Marvel roasts hotdogs for a runaway Dorothy. The echo encourages us to consider the family as a dynamic, often insecure movement between exile and home, composed of all manner of mobile affiliations. Alvin also tells this girl that his disabled daughter, Rose, has had her children taken from her by the state. Like the earlier scene in Alvin's doctor's office, Lynch nods to another intervention into life's vital, intimate processes by larger modern systems of biological administration (doctors, genetic engineers, and now social services). Rose has been pronounced an unfit mother because her children, while being watched by someone else, were nearly harmed in an accidental fire. This allows us to make sense retroactively of a melancholy earlier silent sequence in which Rose looks out her window at night and observes a ball rolling down the sidewalk. A young boy follows after it, picks it up, and pauses. This uncanny movement of the ball, horizontally from frame right to left, recalls the spilling of Elsie Beckmann's ball into an empty frame like this, announcing her murder in Fritz Lang's *M* (1931). Here, the emergence of the boy into the frame only deepens the pangs of absence that Rose feels for her lost children, although Lynch also includes in the tableau a small lawn sprinkler attached to a garden hose. Its faint but persistent flow seems to compensate for human loss.

Similarly, the narrative detail of Rose's haunting by an accidental fire provides precisely the traumatic accident that Lynch's editing will tame, after the fact, in the firefighters' training exercise. He first shows us that we have reason to fear fires, and broken families, balancing that threat with the image of a cheery campfire and its ways of producing temporary attachments. Then he lays bare the mechanisms for domesticating that trauma by folding it into larger dynamic processes in the firefighter training exercise. The burning house, its menace controlled, will resurface as a threat as the brakes on Alvin's rig fail on the decline of a steep hill, sending him speeding out of control. He lands not in the flaming barn but in the bosom of another small community, presided over by Danny Riordan (James Cada). The firemen, in a nice touch, help push the newly stalled rig to Danny's home.

Like Rose's sprinkler, or Alvin's bundle of sticks, the ongoing life—the autumnal harvesting, death, and rebirth—of the Iowa cornfield is a compensatory figure that assuages an earlier loss. Alvin's homeliness in the cornfield, his willingness to expose himself to the elements, is not timeless or ontological. It is a salve for the violence he experienced as a sniper in the war. In one of the film's most affecting scenes, Alvin will accept an invitation for a drink at a local bar from a man who turns out to be another World War II veteran. There, in a sequence shot almost entirely in close-ups, the men trade war stories of the least heroic kind. Their accounts of past trauma seem to spill out of them just by their being in the presence of each other, harvesting memories like adjacent combines. Alvin confesses, for the first time, how as a sniper he accidently shot a fellow soldier and explains how the trauma produces a rift in time: as he gets older, the faces of the dead seem younger, reanimated in memory. Time does not advance only chronologically but is also distended experientially. The traumatic returns, and is managed, in the presence of another, large vital context: another life and another story of lives cut short by larger, here geopolitical, conflicts.

If the environment of *The Straight Story* is organic, it is not an unchanging nature, but nature dynamized by constant motion. Life persists in its movement toward death, a persistence all the more remarkable for the ways its rhythms are warped by trauma and loss and are menaced by intervening forces beyond individuals. Some of these larger, abstract systems contaminate life's most intimate processes, but others provide a network that allows for do-overs and second chances, that domesticates trauma, and that is reanimated following temporary breaks or cessations of the organism's functioning.

The picture of expansive nature, and Alvin's place in it, is further dynamized for the film's spectators by the way it verges on abstraction at times, becoming an experiment in a variously moving image of organic density and superabundant complexity. Michel Chion has observed how the film's first aerial shot of the Iowa cornfield begins as "an unidentified texture" of golden, furrowed lines rather than an identifiable figure. Even more striking is the way Lynch consistently uses Alvin's journey across the landscape as the occasion to stage abstract comparisons between the various speeds and sizes, forces and ages, operating within his image of second nature. So, much as he asks us to compare deer and Deere on the road, Lynch's editing invites comparisons between, say, Alvin's slow and steady movement and the forceful thunder of a passing semi or the bewildering buzzing of a road filled with RAGBRAI (*[Des Moines] Register*'s Annual Great Bicycle Ride Across Iowa) bicyclists; or between Alvin's advanced age and the youth of many of the cyclists; or between the teenage mom-to-be, pregnant for the first time, and Alvin's own dead mother; or, even more abstractly, between Alvin's physical pace and his daughter Rose's mental acuity: "People say she's slow," Alvin notes, "but she has a mind like a bear trap." Emphasizing the varying sizes, speeds, and times of life operating simultaneously, Lynch turns the natural environment into another active, artful garden. For spectators, participating in the teeming life of the image entails recognizing abstract resemblances and differences that animate its terrain of activity and constitute it as a moving picture.

Vital Media: *Inland Empire*

Six Men Getting Sick, *The Grandmother*, and *The Straight Story*, while very different films, suggest that for Lynch, organisms are *mediumistic*. I mean this in two senses: in the general way he twins aesthetic and organic processes, and in the more specific ways in which the films deploy media themselves as sites, channels, conduits, or relays of organic dynamics and psychophysiological currents. This notion has a rich intellectual history in Western modernity, gathering force in the eighteenth century when the scientific discovery of the invisible forces of gravity, magnetism, and electricity spawned a broad discourse that understood earthly, mechanical bodies to be pervaded by a wondrous, ethereal force. This magnetic fluid, in Franz Anton Mesmer's infamous theory, was thought to link embodied life and cosmos in a vast, imponderable network; in it, the mesmerized body was the conduit of vital passage between terrestrial and meteoric orders. Extending eighteenth-century attempts to understand electricity as an immanent force—the spark of life itself—literary Romantics like Coleridge, Shelley, Poe, and Whitman were energized by the confirmation of electromagnetic induction and Morse's invention of the telegraph in the 1830s. These scientific breakthroughs, challenging the static picture of the Newtonian universe of solid particles in motion, led the Romantics to champion electricity as a mode of "techno-utopian thought."[116] For them, electricity and its technological incarnations like the telegraph offered a material metaphor for the transformative power of aesthetic experience, a way of conceptualizing the relationship between sensuous, material existence and consciousness. Moreover, aesthetic electricity was a medium through which the contours of political community could be thought, since electric experience was consistently understood as a kind of depersonalization in which the atomistic self was suspended in estrangement or extended into a larger collective identification.

As Pam Thurschwell has argued, this cultural fascination with the permeability of the borders of mind and bodies, their suggestibility to exterior forces or their vulnerability to mediumistic transmission peaked in the fin-de-siècle explosion of "magical thinking."[117] By this, Thurschwell has in mind the various forms of mediated intimacy or communication believed to collapse distances between bodies and minds, thinking that crossed a range of discourses from the occult investment in spiritualism and telepathy; to the cultural fantasies of electronic simultaneity or disembodiment produced by telegraphs and telephones; to new psychological theories of hysteria, hypnosis, and the corporeal unconscious. On the one hand, such concepts of the self as a kind of mediumistic host to the abstract transmission of psychic energies allowed for the nineteenth-century afterlife of mesmerism; on the other, in their insistence on an uncanny subject never quite present to itself, these theories anticipated the most profound discovery of aesthetic modernism: the boundless terrain of the embodied mind, a medium always different from itself.

Such is the charged psycho-technical landscape of *Inland Empire*, a film that is everywhere preoccupied by the peculiar "liveness" of electronic—specifically, digital—media and the bewildering contours of the worlds it sparks into being. Its inaugural sequence proclaims its medial self-awareness and its strange digital circuits. A beam of projected light illuminates the film's title, and the close-up grooves of a scratchy phonograph stylus announce "AXXon N., the longest-running radio play in history, continuing tonight in the Baltic region, a grey winter day in an old hotel." As inscription, "AXXon N." is a kind of mobile cipher. First heard as a recorded performance, it enacts the kinds of iterative transfers of information across media that shape the world of *Inland*

Empire. The title of an unrealized 2002 Web series from davidlynch
.com, "AXXon N." will later materialize as cryptic text on metal within
the psychic topography of *Inland Empire*'s protagonist, the actress Nikki
Grace (Laura Dern). An "axon" (*uncut* by the doubled, anonymous
"X" or the Kafkaesque abbreviation "N.") is the fiber of a nerve cell
transmitting the body's messages electrically. The graphic and semantic
instability of "AXXon N." is thus a flickering figure for Nikki's iterative
mental circuits and their delayed psychic economies of abreaction.

We now witness, presumably, a first local performance of this longest-
running story: an anonymous, anxious encounter between prostitute and
john in an unrecognizable hotel room. After this scene, the so-called
Lost Girl (Karolina Gruszka), an incarnation or iteration of the prostitute
we've just seen, makes her way toward her eventual intimacy with the
film's protagonist, Nikki Grace, which will consist in their becoming
media for and to each other. For now, the Lost Girl weeps in front of
a television set that moves in and out of static like so many of Lynch's
nested screens, projects future scenes of *Inland Empire* itself, and opens
onto the set of *Rabbits*, an eight-part Web series first distributed on
davidlynch.com (fig. 21). The film's media ecology (projection, pho-
nography, the performing body, radio, television, the Internet) is wildly
impure, upping the ante on Marshall McLuhan's axiom that media always
take as their content another medium, and embedding its characters in

Figure 21. Digital environments for Lost Girls |

a vast digital *combinatoire*, a network of fractal worlds that open onto each other through electricity. Electricity, *Inland Empire* suggests, is the uncanny agent of the infinitely flexible life shared by digital media and consciousness itself.

As Jeffrey Sconce has shown, over the last 150 years the metaphysics of electricity has operated by a durable "series of interrelated metaphors of 'flow,' suggesting analogies between electricity, consciousness, and information that enable fantastic forms of electronic transmutation, substitution, and exchange."[118] In Lynch's case, these analogies have appeared most forcefully in his increasingly public arguments for the compatibility of his theory of embodied consciousness—often metaphorized as either a lightbulb or "an ocean of pure, vibrant consciousness" where "creativity really flows"—and a particular proposition of theoretical physics called "unified field theory," a notion that, for Lynch and others, is compatible with the Vedic practice of Transcendental Meditation (TM).

A practitioner since the 1970s, Lynch has become a vocal proselytizer for TM over the last decade, founding the David Lynch Foundation for Consciousness-Based Education and World Peace and appearing annually as part of a "David Lynch Weekend" fund-raiser for the Maharishi University of Management in Fairfield, Iowa. Commenting on the relationship between "pure consciousness" and unified field theory in his *Catching the Big Fish,* part aesthetic treatise, part New Age self-help book, Lynch loosely paraphrases physicist John Hagelin's theoretical proposal in his manifesto *Manual for a Perfect Government* that "subjective technologies" like meditation can provide "direct experiential access to the laws of nature."[119] In Hagelin's words, unified field theory proposes that subatomic fields of matter reveal "progressively more unified fields of nature's functioning" and that "the entire universe, with all its diverse and multiform properties, is just a cosmic symphony—the vibrational states of a single, underlying, universal, unified field of nature's intelligence."[120] As a concept of mind, unified field theory hinges on a central analogy between the abstract operations of matter at its most fundamental (and theoretical) levels and the deepest, most dynamic and abstract levels of the mind. "Life," Hagelin insists, "derives its special qualities precisely because its roots go deep into the quantum-mechanical realm . . . The abstract nature of the human mind is merely a reflection of the abstract nature of the universe at these fundamental scales."[121]

Comments like these are tricky because they imply that Lynch's interest in TM's compromise between scientific materialism and mental abstraction—one that privileges the indeterminacy and flux of psychic life—entails the recuperation of some suspect mode of romantic transcendence or spiritual unity. Yet *Inland Empire* avoids this risk, chiefly through its materialist exploration of *digital* vitality and through its insistence that the flows of electronic media, information, and consciousness share a basic situational instability. The unformed situation is the intermittent heart of Lynch's digital ecology, producing emotional states of terror and bliss but also less structured, less cognitively interpretable affects that accompany the experience of being brought into uncanny forms of relation and finding oneself in precarious skeins of likeness and difference. In *Inland Empire*, to experience, as its protagonist does, the kind of flickering life the self shares with electronic media is to explore embodied consciousness as an *ethics*. The film insists on consciousness not so much as unbroken "flow" but as a disjunctive encounter with internal difference and the vital medium of recognition of networks of relationship with others—others brought impossibly proximate through the global architecture of Lynch's first digital film. And it is a relentlessly cinematic globality, connecting Hollywood Boulevard to the snowy streets of Lodz, Poland, ground zero for film production in Poland, and home to the renowned Polish National Film School.

A nearly three-hour feature shot entirely with a low-grade digital camera, *Inland Empire* is many things, but it is first and foremost a self-reflexive examination of the strange life of digital technology performed by an artist who has newly fallen in love with cinema in the land of ones and zeroes. The Sony PD-150—a small, cheap, low-definition camera that was already outmoded by the time Lynch first picked it up—is an unsexy love object to be sure, and yet it suits the film's aesthetics of poverty, vulnerability, and indeterminacy. Lynch has happily promoted the notion that *Inland Empire*'s evolution followed the big bang of his encounter with the digital. Even in the few short years since the film's debut, its story of origins has accrued mythic status among Lynch's critics and fans. Made without a complete shooting script, the film began, instead, with a germ, a fragment—a fourteen-page monologue by a victimized woman, which Laura Dern memorized and delivered, and which Lynch filmed with the PD-150 in "about a seventy-minute take," and with no sense of the larger whole to which it might belong.[122] This is an old surrealist lesson in the erotic epistemology of cinema: hallucinate the fragment. In the beginning was a situation, perhaps best described here as "A Woman in Trouble," the ur-situation of melodrama, and the teasing tagline of all promotional materials for *Inland Empire*.

More than any of Lynch's films, *Inland Empire* beggars description, its narrative decentered from the start and later multiply derailed in an intoxicating hash of highly atmospheric situations. *Inland Empire*'s plot, such as it is, concerns an actress named Nikki Grace, who has recently won a starring role in a contrived Hollywood melodrama called *On High in Blue Tomorrows*. In the course of rehearsing *Tomorrows*, Nikki and her costar, Devon Berk (Justin Theroux), learn from their director, Kingsley Stewart (Jeremy Irons), that *Tomorrows* is in fact not an original script but rather a remake of an earlier film called *47*, a "cursed" project, based on a Polish gypsy folktale, abandoned after its two leads were murdered during filming. In *Tomorrows* Nikki plays Susan Blue, a teasing Southern belle who becomes involved in an adulterous relationship with Devon's Billy Side. This fictional act of infidelity is eventually doubled outside the nested film when the "real" Nikki has an affair with Devon, an act that seems to precipitate the narrative's derailing in a bewildering network of situations of variously troubled women who may or may not be Nikki Grace, who saves one of these women—introduced to us early in the film as the "Lost Girl"—by killing a mystery man known as the Phantom (Krzysztof Majchrzak), and, uniting the Lost Girl with her husband and son.

The film's cheery final union, typical of Lynch's endings, is an abrupt putting to death of the film's delirious narrative middle, which grows monstrously vital, undergoing a proliferation of situations that are so teeming as to refuse the kinds of characterological sortings, narrative siftings, and chronological simplifications that would make clear, cognitive sense. From Lynch's enthusiastic remarks about shooting with digital—about its mobility, its constructivist plasticity, its proximity to the contingencies of performance—we can gather that *Inland Empire*'s situational uncertainty is fueled by the technical flexibility of digital life. In more properly Lynchian terms, we might say that digital life is uncanny; generated by abstract algorithms rather than an artist's hand, the digital has no originating signature, nor does it have an end, but is given instead to endless creative refashioning.

Digital's un-homeliness also challenges teleological accounts of cinema itself, since digital's plasticity and supposed freedom from photographic reference marks a kind of return of cinema's repressed roots in nineteenth-century animation techniques. New media theorist Lev Manovich, for example, has posited the advent of digital cinema as the moment that "the history of the moving image thus makes a full circle. *Born from animation, cinema pushed animation to its periphery, only in the end to become one particular case of animation.*"[123] Lynch's own comments on the texture of the PD-150's image describe a similar conviction that the digital instantiates not so much an entirely new kind of image but rather a particular imagistic quality—fantastic and subjective—that returns aesthetically to an earlier moment in the evolution of the moving picture and in his own career: "It's more like a moving painting than it is modern 35mm, there's something about it that gives you room to dream, something magical. What I liked about [digital] video was that it reminded me of '30s films when [the image] wasn't so sharp and was more impressionistic. It made it less real."[124] This, presumably, is why Lynch prefers the relative poverty and imprecision of low-fi video to the illusionistic power of high-end digital reproduction. Like a long tradition of avant-garde artists captivated by the non-naturalistic image, Lynch seeks the reality of the cinematic experience on a phenomenological level, where our involvement in the image deepens as the picture itself becomes less real.

Inland Empire is thus a fine example of the connection between post-filmic technology and post-realist narrative. This affinity, as Garrett Stewart has recently argued, helps explain digital narrative's curious tropism toward narratives of the fantastic and their abiding inorganic temporality, "digitime." In "digitime," time is imaged as a "process malleable, even reversible . . . the feel of time . . . takes shape as a portable interface rather than an organic interval: a phantasmal zone internally convertible without being transversable from one integrated moment to the next . . . Time is . . . differential from the inside out."[125] It is no surprise, then, that many critics have explained the nonlinear, recursive temporality of *Inland Empire* as an enactment of the experiential qualities of a global digital environment: the untimely speed of a series of openings or interfaces to other virtual sites; or the feeling of sudden, often violent connectivity with heretofore unknown space-times; or the sense of algorithmic, nondeterministic causality. For some film and media theorists, of course, this environment has transformed the experience of cinema itself, changes that are taken up directly in the film. Lynch's insertion of *Rabbits* into the network of *Inland Empire* is not only an instance of media convergence but also a knowing commentary on the digital transformation of the cinematic itself into a multimedia event, one that demands both complex forms of storytelling ("puzzle films," game films, modular narratives, database narratives, etc.) and putatively more interactive or "participatory" forms of cross-platform spectatorship.[126]

Lynch, of course, did not need to scrap celluloid to produce "post-realist cinema," any more than Buñuel did, say, or Maya Deren, and he has always understood cinema as a hybrid and impure organism that compels interaction of various kinds. *Inland Empire*, after all, was theatrically distributed and exhibited on film. This should not surprise us, since the digital's plastic powers of animation were always germinating in Lynch's non-digital work. What is specific to *Inland Empire*'s understanding of digital experience is not its post-realism, then, but its privileged relationship to the worldliness and temporality of the female body, and to the broader category of domestic life that is so essential to Lynch's work and its apportioning of gendered behavior. In fact, the film's feminist ethics are based in its attempt to explore a link between the topography of the female body in time and the digital image through their shared "worldliness."

In *Inland Empire* these malleable forms of digital potentiality—and of "digitime" as a portable temporal interface—play out in a series of arresting grotesques of the composited female face and generate some of the film's greatest moments of affective intensity. In one of these moments, an unmotivated cut to a circus poster image of a clown's smiling face is superimposed over, and slowly dissolves into, an image of a solitary Nikki Grace, the film's protagonist, spotlit, on a meandering hillside path. By now, Nikki, a Hollywood actress, has fallen deeply down the ontological rabbit hole of *Inland Empire*'s cursed film-within-the-film, fracturing into several different characters in the process. As Nikki approaches the camera, running in slow motion, her midsection swells, bloats, and swivels until her terrified face jumps quickly into close-up. In another moment, a traumatized Nikki finally confronts the film's mysterious hypnotist, the Phantom, shooting him three times. After the final blast, Lynch cuts to a reaction shot of Nikki, which then explodes into a digitally composited close-up of her utterly distorted look of terror, now layered on top of the Phantom's visage, portions of his glowing hair and beard still visible under Nikki's shocking rictus (fig. 22). We cut back to a slow-motion image of Nikki's pistol, another reaction shot of Nikki, then to another, final digital bit of grotesquerie: now superimposed on the Phantom's face is a powdered white face (echoing the clown poster) with blackened eyes, open red lips, and a dark mouth, from which leaks blood and entrails (fig. 23).

This visceral image, recalling the guts that by now we have seen oozing from the bowels of several women, embodies the way Lynch's digital images in *Inland Empire* consistently blur and collapse identity beyond recognition. At the same time, it underscores the power of the digital grotesque as a cognitive site of resemblance—of doubling and analogy between and across the temporally fractured situations of the film's many troubled girls. We recognize a likeness of situations but also the acute familiarity of a series of reliable interface technologies for coding states of female vulnerability. Nikki's situations, in short, are never properly hers but appear as anticipations and echoes in the film's broader Lost Girl series—extending from Nikki to her alter ego, Susan; to the leggy posse of teenage girls who dance the "Loco-Motion" in some alternate domestic universe; to the hookers on Hollywood Boulevard; to

Figure 22. The female face: composited out of time

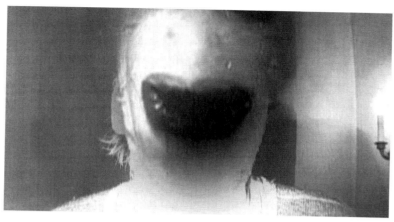

Figure 23. The image as site
of medial recognition

the film's inaugural "Lost Girl," the young prostitute who begins the film proper. She is first introduced to the viewer, and her client, in a hotel room where she asks, anxiously, "This is the room? I don't recognize it," and her head, like that of her john, is vanished into the anonymity of a digital blur. The blur, a reliably modernist photographic technique for coding temporal impossibility, here does the inorganic work of the digital grotesque—citing any number of medial codings of the situation, from the snuff film to the enforced anonymity of the journalistic exposé or the surveillance video reviewed after the crime.

Part of the fascination of these images, like those of Lynch's recent series of digital photographs, "Distorted Nudes," lies in the way their digital unreality—their crude, distorted, almost comical non-naturalism—impinges directly on the body. They summon the affects of disgust and revulsion with the corporeal, as well as the emotional oscillation between horror and humor, that we conventionally associate with the grotesque. For viewers, such grotesques thereby enact on a sensory level *Inland Empire*'s thematic anxieties about the female body in time—a body that is vulnerable to the natural processes of aging and mortality and subject to the pressures of global markets, like Hollywood's own, that capitalize on the commodification of the eternally youthful, ever vital female body. These pressures are evident enough in Nikki's digital grotesques, legible as projections of fundamental fears about embodied life. Think, too, of the strange conversations between the leggy band of teenage girls Nikki encounters in the living room of some alternate domestic universe, for whom the chance of romantic love hinges on having great T and A, bodily currency they mutually display and appraise before busting into a choreographed rendition of Little Eva's "Loco-Motion."

Most illustrative of the temporal vulnerability of the female body is the rather bizarre story Nikki hears late in the film when, apparently stabbed by Doris Side (Julia Ormond), the wife of her fictional lover, Billy, for her fictional infidelity, she collapses on Hollywood Boulevard next to a sidewalk star reading "Dorothy" (for Lynch, the original Lost Girl) and between two other homeless girls, who have taken to sleeping on the street. Nikki has interrupted the girls' debate about whether, from the intersection of Hollywood and Vine, one can or cannot get a bus to Pomona. The African American girl (Helena Chase) asks the time, and the Asian girl (Nae), who speaks accented, subtitled English replies, "After midnight." She then explains that, for "three fifty," she took the bus to Pomona last summer to visit her friend Niko for two weeks:

My friend Niko lives in Pomona and has a blonde wig. She wears it at parties. But she's on hard drugs and turning tricks now. She looks very good in her blonde wig, just like a movie star. Even girls fall in love with her when she's looking so good in her blonde star wig. She blows kisses and laughs, but she has got a hole in her vagina wall. She has torn a hole into her intestine from her vagina. She has seen a doctor, but it is too expensive, and now she knows her time has run out. She score a few more times, and then, like that, she will stay at home with her monkey. She has a pet monkey. This monkey shits everywhere, but she doesn't care. This monkey can scream, it screams like it's in a horror movie. But there are those who are good with animals, who have a way with animals.

On one level the story connects the film's worldly women—prostitutes and stars—through shared vulnerability. Niko and the two Lost Girls whose desperate situation prompts her story, and who, like her, are likely turning tricks, are subject to the same temporal pressures as the dying Nikki Grace, a blonde actress who is also hoping to become a star and whose time, it seems, has also run out. This mutual susceptibility to time is again rendered through the grotesque: first in the account of

Niko's perforated vaginal wall and then, immediately after the story's conclusion, in the image of Nikki, whose ruptured abdomen causes her to vomit blood directly onto one of the Hollywood stars. Like the girls whose stagey version of the "Loco-Motion" happens in a suburban living room, these worldly women also find their movements blocked. The shared promises of Hollywood and romantic love—that, in the words of one of the "Loco-Motion" dancers, "you'll always have a chance with tits like that"—are here betrayed by the facts of destitution and the sheer precariousness of the body.

As in *Six Men Getting Sick*, which pits the organic impossibility of the thrown image against the beholder's experience of pulsation, in *Inland Empire* Lynch sets the temporal warpings of digitime and the limitless body of the feminized digital grotesque against our affective involvement in the thickening texture of media. One effect of this is that we notice a gap between the plasticity of the image and the mortal limits of our bodies. On the other hand, Lynch seems to insist upon the excessive, indeterminate quality shared by bodies and images, which is one way of understanding organisms and media's shared capacity for self-difference. Like the polymorphous uncanniness of the digital, the affective complex of the grotesque is unstable, oscillating between horror and sadistic humor without finally achieving moral or emotional equilibrium. Grotesque affect, we might say, is the embodied yield of the supposedly immaterial digital medium and thus helps to flesh out an ethereal technology.

At the same time, the language of this story and its framing are typical of the film's tendency to structure its images and sounds as sites of cognitive connection, or, better, *recognition*, for characters and viewers alike. In doing so, Lynch's images appeal to what Barbara Stafford has described as the inherently visual component of analogy, an "art of sympathetic thought" that encourages participatory discernment of likeness and connectedness, of "similarity-in-difference."[127] *Inland Empire*'s texture of poetic density is woven chiefly through its imagistic iterations and echoes—the way its happening produces anticipations, fulfillments, and uncanny doublings of earlier narrative situations that have never finally resolved themselves. So, just as we have been encouraged to discern resemblances between the situations of the film's worldly women (how Susan is like Nikki, who is like the Lost Girl, who is like the dancing girls, who are like the prostitutes on Hollywood Boulevard, who are like Niko, who is like Nikki), so the Niko story's narrative placement after the question of the time and the answer "after midnight" is heard as an echo of the Visitor #1's (Grace Zabriskie) claim that she "can't seem to remember if it's today, two days from now, or yesterday. I suppose if it was nine forty-five I'd think it was after midnight." And we have heard variations of the Asian girl's claim that Niko "has a way with animals" twice before—first, as part of another odd comment made backstage by Kingsley's assistant, Freddie (Harry Dean Stanton) to Nikki and Devon. When asked whether he's enjoying himself, Freddie responds, "Well, there's a vast network, an ocean of possibilities. I like dogs. I used to raise rabbits. I've always loved animals. Their nature. How they think. I have seen dogs reason their way out of problems, watched them think through the trickiest of situations." Then, later in the film, when Nikki seems to have transformed into an abused, newly pregnant, working-class housewife who may or may not be the character Susan Blue, she is bewildered to discover one day that her husband tends animals for a circus that performs in traveling shows in the Baltic region. "It was said," explains her husband, "that I have way with animals."

Who or what, in these echoed utterances, are the animals? This last iteration seems to link animality to the feminine, suggesting that the abusive husband's capacity to control and victimize his pregnant wife also qualifies him to tend the domesticated circus animals when he travels, movement from home that she is disallowed. If to be an animal is to be subject to the life of the body, and bodily vulnerability, then Niko's pet monkey, shitting everywhere, befouling the home, is a kind of grotesque double for her own animal abjection, its horror-movie scream an ironic echo of her betrayed star fantasy. Freddie's comments, however, depart from this old equation between female and animal embodiment. For him, animal nature involves a kind of improvisational genius that dogs share with actors, cagey when situations proliferate, at home in performance's creative "ocean of possibilities."

And Freddie's remarks themselves *produce* interpretive openings, not just in their quirky randomness, but in the way, for example, that his line about dogs and rabbits implicates two of Lynch's own creative endeavors: his comic strip, *The Angriest Dog in the World*, and *Rabbits,* a Beckettian sitcom featuring a family of human actors wearing giant rabbit heads and voiced by Laura Elena Harring, Naomi Watts, and Scott Coffey. These same rabbits, of course, show up repeatedly in *Inland Empire* and proved perhaps the most reliable source of critical befuddlement. When we ask ourselves whether or when in this film we have heard about the animals before, and when we begin to experience a dawning sense of similitude between animal situations, which then leads us to another question like "What's up with the rabbits?" we are participating in the unfolding of the film's proliferating network of information. In these ways we become involved in the film's sensory-cognitive continuum, in its capacity for *abstraction*. The point is not to answer finally the question of what it may mean for Niko to be "good with animals," but to see how the question opens itself to situational uncertainty and to a related emotional ambiguity. *Inland Empire*'s rabbits are, interpretively speaking, productive fuckers. They spawn situations. They could mean, virtually, anything.

The Niko sequence "ends" with just this kind of situational disquiet. After Nikki collapses, the African American girl lights her cigarette lighter, holds it in front of Nikki, and whispers, "I'll show you light now. It burns bright forever . . . tomorrow. You on high now, love." We cut to a high-angle shot that slowly cranes out to reveal (as it doubles) the movement of a camera filming this scene, and we hear Kingsley's voice say, "Cut it! Print it!" The viewer senses that we are back on the set of *On High in Blue Tomorrows* and that we have just observed the film-within-a-film's final scene, a hunch that seems confirmed when an emotionally drained (but manifestly alive) Nikki slowly rises to applause from her director and crew. And yet this reading doesn't seem at all certain, doesn't quite fit, and not just because nothing in the clichéd nature of the filmed scenes of *Tomorrows* that we have previously seen has prepared us for this kind of grotesque ending. It's more that between the time of the plot's first clear derailment—which seems to happen during Nikki and Devon's act of adultery—and this, much later attempt to clarify the story, the film has grown monstrously vital, undergoing a proliferation of situations so teeming as to refuse the kinds of characterological sortings, narrative siftings, and chronological simplifications that would make clear, cognitive sense. What we experience instead is a delirious excess of happening over story, milieu over meaning, affect over event. Too much, it seems, has happened, and yet we can't say exactly what, beyond the tremor of happening itself. What's more, like the women in the film, we feel this indeterminacy deeply.

In these ways, *Inland Empire* seems to insist on the excessive, self-differing condition of embodied sensation and digital media alike, a condition with potentially liberating effects. We begin to see this in the way Lynch repeatedly positions women not just as objects within worldly circuits, but as embodied and emotive witnesses of themselves, and of other women, in a community of mediated recognition. Consider how, following the Niko sequence, the dazed Nikki walks off the set toward the exit of the soundstage. She pauses at the building's threshold and looks outside to the surrounding stages. We cut from Nikki, in medium close, to a tight close-up of the crying Lost Girl, whose wet eyes reflect the glow of a television set, in which, the next cut reveals, she watches Nikki in precisely the medium-close shot we ourselves have just seen. A brief shot/reverse-shot sequence between Nikki and the Lost Girl follows, suggesting Nikki's sense of being watched. We return to Nikki in medium close at the threshold of the soundstage, now photographed with a distorting wide-angle lens, but as the camera follows her movement, we realize she is no longer outside in the studio lot but rather in the interior of a dark theater, where she proceeds to watch her battered housewife character at precisely the moment (one we have watched earlier) when she describes going into "a bad time, when I was watching everything go around me while I was standing in the middle. Watching it . . . like in a dark theater before they bring the lights up."

The epistemological vertigo produced by this kind of mise-en-abyme structure is more than a cheap Lynchian mind-fuck. For if *Inland Empire* is replete with women seeing themselves, or other women, as images, its characters also comment on the visual processes of recognition and finding themselves or others unrecognizable. "Is this the room?" the Lost Girl asks in the opening sequence. "I don't recognize it." Nikki Grace, surprised, like us, to find herself suddenly in the person of an abused housewife, abruptly discovers two of the "Loco-Motion" girls in her backyard and says, "Look at me and tell me if you've known me before." Susan/Nikki's question is later globally displaced and asked a third time on a snowy Polish street by the Lost Girl to two other prostitutes. And the Lost Girl's situation is itself unstable: the man who, in the film's first sequence, appears to be her john, she later encounters on the street; only there he treats her as his wife, explaining that he "almost didn't recognize" her and that he's "used to seeing her at our home, not on the street, at night."

Such comments testify to the uncanny effect of the film's circuits of mediated observation: within them, the more these women look at themselves, the less they recognize themselves as distinct selves, appearing instead—to them and to us—to change constantly in echoes, anticipations, or temporal displacements of each other. Or, put another way, as character dissolves into atmosphere and affect, a common situation nonetheless emerges. This is most obvious in the abused housewife's account of male character: "There was this man I once knew. His name was . . . doesn't matter what his name was. A lot of guys change. They don't change, but they reveal. They reveal what they really are. Know what I mean? It's an old story." If the worldliness of women in *Inland Empire* is of the same substance as the worldliness of the digital image, both always uncannily different from themselves, then this vitality is defined against the non-changeability of men and the stasis of the domestic environment.

If the digital grotesque is one environment of situational uncertainty, another is *Inland Empire's* dazzling architecture of experience, its profusion of thresholds, open doors, stairways, alleys, streets, and halls that link the variety of homes through which Nikki Grace passes. Lynch's late-surrealist living room is a mise-en-scène of transition and passage, of movement away from the conservatism of the domestic. This is most obvious in the film's deployment of the modest ranch house on the so-called Smithy (Smithee?) set, where Nikki and Devon first read the cursed script of 47 only to be interrupted by an intruder we later find out to be another version of Nikki herself (fig. 24). The home's decor recalls the dilapidated modernity of so many of Lynch's domestic scenes, whose once au courant trappings have assumed the stalled temporality of vaguely mid-century kitsch. But over the next half hour of film time, this tableau of seemingly stilled domestic time will host or find some form of psychic adjacency to a dizzying multiplicity of space-times. Here, Nikki, in a past or future self, will both find her husband sleeping in the same bedroom in which she and Devon first made love and, later, announce to him that she is pregnant. Here, momentarily, Nikki will be taken by the troupe of dancing girls to Poland, which, it turns out, is just down the way and whose scenes are somehow also playing on the Lost Girl's

Figure 24. The Smithy set and the architecture
of experience

TV set. Here, Nikki will return to follow the instructions of the Lost Girl, who tells her that she can be made to see by burning a hole in silk with a cigarette and peering through the opening. Here, having created this visionary aperture, Nikki will see the Lost Girl abused by her husband/ john and see her own husband, or her other housewife-self's husband, on the streets of Lodz, Poland, and with his own, other wife, who can't give him children. Here, Nikki's cigarette will also burn an opening into the living room of the set of *Rabbits* (fig. 25). Here, on the *Rabbits* set, now spatially proximate to *Inland Empire*'s living room, she will later receive a phone call from Billy. And here also is the stage where the girls do the "Loco-Motion."

How, or by what kind of logic, can we understand everything that manages to happen here, defying causality and the laws of organic life? How, in this Lynchian room, do such "unrelated things live together"? In her suggestive discussion of *Inland Empire*, Amy Taubin has offered a materialist reading: that Lynch's newly global rooms in fact house a new digital gestalt in which "meaning is a matter of adjacent data."[128] Most of the film's scenes, Taubin notes, "begin and end with entrances and exits that connect two spaces that, in terms of real-world geography, could not be contiguous but become so simply because they reside in the 'select' bin on Lynch's Avid hard drive."[129] Extending Taubin's claim a bit, we

Figure 25. Rabbits and the Lynchian sitcom |

might say that the work of *Inland Empire* is to produce the feeling of unformed situations, an experience that Lynch codes as both specifically cinematic and surprisingly feminist. The global electronic environment of *Inland Empire* might be best described as an exploration of the virtual landscape that lies within the cinematic concept of "a girl in trouble." Lynch's digital poetics of the micro-situation grows, inorganically, from a succession of interrelated fragments that "live together" as so many incipiencies, variations, or riffs on the cinema's expressive powers for coding states of female distress. Like the cursed film *47*, or the Smithy set, these states will remain unfinished, always *in potentia*.

To explore this kind of potential requires Lynch's characters, and their bodies, to become inorganic. I read this less as a denial of embodied finitude than as a subversive sense of "domestic abuse," one at the heart of surrealist activity. Think of the way the threshold situations themselves do violence to codified scenes of domesticity, whose most reified form in mass media might well be the sitcom. Having converged into the digital texture of *Inland Empire*, the surreal mise-en-scène of Lynch's Web-based sitcom, *Rabbits*—with its alienated gestures and voices, its obscure non sequiturs, and its dislocated laugh track, failing to synchronize emotion and narrative—works as a microcosm of the way *Inland Empire* uses the architectural uncanny to defamiliarize the domestic, returning it to a space of virtuality. The domestic becomes virtual, and strange, when the scenes, bodies, and behaviors that comprise its proper operation lose the codes or habits that inscribe them as fetishes and make them individually or culturally recognizable. The coercive terrain of the domestic is loosened in *Inland Empire* the more the stories of its worldly women are returned to a space of emergence, the more the codified dimensions of felt life that we call "emotions" are scrapped for unstructured affects that seem more atmospheric—in the air, rather than walled firmly in the self.

Domestic abuse is therefore also affirmed in *Inland Empire* as that which happens in the feeling body when the kinds of turbulent emotions that seem most proper to the self are expropriated, delinked from specific individuals, characters, or situations, and somehow transmitted between them. Part of the affective experience of domestic abuse is to find a once-known person growing unrecognizably violent, to find one's most intimate relations pervaded by a threatening foreignness. In *Inland Empire*, while this intimate foreignness is surely linked to female victimization, it is also the precondition for Lynch's mediumism, which requires that affect be transmissible, always un-homelike.

This kind of mediumistic transmission across psychic borders has a strong romantic pedigree and appears throughout *Inland Empire* in various guises—in the Phantom's hypnotism, in Visitor #1's obscure reference to "the magic," in the discourse of acting, and in its investment in a communal body electric that is most evident in the film's closing sequences. Nikki, after shooting the Phantom, enters room 47 and is bathed in a blue light as the strains of Lynch's song "Polish Poem" swell on the sound track: "I sing this poem to you . . . / On the other side, I see . . . / / . . . I can see it there." The lyrics—globally available today as MP3 downloads on the recently revamped davidlynch.com, now the "David Lynch Music Factory," an online music store for Lynch's past and present collaborations—strain toward their current condition of electronic transmission as they cross the time-spaces of the film. As the poem is sung, we cut to a reaction shot of the Lost Girl, who, facing her glowing television set, first watches two of the dancing girls run exuberantly toward her and then, herself bathed in electric blue light, watches Nikki enter her room, kiss her, and disappear. Echoing the disorienting mise-en-abyme structures we have seen before, Lynch shoots this reunion both from within the space of the Lost Girl's hotel room and as seen on her own television screen. The kiss frees the Lost Girl, who leaves her room to emerge at last in the Lynchian room of the Smithy set, where she embraces her husband (also played by Peter J. Lucas) and son. We fade back to the blue light, which becomes dazzlingly white as we cut to a close-up of Nikki, and hear, with her, the tinny sound of recorded cheers before dissolving to a close-up of the Visitor, now smiling warmly. We have, it seems, returned to the opening sequence with the Visitor, except that the earlier atmosphere of domestic and psychic disquiet has become much more homelike. Now Nikki watches herself sitting peacefully on the couch as the song concludes "Something is happening. / Something is happening," and we cut to black.

The lyric voice, the pulse of electric light, the soft glow of the television screen—all vital media through which passes a pervasive feeling of relatedness, of a sensual community that happens through and across the unbounded situations of the digital image. In uniting, impossibly, the film's separated Lost Girls, and returning them to happy homes, this sequence smacks of Lynch's penchant for transcendent endings and the final unions of comedy.

This is not, however, the end of the movie, since Lynch's romanticism, and its affects, are always mass-mediated products of a more materialist magic—the synchronization of an image—a sound situation from a swarming *electronic* field of audiovisual virtuality. How else to describe what happens in the final moments of *Inland Empire* as the credits run, when, after Nikki finds herself at home, her house becomes populated with various incarnations of *Inland Empire*'s stories, past and future, strewn with design elements of a much broader Lynch kit? First to enter is a girl on crutches with one false leg. She has sprung to life from the monologue of Nikki Grace's battered housewife character, who had made passing reference to the Phantom's one-legged sister, who might have become another girl in trouble, and has been briefly glimpsed on the streets of Lodz. Admiring the vast living room and pronouncing it "Suh-WEET!" this virtual person looks over to another, Niko, who at this point has had no existence outside of a story of another Lost Girl told by a homeless teenager to a dying Nikki on the Hollywood Walk of Fame. Now Niko has emerged from the story, pet monkey in tow, to join the party. Niko shoots a knowing glance at a seated Laura Elena Harring, one of the costars of Lynch's *Mulholland Dr.* and the voice of one of the characters in *Rabbits*. Harring, smiling and as gorgeous as ever, blows a kiss to Laura Dern, who returns the favor as the center of this living room fills with the "Loco-Motion" girls, who are then supplemented by another group of African American dancers, who lead this room's collection of eccentrics in an ecstatic, lip-synched version of Nina Simone's "Sinnerman" that lasts through the final credits. Rarely has a film ended with such an aggressive, affirmative declaration of the power of its own artifice. The denizens of this final interior—incarnated stories of *Inland Empire* and actors from the worlds of Lynch's other films—are, alike, the inchoate stuff of vital media. This is perhaps why Lynch chooses to include, as part of this final dance number, a lumberjack vigorously sawing a log. Returning us to the mysteries of the Montana forests that prompted Lynch's fascination with organic process in the first place, this is a densely coded figure of intermediality in a forest of code: a metaphor for sleep; a reference to Michael J. Anderson's miked act of log-sawing in Lynch's 1989 Brooklyn Academy of Music performance piece, *Industrial Symphony No. 1,* which itself recalled the chipper sounds of radio station WOOD that tuned us into another, sunny day in *Blue Velvet*'s Lumberton; the image had another life on davidlynch.com. There, with Lynch himself brandishing the saw, log-sawing functioned for a while as a stand-in for whatever part of the site was "under construction." Log-sawing, like *Inland Empire* itself, is a digital work in progress, the fundamental Lynchian dynamic: organic becoming in media.

Lynch's late-surrealist living rooms and their fluid digital substance are easily dismissed as an affront to the way finite human bodies actually experience the world. So much depends on how we understand what it means for bodies and culture to be plastic. My answer has been to think of the plasticity of the mediated organism as primarily a kind of surrealist anthropology. Lynch's picture of vital media shares the surrealists' view of both human nature and human culture as disruptively inorganic—powerfully structured by an inhuman assemblage of codes, forces, and prosthetic accoutrement that are subject to infinitely plastic dynamism. If his work compels us, if it is important at all, it is so mostly because it recalls to us life's myriad ways of being never fully itself.

Notes

1. Andrew Ross, qtd. in "(Why) Is David Lynch Important? A *Parkett* Inquiry," *Parkett* 28 (1991): 153–62.

2. Fredric Jameson, "Nostalgia for the Present," *South Atlantic Quarterly* 88, no. 2 (1989); Slavoj Žižek, "The Lamella of David Lynch," in *Reading Seminar XI: Lacan's Four Fundamental Concepts of Psychoanalysis,* ed. Richard Feldstein, Bruce Fink, and Maire Jaanus (Albany: SUNY Press, 1995), 205–20; and Slavoj Žižek, *The Art of the Ridiculous Sublime: On David Lynch's* Lost Highway (Seattle: Walter Chapin Simpson Center for the Humanities, 2000).

3. Roland Barthes, "Plastic," in *Mythologies*, trans. Annette Lavers (New York: Farrar, Straus, and Giroux), 97.

4. Chris Rodley, ed., *Lynch on Lynch* (London: Faber and Faber, 2005), 4–5.

5. David Lynch, interview with Kristine McKenna, in *David Lynch: The Air Is on Fire* (Paris: Fondation Cartier pour l'art contemporain, 1997), 28.

6. See Julie H. Reiss, *From Margin to Center: The Spaces of Installation Art* (Cambridge: MIT Press, 2001).

7. Élie Faure, "Cineplastics," in *French Film Theory and Criticism*, vol. 1, 1907–1928, ed. and trans. Richard Abel (Princeton, N.J.: Princeton University Press, 1988), 260–61.

8. Interview with John Powers, 1986, qtd. in Guy Maddin, "I'm Shockingly Unchanged since I Picked up a Camera," in *The Young, the Restless, and the Dead: Interviews with Canadian Filmmakers,* ed. George Melnyk (Waterloo, Ont.: Wilfrid Laurier University Press), 45.

9. Alan Weintraub, *Lloyd Wright: The Architecture of Frank Lloyd Wright Jr.* (New York: Harry N. Abrams, 1998).

10. David Lynch, interview with Kathrin Spohr, *form* 158, no. 2 (1997): 44–45.

11. Diana Fuss, *The Sense of an Interior: Four Writers and the Rooms That Shaped Them* (Routledge: New York, 2004), 9.

12. Walter Benjamin, *The Arcades Project*, trans. Howard Eiland and Kevin McLaughlin (Cambridge: Belknap Press, 1999), 220.

13. See Anthony Vidler, *Warped Space: Art, Architecture, and Anxiety in Modern Culture* (Cambridge: MIT Press, 2001).

14. Ibid., viii.

15. Rodley, *Lynch on Lynch*, 10.

16. Michel Chion, *David Lynch* (London: British Film Institute, 1992), 31.

17. Anthony Vidler, *The Architectural Uncanny: Essays in the Modern Unhomely* (London: MIT Press, 1994), 217.

18. Lynch, qtd. in Greg Olson, *David Lynch: Beautiful Dark* (Lanham, Md.: Scarecrow Press, 2008), 223–24.

19. See Joe Kember, "David Lynch and the Mug Shot: Face Working in *The Elephant Man* and *The Straight Story*," in *The Cinema of David Lynch*, ed. Erica Sheen and Annette Davison (London: Wallflower, 2004), 29–34.

20. Pauline Kael, "Out There and In Here," *New Yorker*, Sept. 22, 1986, 99–103.

21. Fredric Jameson, "Nostalgia for the Present," in *Postmodernism; or, The Cultural Logic of Late Capitalism* (Durham, N.C.: Duke University Press, 1991), 295; my emphasis.

22. Ibid.

23. Richard Allen, *Hitchcock's Romantic Irony* (New York: Columbia University Press, 2007), 15. For a powerful reading of queer negativity in Hitchcock, see Lee Edelman, "Hitchcock's Future," in *Alfred Hitchcock: Centenary Essays*, ed. Richard Allen and Sam Ishii-Gonzalès (London: British Film Institute, 1999).

24. Silvia Lavin, *Form Follows Libido: Architecture and Richard Neutra in a Psychoanalytic Culture* (Cambridge: MIT Press, 2004), 4–5.

25. Yoke-Sum Wong, "Modernism's Love Child: The Story of Happy Architectures," *Common Knowledge* 14, no. 3 (2008): 456.

26. Ibid.

27. Clement Greenberg, "The Avant-Garde and Kitsch," in *Art and Culture: Critical Essays* (Boston: Beacon Press, 1961), 15, 106–7.

28. Rodley, *Lynch on Lynch*, 110; emphasis in original.

29. See Michael Atkinson, *Blue Velvet* (London: British Film Institute, 1997), 34.

30. David Lynch, *Catching the Big Fish: Meditation, Consciousness, and Creativity* (New York: Penguin, 2006), 15.

31. Wong, "Modernism's Love Child," 448.

32. Lucy Fischer, *Designing Women: Cinema, Art Deco, and the Female Form* (New York: Columbia University Press, 2003).

33. Ibid., 19–20.

34. David Chute, "Out to Lynch," *Film Comment* 22, no. 5 (1986): 34.

35. Baudrillard, qtd. in Fischer, *Designing Women*, 10.

36. Michael Moon, "A Small Boy and Others: Sexual Disorientation in Henry James, Kenneth Anger, and David Lynch," in *A Small Boy and Others: Imitation and Initiation in American Culture from Henry James to Andy Warhol* (Durham, N.C.: Duke University Press, 1998), 21.

37. Laura Mulvey, "The Pre-Oedipal Father: The Gothicism of *Blue Velvet*," in *Modern Gothic: A Reader*, ed. Victor Sage and Allan Lloyd Smith (New York: Manchester University Press, 1996), 55.

38. Chute, "Out to Lynch," 33.

39. Ibid., 32.

40. Ibid., 35.

41. *Lost Highway* press kit, online at www.lynchnet.com/lh/lhpress.html.

42. Ibid.

43. Ibid.

44. Ibid.

45. Jean Baudrillard, *The System of Objects*, trans. James Benedict (London: Verso, 1996).

46. Ibid., 37.

47. Christian Louboutin, qtd. in Nicolas Smirnoff, Art Is Alive: FETISH = David Lynch/Christian Louboutin, July 19, 2007, http://artisnotdead.blogspot.com/2007/07/fetish-david-lynchchristian-louboutin.html.

48. Vivian Sobchack, "Lounge Time: Post-War Crises and the Chronotope of Film Noir," in *Refiguring Film Genres*, ed. Nick Browne (Berkeley: University of California Press, 1998), 166.

49. Beatriz Colomina, AnnMarie Brennan, and Jeannie Kim, eds., *Cold War Hothouses: Imagining Postwar Culture from Cockpit to Playboy* (New York: Princeton Architectural Press, 1994), 14.

50. Ibid., 19.

51. See Chion's indispensable "Lynch Kit," in Michel Chion, *David Lynch* (London: British Film Institute, 1992), 161–98.

52. Baudrillard, *System of Objects*, 48.

53. Ibid., 25.

54. Ibid., 26, 29.

55. On hard-core pornography as a Foucauldian technology of "speaking sex" and visualizing the "truth" of female sexuality, see Linda Williams, *Hard Core: Power, Pleasure, and the "Frenzy of the Visible"* (Berkeley: University of California Press, 1989).

56. Frances Ferguson, *Pornography, the Theory: What Utilitarianism Did to Action* (Chicago: University of Chicago Press, 2004).

57. Susan Sontag, "The Pornographic Imagination," in *Styles of Radical Will* (New York: Picador, 1966), 49.

58. Barry Gifford, review of *Blue Velvet*, in *Devil Thumps a Ride and Other Unforgettable Films* (New York: Grove Press, 1988), 22.

59. See Allen, *Hitchcock's Romantic Irony*.

60. David Foster Wallace, "David Lynch Keeps His Head," in *A Supposedly Fun Thing I'll Never Do Again: Essays and Arguments* (Boston: Little, Brown, 1997), 161.

61. Ibid., 199.

62. Martha P. Nochimson, *The Passion of David Lynch: Wild at Heart in Hollywood* (Austin: University of Texas Press, 1997), and Todd McGowan, *The Impossible David Lynch* (New York: Columbia University Press, 2007).

63. Noël Carroll, "Film, Emotion, and Genre," in *Passionate Views: Film, Cognition, and Emotion*, eds. Carl Plantinga and Greg M. Smith (Baltimore: Johns Hopkins University Press, 1999), 27.

64. For a smart recent attempt to rethink Lynch as primarily a filmmaker preoccupied with pre-personal states of affect and intensity, and with the cinema's powers as a machine that doesn't represent and code bodies so much as *produce* them, in states of becoming and qualitative transformation, see Elena Del Rio's chapter "Powers of the False" in *Gilles Deleuze and the Cinemas of Performance: Powers of Affection* (Edinburgh: Edinburgh University Press, 2009).

65. Rodley, *Lynch on Lynch*, 204.

66. Ibid.

67. See, respectively, Ernst Bloch and Fredric Jameson, qtd. in Sianne Ngai, *Ugly Feelings* (Cambridge: Harvard University Press, 2004), 210.

68. Chion, *David Lynch*, 123.

69. See Gifford's interview with Thomas McCarthy in Barry Gifford, *The Rooster Trapped in the Reptile Room: The Barry Gifford Reader* (New York: Seven Stories Press, 2003), 7.

70. Chion, *David Lynch*, 134.

71. Henri Bergson, "Laughter" (*Le Rire*) [1900], in *Comedy*, ed. Wylie Sypher (Baltimore: Johns Hopkins University Press, 1980), 97.

72. Simon Critchley, *On Humor* (London: Routledge, 2002), 41–52.

73. Thomas Elsaesser, "Tales of Sound and Fury: Observations on the Family Melodrama" (1972), reprt. in *Imitations of Life: A Reader on Film and Television Melodrama*, ed. Marcia Landy (Detroit: Wayne State University Press, 1991), 69.

74. Paul Willeman, "The Sirkian System" (1971), in *Looks and Frictions: Essays in Cultural Studies and Film Theory* (Bloomington: Indiana University Press, 1994), 88.

75. Peter Brooks, *The Melodramatic Imagination: Balzac, Henry James, Melodrama, and the Mode of Excess* (New Haven, Conn.: Yale University Press, 1976).

76. Christine Gledhill, "The Melodramatic Field," qtd. in Williams, "Melodrama Revised," in *Refiguring American Film Genres: History and Theory*, ed. Nick Browne (Berkeley: University of California Press, 1998), 48.

77. Chion, *David Lynch*, 144–45.

78. Ibid., 142.

79. Henry Jenkins, "'Do You Enjoy Making the Rest of Us Feel Stupid?': alt.tv.twinpeaks, the Trickster Author, and Viewer Mastery," in *Fans, Bloggers, and Gamers: Exploring Participatory Culture* (New York: New York University Press, 2006), 115–33.

80. Elsaesser, "Tales of Sound and Fury," 76.

81. Todd McGowan, *The Impossible David Lynch* (New York: Columbia University Press, 2007), 142.

82. Steve Neale, "Melodrama and Tears," *Screen* 27, no. 6 (1986): 22.

83. Susan Sontag, "The Decay of Cinema," *New York Times Magazine*, Feb. 25, 1996, 60–61.

84. Ibid.

85. "A Decade in the Dark: 2000–2009," *Film Comment* 46, no.1 (2010): 26–43.

86. Susan Sontag, "Bergman's *Persona*," in *Styles of Radical Will* (New York: Picador, 1966), 124.

87. Ibid., 132.

88. Ibid., 142.

89. For a superb rethinking of these art-cinematic categories and their histories and politics, see Mark Betz, *Beyond the Subtitle: Remapping European Art Cinema* (Minneapolis: University of Minnesota Press, 2009).

90. Lynch, qtd. in Tad Friend, "Creative Differences," *New Yorker*, Sept. 6, 2009, 59.

91. Warren Buckland, "'A Sad, Bad, Traffic Accident': The Televisual Prehistory of David Lynch's Film *Mulholland Drive*," *New Review of Film and Television Studies* 1, no. 1 (2003): 131–47.

92. Charles Sanders Peirce, *The Essential Peirce: Selected Philosophical Writings,* vol. 1, ed. Nathan Houter and Christian Kloesel (Bloomington: Indiana University Press, 1992).

93. Mary Ann Doane, "The Indexical and the Concept of Medium Specificity," *differences* 18, no. 1 (2007): 136.

94. On the erotics of telephony, see Avital Ronell, *The Telephone Book: Technology, Schizophrenia, Electric Speech* (Lincoln: University of Nebraska Press, 1989), and Ellis Hanson, "The Telephone and Its Queerness," in *Cruising the Performative: Interventions into the Representation of Ethnicity, Nationality, and Sexuality,* ed. Sue-Ellen Case et al. (Bloomington: Indiana University Press, 1995), 34–58.

95. George Toles, "Auditioning Betty in *Mulholland Drive*," *Film Quarterly* 58, no. 1 (2004): 9.

96. Ibid., 11.

97. Christian Metz, *The Imaginary Signifier: Psychoanalysis and the Cinema,* trans. Celia Britton et al. (Bloomington: Indiana University Press, 1982), 70.

98. Paul de Man, "Anthropomorphism and Trope in the Lyric," in *The Rhetoric of Romanticism* (New York: Columbia University Press, 1984), 256.

99. Daniel Tiffany, *Toy Medium: Materialism and Modern Lyric* (Berkeley: University of California Press, 2000), 15.

100. Ibid., 71.

101. Rosalind Krauss, "The Photographic Conditions of Surrealism," in *The Originality of the Avant-Garde and Other Modernist Myths* (Cambridge: MIT Press, 1986), 87–118.

102. Malcolm Turvey, *Doubting Vision: Film and the Revelationist Tradition* (Oxford: Oxford University Press, 2008).

103. Rodley, *Lynch on Lynch,* 10.

104. D. N. Rodowick, *The Virtual Life of Film* (Cambridge: Harvard University Press, 2007), 31–46; Rosalind Krauss, "*A Voyage on the North Sea*": Art in the Age of the Post-Medium Condition (London: Thames and Hudson, 1999), 9–64.

105. Chion, *David Lynch,* 44–45.

106. Ibid., 10.

107. Tom Gunning, "Moving Away from the Index: Cinema and the Impression of Reality," *differences* 18, no. 1 (2007): 29–52.

108. For a compelling return to Fried's canonical essay "Art and Object-hood" (1967) as part of a broader 1960s interest in time, technology, and medial impurity, see Pamela M. Lee, *Chronophobia: On Time in the Art of the 1960s* (Cambridge: MIT Press, 2004).

109. Michel Chion, *Audio-Vision: Sound on Screen*, ed. and trans. Claudia Gorbman (New York: Columbia University Press, 1994), 63.

110. Walter Benjamin, "Franz Kafka," in *Illuminations*, ed. Hannah Arendt, trans. Harry Zohn (New York: Schocken Books, 1969), 122.

111. Ibid., 130.

112. Esther Leslie, *Hollywood Flatlands: Animation, Critical Theory, and the Avant-Garde* (London: Verso, 2001), 19.

113. Thomas Lamarre, *The Anime Machine: A Media Theory of Animation* (Minneapolis: University of Minnesota Press, 2009), xxvi.

114. Ibid.

115. Rodley, *Lynch on Lynch*, 248.

116. Paul Gilmore, "Romantic Electricity, or the Materiality of Aesthetics," *American Literature* 76, no. 3 (2004): 485.

117. Pamela Thurschwell, *Literature, Technology, and Magical Thinking, 1880–1920* (Cambridge: Cambridge University Press, 2001).

118. Jeffrey Sconce, *Haunted Media: Electronic Presence from Telegraphy to Television* (Durham, N.C.: Duke University Press, 2000), 7.

119. John Hagelin, *Manual for a Perfect Government: How to Harness the Laws of Nature to Bring Maximum Success to Governmental Administration* (Fairfield, Ia.: Maharishi Institute of Management Press, 1988), 40.

120. Ibid., 48.

121. Ibid. 43.

122. Lynch, *Catching the Big Fish*, 140.

123. Lev Manovich, *The Language of New Media* (Cambridge: MIT Press, 2002), 302; Manovich's emphasis.

124. Qtd. in Mike Figgis, "Into the Abstract," *Sight and Sound* 17, no. 3 (2007): 19.

125. Garrett Stewart, *Framed Time: Toward a Postfilmic Cinema* (Chicago: University of Chicago Press, 2007), 7–8.

126. See Kristen Daly, "Cinema 3.0: The Interactive Image," *Cinema Journal* 50, no. 1 (2010): 81–98.

127. Barbara Maria Stafford, *Visual Analogy: Consciousness and the Art of Connecting* (Cambridge: MIT Press, 2001).

128. Amy Taubin, "The Big Rupture: David Lynch, Richard Kelly, and the New Cinematic Gestalt," *Film Comment* 43, no. 1 (2007): 54.

129. Ibid.

Interviews with David Lynch |

From *form* 158, no. 2 (1997): 44–45; interviewed by Kathrin Spohr in Santa Monica, California.

KATHRIN SPOHR: You're internationally known as a film director, actor, and creator of the meanwhile legendary *Twin Peaks* TV series. But your passion lies not only with cinema and television. You've composed music with Angelo Badalamenti. You're a writer. And a painter . . . Recently your pictures were on show in Paris. And now we find that you've been designing furniture for some time. What else can we expect to find you doing?

DAVID LYNCH: Don't worry. I don't want to appear like some all-round talent. Not at all. I just inevitably get involved in different things.

I started out being a painter. And like many painters I was looking for a new challenge. Because it is not easy to make money with art. After all, just to build canvas stretchers, and stretch a canvas you get involved with a lot of tools. And one thing always leads to another. Pretty soon I was building things.

It's a special outlook. You build your own world. And, in my case, my father always had a workshop in the house, and I was taught how to use tools and spent a lot of time in the shop building things, so it all got started at a young age.

KS: So furniture design is nothing new for you?

DL: Right. I've always been interested in it.

KS: Is there a particular element that connects all of your creative activities?

DL: Well, film brings most mediums together. Painting, building, furniture, or working with Angelo in music is like an avenue and is initially its own thing. Sure, you can get lost in those specific things completely. And if you get an idea for some table or some piece of furniture, it's pretty thrilling.

KS: In April, you are presenting a collection at the world's most important and famous furniture exhibition, the Salone del Mobile in Milan. The furniture will be produced. Are you planning a second career as a designer?

DL: Yes . . . I've got many ideas.

KS: And when did you start designing furniture?

DL: Well, when I started I never really thought of myself as a furniture designer. I would just get an idea and build something.

In art school I started building things based on my own designs. And then things kind of went from there. But now, I'd like to get hooked up with a company that could produce my stuff. When somebody is interesting in following through, then ideas really start flowing, and you need an outlet, and people to back you.

KS: You actually started building things while a student in the Sixties?

DL: Yes, right. During the decade of change . . .

KS: Well, what about the tables that show up in Milan. How old are they?

DL: The "Espresso Table" is about five years old. The others are newer.

KS: People often associate violence, some special desires and nightmares with your movies. In this context, it seems to be a far cry from design.

DL: That could be, but films, paintings, furniture, etc. are all based on ideas. You get an idea. And then you're hooked.

Not to forget: I love building. And building is as important as designing, because many times design grows as one is building.

KS: It's not very common for directors to design furniture for their movies themselves.

DL: Could be, but sometimes I see a need for a certain piece of furniture in a certain place. It'd take too much time to search for a specific piece. And it's more fun for me to build it on my own.

KS: Have you ever attempted to sell your furniture?

DL: Well, years ago I sold my first little table to Skank World, on Beverly Drive. Skank World is a small place featuring 50s design and furniture—I love the place. But people don't normally go there to buy new furniture. So, it didn't work out. But since then I haven't worked on selling my furniture. Till now, that is. [. . .]

KS: It's obvious from your movies that wood attracts you. In your office there is a perfectly equipped carpentry workshop. At the premier of *Lost Highway* here in Los Angeles you held a speech in which wood functioned as a metaphor for quality of content in films. How did you come up with such an association?

DL: Well, wood is a very special material, and since the dawn of time people have been chopping down trees and working with wood. Most wood will take a nail and not split apart. And wood can be cut with a saw and carved with chisels and smoothed. It has this beautiful grain, there's something that goes right to your soul.

KS: Isn't such praise of wood and handicrafts a little anachronistic nowadays?

DL: I've always been interested in industrial structures and materials. Plastic has a place and it's a really cool thing. But it's two or three steps removed from something that's organic. So, wood talks to you and you can relate to it. It's such a pleasant material and so user-friendly, really. There're so many different types of wood—quite amazing. Wood is more than just a material.

KS: What role does architecture play in your movies?

DL: Architecture or space is all around us. But capturing space in a really pleasing way is an art form in its own right. And there're very few people who can do it. Most homes, generally speaking, and especially in the modern U.S. approach, more or less destroy something inside.

They're devoid of design. I think they suck happiness away from people, and it's really hard to live in those kind of places.

I always go by ideas. The idea for the red room in *Twin Peaks* just popped into my head. The floor has the same pattern as the floor in the lobby in Henry Spencer's apartment in *Eraserhead*. I liked that pattern.

KS: While watching *The Elephant Man*, I was struck by a scene in which the Elephant Man constructs a perfect model of a church. Did you design that church?

DL: No, Stewart Craig, the production designer, made it. It was based on Victorian cardboard kits they used to sell and a church near the London Hospital.

KS: You wrote the screenplay to *Lost Highway* together with Barry Gifford. And you said that *Lost Highway* is "a world where time is dangerously out of control." How is this idea expressed in the set design?

DL: The film deals with time: it starts back at one place and moves forward or backwards, or stands still, relatively speaking. But, time marches on and films compact time, or prolong time in different ways. There are sequences built with time in mind, as is the music. So, I guess it really probably has more to do with the story and the editing than with the elements and the set design.

KS: In the screenplay there's no mention of the set design at all. When do you usually start to put such ideas to paper?

DL: They never go on paper. When you get an idea many things come with the idea, most things. And pictures form: In your mind and those pictures and the mood that comes, and the light, and many things you remember and you stay as true to those things as you can. When you're working on a location you might have pictures of a different place in your mind, so you look around for the closest thing to it that you can find.

KS: During *Eraserhead* you were living in the rooms in which you shot the film; in *Lost Highway* your house is part of the scenery. Why do you prefer to use your private space?

DL: If you love the world of the movie so much, you want to be in the middle of things. So, it's great if, while shooting a film, you're always living in the places, and spend as much time there as possible. That way, the world reveals itself more.

KS: And, as far as I know, your house was designed by Lloyd Wright, son of Frank Lloyd Wright.

DL: Correct. Lloyd Wright designed the house that I live in, the Beverly Johnson House, in the Sixties. Lloyd Wright's son, Eric Wright, supervised the building work for his father. 25 years later, Eric designed a pool and a pool house on the property in the spirit of his father's work.

KS: And you believe that your house has an influence on your work?

DL: Wright is a great architect. The house has quite a feel of pure Japanese architecture, but also of American modernity, a bit of both. The whole space is just pleasing, gives me a good feeling. So it affects my whole life to live inside of it. And then, sometimes I see things, shapes or something that would go inside of it and that leads to furniture or film.

KS: In your house things are very carefully arranged. You've designed boxes which conceal the phone and the video system. Why do you hide these devices? Do you find technology somehow threatening?

DL: It's a double-edged sword. Technology doesn't threaten me in general. It could, though. It all depends on how it is used. But if it leads to a better standard of living then I think it's really O.K.

KS: So why do you hide your video system, for example?

DL: Well, I could hide everything to keep rooms as pure as possible. You have electronic equipment that works, it's state of the art stuff, but the boxes it comes in are really boring. A lot of thought has gone into the front, but not into the other side.

KS: Perhaps those sides are more interesting for precisely that reason. They aren't designed as consciously as the front.

DL: But they're always more boring.

KS: You've' said that you're ideas often occur in the form of daydreams. Is the Beverly Johnson House the house of your dreams?

DL: It's a beautiful place. Architecture is something to always think about. Design influences my life. I need pleasing spaces. Often my mind drifts in that direction, but I'm not an architect. Although I really appreciate the great architects, and the difference a great design can make to a person.

KS: Who are the architects you admire most?

DL: From Bauhaus, all the students of the Bauhaus School, and Pierre Chareau, he did the House of Glass in Paris, Ludwig Mies van de Rohe, all the Wright family, Rudolph Michael Schindler and Richard Neutra. I like really beautifully designed, minimal things.

KS: Did you ever dream of furniture?

DL: I day-dream of furniture, yes.

KS: Do you think the spirit of the so-called "American dream" produces a special kind of furniture?

DL: Different cultures produce different things for one reason or another. But a great design is recognized everywhere.

KS: You say you were inspired by Ray and Charles Eames. What is it you most appreciate about their work?

DL: The design. I love Ray and Charles Eames, yes.

KS: Their entire oeuvre?

DL: Yes, I like their designs.

KS: Did you ever meet the Eameses?

DL: I had lunch with Charles Eames, he came to the American Film Institute in 1970 or '71 and took part in a lunch with all of the students. And I sat at his table. He was one of the most intelligent, down to earth, greatest persons I ever met. He was just a pure, kind of happy person, somehow childlike, enjoying life. The kind of guy you'd like right away.

KS: Vladimir Kagan, the New York designer, is also a source of inspiration for you.

DL: He's very old now, maybe around 80. He was kind of famous in the 50s, and his designs are coming back into vogue now, as is the work of Charlotte Perriand, who worked together with Le Corbusier and Pierre Jeanneret. They're getting recognition again. And rightly so.

KS: In Europe, incidentally, the work of the Eameses is much more admired than it is in the U.S. Any idea why?

DL: Because Europeans appreciate the finer things.

KS: Do you like German design?

DL: Yes. German design is usually very pure, and sparse, and solid and functional. And those are exactly the features I like.

KS: In other words, you like the technical aspects of German design?

DL: No, in many cases the look and materials. The Germans are known for very good craftsmanship, and so if the thing is built, you know it's going to work. That's for sure.

KS: For many years now, you have worked with Patricia Norris. She designs your productions. Does she influence your own design work?

DL: She is production designer and in charge of the costume design. With regard to the costumes, I hardly ever say anything to her, the things just blow right out of her. But when it comes to set design. Well, we always talk about everything.

I try to get her in tune with the thing I'm tuning into and so the thing flows, and then we just keep a constant dialogue going. But the design of each and everything is important if the whole film is to hold together.

KS: Are there any other architects or designers involved?

DL: No. Only her.

KS: Are you able to compromise when the locations or interiors that you imagined for your set simply can't be found?

DL: No. There's no compromise possible. You keep looking until you find the place that will work for the story. And that holds for the objects, too. Many places are painted or rearranged, new furniture is brought in. You can't make compromises. Compromises kill the film.

From "Into the Abstract," *Sight and Sound* 17, no. 3 (2007); interviewed by Mike Figgis in Lodz, Poland, 2007.

MIKE FIGGIS: [*Inland Empire*] is your longest film by some way.

DAVID LYNCH: By a few minutes. I don't know what my second-longest film is. It's not a conscious thing on my part.

My whole process begins when somewhere along the line I catch an idea. That idea is everything to me then. You catch a film idea and you fall in love with it for two reasons. One is the idea itself and the second is how cinema can translate it. And then you just stay true to that idea and go. It keeps talking to you and you don't walk away from anything until it feels correct based on that idea. That's it.

MF: These ideas spawn other ideas. Did you have the complete film in mind when you started?

DL: No. I always use the analogy of fishing. You catch an idea, and even if it's just a tiny fish of an idea, a fragment, if you focus on it and desire more they'll swim in to you over time.

MF: That means you have to have a particular type of focus throughout the process of making the film. It's different from the studio convention.

DL: For sure. Usually in a studio they come in with a script. By the time the script is finished and whoever wrote it presents it to the system then it's one big idea and many little parts. All that catching of ideas and waiting has already occurred. But if you read that script it's just like getting ideas again. It all comes alive in your mind and you see it. So you stay true to that.

The script to me is like a blueprint, it's not the finished house. There are millions of stories where once you start seeing the house, you say wait a minute, it would be better to have a slow curve instead of a hard edge and we need a fireplace here. There are certain things that the seeing of it conjures up and there are happy accidents that happen along the way that you need to be on guard for. Who's to say whether the waiting for the final piece could open up another whole thing that was meant to be? The idea is that it's not finished until it's finished: when the whole feels correct, you say it's done. Like with a painting.

MF: Do you approach painting in the same way?

DL: Painting is different because there's no script. So if you've got a bunch of canvases ready to go, some paint and a place to work, all you need is to catch an idea to get you started. Then it's action and reaction: the paint starts talking to you, the beautiful process begins, and a whole bunch of different things happen. More often than not there's a point in the action and reaction where the reaction is to destroy the thing: it's pretty much bullshit surface baloney, and you just want to destroy it and get past it. The destruction is much more free, so you might just start building on the thing that was destroyed, another thing comes out and that's the way it can grow. You can break through to something else, but if you're not up for destroying you can't get there.

MF: So you need a starting point.

DL: Exactly. The idea happens in a second, but if you really focus on just that fragment you might find you can write pages. I'm in awe of ideas: they seem to come from outside us and then suddenly they enter our conscious mind. It's a gift.

MF: I have the feeling that your films zoom in on portals way under the surface.

DL: There are two things. There's a surface, which is beautiful, but it's the surface. When we see a person we see the surface, but as they begin to talk we get glimpses of something more. Cinema can say things that words can't really articulate. A great poet might articulate abstractions with words but cinema does it with pictures flowing together in sequences. It's magical, it goes into the abstract. I love the idea of going deeper into a world or a character.

MF: What made you concentrate on film rather than painting or writing?

DL: I've told the story of the reason I got into film a million times. I was working on a painting of a garden at night at the Pennsylvania Academy of the Fine Arts. The plants in the dark night painting began to move and I heard a wind. I thought, "Oh, this is interesting. A moving painting." That was the thought that started it.

There was an experimental painting and sculpture contest at the end of each year, so I built a moving painting, a sculptured screen. I went to a camera shop and got a camera that took single frames and asked the guys there how to light the thing and they told me. That would have been the end of it, but then some guy commissioned me to do one for his home. I got a used Bolex, beautiful, with a leather case, single frames. I worked for two months on the animation but I didn't realize the camera had a broken take-up spool. When I went to get the film developed it was one continuous blur—everyone thought I would be upset but something inside made me happy. I called the guy and told him what had happened and he told me to keep the rest of the money and do whatever I wanted to and give him a print. By then I'd been getting ideas about live action combined with animation. So I made a completely different kind of film out of that supposed disaster and it was actually a gift. A gift beyond the beyond. I don't remember what your question was.

MF: With *Inland Empire* you worked on video and not even high-def. Did you like it?

DL: I liked video. I always say I like bad quality, though I don't know exactly what I mean by that. I used a Lumière brothers camera and really early-days emulsion. It's more like a moving painting than modern 35mm, there's something about it that gives you room to dream, something magical. What I liked about this video was that it reminded me of 1930s films when it wasn't so sharp and was more impressionistic. It made it less real. Then we did tests from that to film using a machine called the Alchemist. At first I was just experimenting but once I'd locked into some scenes I didn't want to change my camera. Next time

I might see what the state-of-the-art small camera is and lock into that. It'll probably be high-def but I could degrade it if I wanted.

MF: You operated the camera on this film. Had you done that before?

DL: Not much. As you know, if you've got the camera then you're going to do something you wouldn't do if you're back here behind two people and you don't have the hands on. So I don't want to go back to having an operator—I just love being in there. We need to do what's feeling correct now, no matter what, and the digital is giving us that chance more and more. Small crew. Long takes. Feel it and you're staying true to the idea more than ever.

MF: 35mm developed towards perfect reproduction but I felt it was getting in the way of the image. Did you find it liberating to move away from that?

DL: Very much. You see what you've got and if you don't like it you can pop another 40-watt bulb over there. Because you don't need giant lamps and you can work with what's there 90 percent of the time, you can move around the set. This freedom is unbelievable. In my mind, that's the way it's supposed to be.

Film is beautiful and I really respect cinematographers for getting better and better images. But what it really comes down to is getting the image that's true to the idea. Great cinematographers will help you get whatever it is you want in the best possible way, even if it goes against all the rules and is technically bad.

Film is beautiful, but having had this experience I would die if I had to go that slow ever again. It's not slow in a good way. It's death, death, death. I can hardly stand even thinking about it.

Note: Only the films discussed in this book, and one that is not, *Dune*, are listed here. Michel Chion's second edition of *David Lynch* (2008), from which the information below is culled, offers a more complete filmography that covers the vast terrain of Lynch's artistic production: short films, television, exhibitions of visual art and installations, Internet-based media distributed on davidlynch.com, advertising spots, music albums, and collaborations.

Six Men Getting Six (1967; multimedia installation: 16mm animation loop and three-dimensional sculpted screen)
USA
Script: David Lynch
Animation: David Lynch
Format: 16mm, color
1 min.

The Grandmother (1970)
USA
Producer: David Lynch, financed by an American Film Institute grant
Director: David Lynch
Script: David Lynch
Animation: David Lynch
Music and Music Effects: Tractor
Script Consultants: Margaret Lynch, C. K. Williams
Still Photography: Doug Randall
Sound Editing and Mixing: Alan Splet
Sound Effects: David Lynch, Margaret Lynch, Robert Chadwick, Alan Splet
Cast: Richard White (Boy), Dorothy McGinnis (Grandmother), Virginia Maitland (Mother), Robert Chadwick (Father)
Format: 16mm, color (part animation)
34 min.

Eraserhead (1977)
USA
Producer: David Lynch and the American Film Institute for Advanced
    Studies
Distribution: Libra Films
Director: David Lynch
Assistant to the Director: Catherine Coulson
Script: David Lynch
Editor: David Lynch
Cinematography: Frederick Elmes and Herbert Cardwell
Special Effects Photography: Frederick Elmes
Sound Effects: David Lynch and Alan Splet
Sound Recording and Mixing: Alan Splet
Music: David Lynch
Art Direction: David Lynch
Production Manager: Doreen G. Small
Principal Cast: Jack Nance (Henry Spencer), Charlotte Stewart (Mary X),
    Allen Joseph (Mr. Bill X), Jeanne Bates (Mrs. X), Judith Anna Roberts
    (Beautiful Girl across the Hall), Laurel Near (Lady in the Radiator), Jack
    Fisk (Man in the Planet)
Format: 35mm, black and white
88 min.

The Elephant Man (1980)
USA
Production: Brooksfilms
Producer: Jonathan Sanger
Executive Producer: Stuart Cornfeld
Distribution: Paramount
Director: David Lynch
Screenplay: Christopher De Vore, Eric Bergren, and David Lynch (based on
    The Elephant Man and Other Reminiscences, by Sir Frederick Treves, and
    The Elephant Man: A Study in Human Dignity, by Ashley Montagu)
Photography: Freddie Francis
Music: John Morris
Editor: Anne V. Coates
Production Design: Stuart Craig
Costumes: Patricia Norris
Makeup: Christopher Tucker
Art Director: Bob Cartwright
Sound Design: Alan Splet
Principal Cast: Anthony Hopkins (Frederick Treves), John Hurt (John
    Merrick), Anne Bancroft (Madge Kendal), Sir John Gielgud (Carr Gomm),
    Freddie Jones (Bytes), Michael Elphick (Night Porter)

Format: 35mm, black and white
124 min.

Dune (1984)
USA
Production: Dino De Laurentiis Corporation
Producer: Raffaella De Laurentiis
Distribution: Universal
Director: David Lynch
Screenplay: David Lynch, based on the novel by Frank Herbert
Photography: Freddie Francis
Editor: Antony Gibbs
Production Design: Anthony Masters
Costume Design: Bob Ringwood
Special Effects: Kit West, Barry Nolan, Albert J. Whitlock
Mechanical Creatures: Carlo Rambaldi
Music: Toto and Brian Eno
Sound Designer: Alan Splet
Principal Cast: Kyle MacLachlan (Paul Atreides), Viginia Madsen (Princess
    Irulan), Kenneth McMillan (Baron Harkonnen), Jack Nance (Nefud),
    Patrick Stewart (Gurney Halleck), Sting (Feyd Rautha), Dean Stockwell
    (Doctor Wellington Yueh), Max Von Sydow (Doctor Kynes), Sean Young
    (Chani)
Format: 35mm, color
136 min.

Blue Velvet (1986)
USA
Production: Dino De Laurentiis Entertainment Group
Producers: Fred Caruso and Richard Roth
Distribution: Dino De Laurentiis Entertainment Group
Director: David Lynch
Screenplay: David Lynch
Music: Angelo Badalamenti
Photography: Frederick Elmes
Production Design: Patricia Norris
Editing: Duwayne Dunham
Sound Design: Alan Splet
Principal Cast: Kyle MacLachlan (Jeffrey Beaumont), Isabella Rossellini
    (Dorothy Vallens), Dennis Hopper (Frank Booth), Laura Dern (Sandy
    Williams), Dean Stockwell (Ben)
Format: 35mm, color
120 min.

Wild at Heart (1990)
Germany, USA
Production: Polygram Filmproduktion GmbH/Propaganda Films
Distribution: The Samuel Goldwyn Company
Director: David Lynch
Screenplay: David Lynch, based on the novel by Barry Gifford
Producers: Monty Montgomery, Steve Golin, Sigurjon Sighvatsson
Photography: Frederick Elmes
Music: Angelo Badalamenti
Editor: Duwayne Dunham
Production Design: Patricia Norris
Sound Design: Randy Thom
Principal Cast: Nicolas Cage (Sailor Ripley), Laura Dern (Lula Pace
    Fortune), Willem Dafoe (Bobby Peru), J. E. Freeman (Marcello Santos),
    Crispin Glover (Dell), Diane Ladd (Marietta Fortune), Isabella Rossellini
    (Perdita Durango), Harry Dean Stanton (Johnnie Farragut), Grace
    Zabriskie (Juana Durango), W. Morgan Sheppard (Mr. Reindeer)
Format: 35mm, color
124 min.

Twin Peaks: Fire Walk with Me (1992)
USA
Production: Twin Peaks Productions, Inc.
Executive Producers: Mark Frost and David Lynch
Producers: Francis Bouygues, Gregg Fienberg, and John Wentworth
Distribution: New Line Cinema
Director: David Lynch
Screenplay: David Lynch and Robert Engels
Photography: Ron Garcia
Music: Angelo Badalamenti
Editor: Mary Sweeney
Production Design and Costumes: Patricia Norris
Sound Design: David Lynch
Principal Cast: Sheryl Lee (Laura Palmer), Ray Wise (Leland Palmer),
    Grace Zabriskie (Sarah Palmer), Madchen Amick (Shelly Johnson), Dana
    Ashbrook (Bobby Briggs), David Lynch (Gordon Cole), Phoebe Augustine
    (Ronette Pulaski), Pamela Gidley (Teresa Banks), Harry Dean Stanton
    (Carl Rodd), Chris Isaak (Special Agent Chester Desmond), James
    Marshall (James Hurley), Kyle MacLachlan (Special Agent Dale Cooper),
    Kimberly Ann Cole (Lil)
Format: 35 mm, color
135 min.

Lost Highway (1997)
France, USA
Production: Ciby 2000, Asymmetrical Productions
Producers: Deepak Nayar, Tom Sternberg, Mary Sweeney
Distribution: October Films
Director: David Lynch
Screenplay: David Lynch and Barry Gifford
Photography: Peter Deming
Music: Angelo Badalamenti
Editor: Mary Sweeney
Production and Costume Design: Patricia Norris
Sound Design: David Lynch
Principal Cast: Bill Pullman (Fred Madison), Patricia Arquette (Renée
  Madison/Alice Wakefield), Balthazar Getty (Pete Dayton), Robert Blake
  (Mystery Man), Robert Loggia (Mr. Eddie/Dick Laurent)
Format: 35mm, color
134 min.

The Straight Story (1999)
USA, France, UK
Production: Walt Disney Pictures, a Picture Factory production in association
  with Le Studio Canal Plus and FilmFour
Executive Producers: Pierre Edelman and Michael Polaire, in association
  with Alain Sarde
Distribution: Buena Vista
Producers: Mary Sweeney, Neal Edelstein
Director: David Lynch
Screenplay: Mary Sweeney and John Roach
Photography: Freddie Francis
Music: Angelo Badalamenti
Editor: Mary Sweeney
Production Design: Jack Fisk
Costume Design: Patricia Norris
Sound Design: David Lynch
Principal Cast: Richard Farnsworth (Alvin Straight), Sissy Spacek (Rose
  Straight), Harry Dean Stanton (Lyle Straight), Everett McGill (Tom the
  John Deere Dealer), James Cada (Danny Riordan)
Format: 35mm, color
111 min.

Mulholland Dr. (2001)
France, USA
Production: Les Films Alain Sarde, Asymmetrical Productions
Executive Producer: Pierre Edelman

Producers: Mary Sweeney, Alain Sarde, Neal Edelstein, Michael Polaire,
    Tony Krantz
Distribution: Universal
Director: David Lynch
Writer: David Lynch
Photography: Peter Deming
Music: Angelo Badalamenti, with David Lynch and John Neff
Editor: Mary Sweeney
Production Design: Jack Fisk
Costume Design: Amy Stofsky
Sound Design: David Lynch
Principal Cast: Naomi Watts (Betty Elms/Diane Selwyn), Laura Elena
    Harring (Rita/Camilla Rhodes), Justin Theroux (Adam Kesher), Ann Miller
    (Coco Lenoix), Michael J. Anderson (Mr. Roque), Melissa George (Camilla
    Rhodes)
Format: 35 mm, color
147 min.

Inland Empire (2006)
France, Poland, USA
Production: StudioCanal, Camerimage, Fundacja Kultury, and Asymmetrical
    Productions
Executive Producers (Poland): Ewa Pusazczynska, Marek Zydowicz
Producers (Poland): Kazimierz Suvala, Janusz Hetman, Michal Stopowski
Producers: David Lynch, Mary Sweeney, Jeremy Alter, Laura Dern
Distribution: 518 Media, Absurda
Director: David Lynch
Writer: David Lynch
Photography: David Lynch
Editor: David Lynch
Art Direction: Christina Ann Wilson
Set Decoration: Melanie Rein
Costume Design: Karen Baird and Heidi Bivens
Sound Design: David Lynch
Principal Cast: Laura Dern (Nikki Grace/Susan Blue), Jeremy Irons (Kingsley
    Stewart), Justin Theroux (Devon Berk/Billy Side), Karolina Gruszka (Lost
    Girl), Jan Hencz (Janek), Krzysztof Majchrzak (Phantom), Grace Zabriskie
    (Visitor #1), Peter J. Lucas (Piotrek Król), Harry Dean Stanton (Freddie
    Howard), Diane Ladd (Marilyn Levens)
Format: Digital videotape, color
179 min.

What follows includes works cited in the text as well as work on Lynch that proved essential to my argument even if not cited directly. This bibliography represents only a selection of the large body of work on Lynch. More extensive bibliographies can be found online at UC Berkeley's Media Resources Center (http://www.lib.berkeley.edu/MRC/lynch.html), the City of Absurdity website (www.cityofabsurdity.com), and in Michel Chion's *David Lynch*, which lists much of the vast work on Lynch written in the French language.

"A Decade in the Dark: 2000–2009." *Film Comment* 46, no. 1 (2010): 26–43.

Allen, Richard. *Hitchcock's Romantic Irony*. New York: Columbia University Press, 2007.

Andrews, David. "An Oneiric Fugue: The Various Logics of *Mulholland Drive*." *Journal of Film and Video* 56, no. 1 (2004): 25–40.

Atkinson, Michael. *Blue Velvet*. London: British Film Institute, 1997.

Barker, Jennifer M. "Out of Sync, Out of Sight: Synaesthesia and Film Spectacle." *Paragraph* 31, no. 2 (2008): 236–51.

Barney, Richard A. *David Lynch: Interviews*. Jackson: University Press of Mississippi, 2009.

Barthes, Roland. "Plastic." In *Mythologies*, translated by Annette Lavers, 97–99. New York: Farrar, Straus, and Giroux, 1972.

Baudrillard, Jean. *The System of Objects*. Translated by James Benedict. London: Verso, 1996.

Benjamin, Walter. *The Arcades Project*. Translated by Howard Eiland and Kevin McLaughlin. Cambridge: Belknap Press, 1999.

———. "Franz Kafka." In *Illuminations*, edited by Hannah Arendt, translated by Harry Zohn, 114–45. New York: Schocken Books, 1969.

Bergson, Henri. "Laughter" (*Le Rire*) (1900). In *Comedy*, edited by Wylie Sypher, 59–190. Baltimore: Johns Hopkins University Press, 1980.

Betz, Mark. *Beyond the Subtitle: Remapping European Art Cinema*. Minneapolis: University of Minnesota Press, 2009.

Biga, Tracy. Review of *Blue Velvet*. *Film Quarterly* 41, no. 1 (1987): 44–49.

Brooks, Peter. *The Melodramatic Imagination: Balzac, Henry James, Melodrama, and the Mode of Excess*. New Haven, Conn.: Yale University Press, 1976.

Buckland, Warren. "'A Sad, Bad, Traffic Accident': The Televisual Prehistory of David Lynch's Film *Mulholland Drive*." *New Review of Film and Television Studies* 1, no. 1 (2003): 131–47.

Carroll, Noël. "Film, Emotion, and Genre." In *Passionate Views: Film, Cognition, and Emotion*, edited by Carl Plantinga and Greg M. Smith, 21–47. Baltimore: Johns Hopkins University Press, 1999.

Chion, Michel. *Audio-Vision: Sound on Screen*. Edited and translated by Claudia Gorbman. New York: Columbia University Press, 1994.

———. *David Lynch*. London: British Film Institute, 1992.

———. *David Lynch*. 2nd edition. London: British Film Institute, 2008.

Chute, David. "Out to Lynch." *Film Comment* 22, no. 5 (1986): 32–35.

Colomina, Beatriz, AnnMarie Brennan, and Jeannie Kim, eds. "Cold War Hothouses." In *Cold War Hothouses: Imagining Postwar Culture from Cockpit to Playboy*, 10–21. New York: Princeton Architectural Press, 1994.

Creed, Barbara. "A Journey through *Blue Velvet*: Film, Fantasy and the Female Spectator." *New Formations* 6, no. 2 (1988): 97–118.

Critchley, Simon. *On Humor*. London: Routledge, 2002.

Daly, Kristen. "Cinema 3.0: The Interactive Image." *Cinema Journal* 50, no. 1 (2010): 81–98.

Delorme, Stéphane. "David Lynch: Inland on Fire." *Art Press* 331 (Feb. 2007): 19–25.

Del Rio, Elena. "Powers of the False." In *Gilles Deleuze and the Cinemas of Performance: Powers of Affection*, 178–207. Edinburgh: Edinburgh University Press, 2009.

De Man, Paul. "Anthropomorphism and Trope in the Lyric." In *The Rhetoric of Romanticism*, 239–62. New York: Columbia University Press, 1984.

Devlin, William J., and Shai Biderman, eds. *The Philosophy of David Lynch*. Lexington: University Press of Kentucky, 2011.

Doane, Mary Anne. "The Indexical and the Concept of Medium Specificity." *differences* 18, no. 1 (2007): 128–52.

Edelman, Lee. "Hitchcock's Future." In *Alfred Hitchcock: Centenary Essays*, edited by Richard Allen and Sam Ishii-Gonzalès, 239–62. London: British Film Institute, 1999.

Elsaesser, Thomas. "Tales of Sound and Fury: Observations on the Family Melodrama" (1972). Reprinted in *Imitations of Life: A Reader on Film and Television Melodrama*, edited by Marcia Landy, 68–91. Detroit: Wayne State University Press, 1991.

Faure, Élie. "Cineplastics." In *French Film Theory and Criticism*, vol. 1, 1907–1928, edited and translated by Richard Abel, 260–61. Princeton, N.J.: Princeton University Press, 1988.

Ferguson, Frances. *Pornography, the Theory: What Utilitarianism Did to Action*. Chicago: University of Chicago Press, 2004.

Figgis, Mike. "Into the Abstract." *Sight and Sound* 17, no. 3 (2007): 18–19.

Fischer, Lucy. *Designing Women: Cinema, Art Deco, and the Female Form*. New York: Columbia University Press, 2003.

Friend, Tad. "Creative Differences." *New Yorker*, Sept. 6, 2009, 56–67.

Fuss, Diana. *The Sense of an Interior: Four Writers and the Rooms That Shaped Them*. Routledge: New York, 2004.

Gifford, Barry. Review of *Blue Velvet*. In *Devil Thumbs a Ride and Other Unforgettable Films*, 21–22. New York: Grove Press, 1988.

———. *The Rooster Trapped in the Reptile Room: The Barry Gifford Reader*. Edited by Thomas McCarthy. New York: Seven Stories Press, 2003.

Gilmore, Mikal. "*Lost Highway*—The Lost Boys: Betrayal, Sex, Murder, Deception, and Nine Inch Nails." *Rolling Stone*, March 6, 1997.

Gilmore, Paul. "Romantic Electricity, or the Materiality of Aesthetics." *American Literature* 76, no. 3 (2004): 467–94.

Gleyzon, François-Xavier, ed. *David Lynch in Theory*. Prague: Litteraria Pragensia Books, 2010.

Godwin, K. G. "*Eraserhead*: The Story behind the Strangest Film Ever Made, and the Cinematic Genius Who Directed It." *Cinefantastique* 14, no. 4 and 15, no. 5. Special Double Issue (1984): 41–72.

Greenberg, Clement. "The Avant-Garde and Kitsch." In *Art and Culture: Critical Essays*, 3–21. Boston: Beacon Press, 1961.

Gunning, Tom. "Moving Away from the Index: Cinema and the Impression of Reality." *differences* 18, no. 1 (2007): 29–52.

Hagelin, John. *Manual for a Perfect Government: How to Harness the Laws of Nature to Bring Maximum Success to Governmental Administration*. Fairfield, Ia.: Maharishi Institute of Management Press, 1988.

Hanson, Ellis. "The Telephone and Its Queerness." In *Cruising the Performative: Interventions into the Representation of Ethnicity, Nationality, and Sexuality*, edited by Sue-Ellen Case et al., 34–58. Bloomington: Indiana University Press, 1995.

Hoberman, J., and Jonathan Rosenbaum. *Midnight Movies*. New York: Da Capo, 1983.

Holladay, William E., and Stephen Watt. "Viewing the Elephant Man." *PMLA* 104, no. 5 (1989): 868–81.

Jameson, Fredric. "Nostalgia for the Present." In *Postmodernism; or, The Cultural Logic of Late Capitalism*, 279–96. Durham, N.C.: Duke University Press, 1991.

Jenkins, Henry. "'Do You Enjoy Making the Rest of Us Feel Stupid?': alt .tv.twinpeaks, the Trickster Author, and Viewer Mastery." In *Fans, Bloggers, and Gamers: Exploring Participatory Culture*, 115–33. New York: New York University Press, 2006.

Kael, Pauline. "Out There and In Here." *New Yorker*, Sept. 22, 1986, 99–103.

Kaleta, Kenneth C. *David Lynch*. New York: Twayne, 1993.

Kember, Joe. "David Lynch and the Mug Shot: Face Working in *The Elephant Man* and *The Straight Story*." In *The Cinema of David Lynch*, edited by Erica Sheen and Annette Davison, 29–34. London: Wallflower, 2004.

Krauss, Rosalind. "The Photographic Conditions of Surrealism." In *The Originality of the Avant-Garde and Other Modernist Myths*, 87–118. Cambridge: MIT Press, 1986.

———. *"A Voyage on the North Sea": Art in the Age of the Post-Medium Condition*. London: Thames and Hudson, 1999.

Lamarre, Thomas. *The Anime Machine: A Media Theory of Animation*. Minneapolis: University of Minnesota Press, 2009.

Lavery, David, ed. *Full of Secrets: Critical Approaches to* Twin Peaks. Detroit: Wayne State University Press, 1995.

Lavin, Silvia. *Form Follows Libido: Architecture and Richard Neutra in a Psychoanalytic Culture*. Cambridge: MIT Press, 2004.

Layton, Lynn. "*Blue Velvet*: A Parable of Masculine Development." *Screen* 25, no. 4 (1994): 374–93.

Lee, Pamela M. *Chronophobia: On Time in the Art of the 1960s*. Cambridge: MIT Press, 2004.

Leslie, Esther. *Hollywood Flatlands: Animation, Critical Theory, and the Avant-Garde*. London: Verso, 2001.

Lippit, Akira Mizuta. "David Lynch's Wholes," November 13, 2011. Accessed December 5, 2011. http://flowtv.org/2011/11/david-lynchs-wholes/.

Love, Heather. "Spectacular Failure: The Figure of the Lesbian in *Mulholland Drive*." *New Literary History* 35 (2004): 117–32.

Lynch, David. *Catching the Big Fish: Meditation, Consciousness, and Creativity*. New York: Penguin, 2006.

———. *David Lynch: The Air Is on Fire*. Exhibition catalogue. Paris: Fondation Cartier pour l'art contemporain, 1997.

———. *Images*. Hyperion, 1994.

———. Interview with Kathrin Spohr. *form* 158, no. 2 (1997): 44–45.

Mactaggart, Allister. *The Film Paintings of David Lynch: Challenging Film Theory*. Bristol: Intellect Books, 2010.

Maddin, Guy. "I'm Shockingly Unchanged since I Picked up a Camera." In *The Young, the Restless, and the Dead: Interviews with Canadian Filmmakers*, edited by George Melnyk, 39–54. Waterloo, Ont.: Wilfrid Laurier University Press.

Manovich, Lev. *The Language of New Media*. Cambridge: MIT Press, 2002.

McCarthy, Tom. "His Dark Materials." *Guardian*, Jan. 8, 2010.

McGowan, Todd. *The Impossible David Lynch*. New York: Columbia University Press, 2007.

Metz, Christian. *The Imaginary Signifier: Psychoanalysis and the Cinema*. Translated by Celia Britton et al. Bloomington: Indiana University Press, 1982.

Moon, Michael. "A Small Boy and Others: Sexual Disorientation in Henry James, Kenneth Anger, and David Lynch." In *A Small Boy and Others: Imitation and Initiation in American Culture from Henry James to Andy Warhol*, 15–30. Durham, N.C.: Duke University Press, 1998.

Mulvey, Laura. "The Pre-Oedipal Father: the Gothicism of *Blue Velvet*." In *Modern Gothic: A Reader*, edited by Victor Sage and Allan Lloyd Smith, 38–57. New York: Manchester University Press, 1996.

Naha, Ed. *The Making of Dune*. New York: Berkeley Books, 1984.

Naremore, James. *More Than Night: Film Noir in Its Contexts*. 2nd ed. Berkeley: University of California Press, 2008.

Neale, Steve. "Melodrama and Tears." *Screen* 27, no. 6 (1986): 6–22.

Ngai, Sianne. *Ugly Feelings*. Cambridge: Harvard University Press, 2004.

Nochimson, Martha. *David Lynch: Wild at Heart in Hollywood*. Austin: University of Texas Press, 1997.

———. "*Inland Empire*." *Film Quarterly* 60, no. 4 (2007): 10–14.

———. *The Passion of David Lynch: Wild at Heart in Hollywood*. Austin: University of Texas Press, 1997.

Olson, Greg. *David Lynch: Beautiful Dark*. Lanham, Md.: Scarecrow Press, 2008.

Peirce, Charles Sanders. *The Essential Peirce: Selected Philosophical Writings*, vol. 1, edited by Nathan Houter and Christian Kloesel. Bloomington: Indiana University Press, 1992.

Pfeil, Fred. "Home Fires Burning: Family Noir in *Blue Velvet* and *Terminator 2*." In *Shades of Noir*, edited by Joan Copjec, 227–60. London: Verso, 1993.

Reiss, Julie H. *From Margin to Center: The Spaces of Installation Art*. Cambridge: MIT Press, 2001.

Rhodes, Eric Bryant. Review of *Lost Highway*. *Film Quarterly* 51, no. 3 (1998): 57–61.

Rodley, Chris, ed. *Lynch on Lynch*. London: Faber and Faber. 2005.

Rodowick, D. N. *The Virtual Life of Film*. Cambridge: Harvard University Press, 2007.

Ronell, Avital. *The Telephone Book: Technology, Schizophrenia, Electric Speech*. Lincoln: University of Nebraska Press, 1989.

Sammon, P. M. "David Lynch's Dune." *Cinefantastique* 14, no. 4 and 15, no. 5 (1984): 28–91.

Sconce, Jeffrey. *Haunted Media: Electronic Presence from Telegraphy to Television*. Durham, N.C.: Duke University Press, 2000.

Shattuc, Jane M. "Postmodern Misogyny in *Blue Velvet*." *Genders* 13 (1992): 73–89.

Sheen, Erica, and Annette Davison, eds. *David Lynch: American Dreams, Nightmare Visions*. London: Wallflower Press, 2004.

Smith, Murray. "A Reasonable Guide to Horrible Noise (Part 2): Listening to *Lost Highway*." In *Film Style and Story: A Tribute to Torben Groudal*, 153–70. Copenhagen: Museum Tusculanum Press, 2003.

Sobchack, Vivian. "Lounge Time: Post-War Crises and the Chronotope of Film Noir." In *Refiguring Film Genres*, edited by Nick Browne, 129–70. Berkeley: University of California Press, 1998.

Sontag, Susan. "Bergman's *Persona*." In *Styles of Radical Will*, 123–46. New York: Picador, 1966.

———. "The Pornographic Imagination." In *Styles of Radical Will*, 35–73. New York: Picador, 1966.

———. "The Decay of Cinema." *New York Times Magazine*, Feb. 25, 1996.

Spies, Werner, ed. *David Lynch: Dark Splendor*. Berlin: Hatje Cantz, 2010.

Stafford, Barbara Maria. *Visual Analogy: Consciousness and the Art of Connecting*. Cambridge: MIT Press, 2001.

Stewart, Garrett. *Framed Time: Toward a Postfilmic Cinema*. Chicago: University of Chicago Press, 2007.

Taubin, Amy. "The Big Rupture: David Lynch, Richard Kelly, and the New Cinematic Gestalt." *Film Comment* 43, no. 1 (2007): 54–59.

Thurschwell, Pamela. *Literature, Technology, and Magical Thinking, 1880–1920*. Cambridge: Cambridge University Press, 2001.

Tiffany, Daniel. *Toy Medium: Materialism and Modern Lyric*. Berkeley: University of California Press, 2000.

Toles, George. "Auditioning Betty in *Mulholland Drive*." *Film Quarterly* 58, no. 1 (2004): 2–13.

Turvey, Malcolm. *Doubting Vision: Film and the Revelationist Tradition*. Oxford: Oxford University Press, 2008.

Ujica, Andrei, and Boris Groys. "On the Art of David Lynch." In Lynch, *David Lynch: The Air Is on Fire*, 106–209, 377–84.

Vidler, Anthony. *The Architectural Uncanny: Essays in the Modern Unhomely*. London: MIT Press, 1994.

———. *Warped Space: Art, Architecture, and Anxiety in Modern Culture*. Cambridge: MIT Press, 2001.

Wallace, David Foster. "David Lynch Keeps His Head." In *A Supposedly Fun Thing I'll Never Do Again: Essays and Arguments*, 146–212. Boston: Little, Brown, 1997.

Weintraub, Alan. *Lloyd Wright: The Architecture of Frank Lloyd Wright, Jr.* New York: Harry N. Abrams, 1998.

"(Why) Is David Lynch Important? A *Parkett* Inquiry." *Parkett* 28 (1991): 153–62.

Willeman, Paul. "The Sirkian System" (1971). In *Looks and Frictions: Essays in Cultural Studies and Film Theory*, 87–98. Bloomington: Indiana University Press, 1994.

Williams, Linda. *Hard Core: Power, Pleasure, and the "Frenzy of the Visible."* Berkeley: University of California Press, 1989.

———. "Melodrama Revised." In *Refiguring American Film Genres: History and Theory*, edited by Nick Browne, 42–88. Berkeley: University of California Press, 1998.

Willis, Sharon. "Do the Wrong Thing: David Lynch's Perverse Style." In *High Contrast: Race and Gender in Contemporary Hollywood Film*, 131–57. Durham, N.C.: Duke University Press, 1997.

Wong, Yoke-Sum. "Modernism's Love Child: The Story of Happy Architectures." *Common Knowledge* 14, no. 3 (2008): 445–71.

Wood, Bret. "Organic Phenomena." *Art Papers* (Focus on Art and Film) 22, no. 5 (1998): 16–21.

Žižek, Slavoj. *The Art of the Ridiculous Sublime: On David Lynch's Lost Highway*. Seattle: Walter Chapin Simpson Center for the Humanities, 2000.

———. "The Lamella of David Lynch." In *Reading Seminar XI: Lacan's Four Fundamental Concepts of Psychoanalysis*, edited by Richard Feldstein, Bruce Fink, and Maire Jaanus, 205–20. Albany: SUNY Press, 1995.

aesthetics: of collecting, 42–43; counter-cultural, 45–46; and electricity, 134–35; and environments, 4–5; and Lynch's signature, 54, 56; and MTV, 71; of modernity, 64; organic, 119, 125, 134; and painting, 4–5, 114–15; of plastic, 1–8; and politics, 30; pop, 45; postmodern, 2, 30, 62–63, 65; post-Romantic, 30; self-reflexive, 38–39; and taste in *Blue Velvet*, 28–47

affect: and the close-up, 21; and cognitivist film theory, 64; countercultural, 30; in *film noir*, 37; and impersonality in *Mulholland Dr.*, 96–111; instability of, 4, 21, 40, 61, 82, 122; lyric, 109–11; mediated, 6, 63–111; and melodrama in *Fire Walk with Me*, 79–94; modernist, 63–64; and motion, 115; perverse, 118; pornographic, 60; postmodern, 30, 62–63; pre-personal, 157; and psychoanalysis, 63; and sincerity, 6, 62–63; transmission of, in *Wild at Heart*, 65–78; and unstable situations in *Inland Empire*, 151–54. *See also*, anxiety; black humor; irony; grotesque; melodrama

All That Heaven Allows, 82

Alphabet, The, 114, 122

American Film Institute, 28, 114, 119, 120, 166

Anderson, Michael J., 154

Anger, Kenneth, 44

Angriest Dog in the World, The, 12, 146

animals: and aggression, 70; and domestic life, 14, 119–20, 146–47; and the human, 20–28, 77–78; in *Inland Empire*, 146–47; and the natural world, 127–34; passion of, 33; suffering of, 90

animation: and absence, 1, 82–84; cel, 7, 119–24, 169; and the avant-garde, 121–22; and cinema's heterogeneity, 114–16; and digital technologies, 140–41; of Laura Palmer, 82–84, 93; lyric, 109–11; and non-naturalism, 121; and things, 14, 73

Antonioni, Michelangelo, 10

anxiety: and architecture, 11; the domestication of, in *The Straight Story*, 131–33; and kitsch, 3; and off-screen space, 101; and the uncanny, 19; in *Wild at Heart*, 65–78; in Winkie's diner, 102

architecture: Bauhaus, 32; Beverly Johnson House, 8–9, 48–49, 165; of *Blue Velvet*, 28; cinema as, 5–6, 9, 18, 163–64; Congrès Internationaux d'Architecture Moderne, 31; of experience in *Inland Empire*, 149–50; House of Glass, 10; mid-century, 31–32, 55, 81; modernist, 9–10, 31–32, 50, 165; and self-reflexivity, 38–39; urban in *Eraserhead*, 18–19

art cinema: 50, 60, 63, 94–97

art deco: 39–42

Asymmetrical Productions, 48, 117

Autobiography of Special Agent Dale Cooper: My Life, My Tapes, The, 83

Bacon, Francis, 26, 33, 56

Badalamenti, Angelo, 73, 85, 162

Balázs, Béla, 112

Barthes, Roland, 2, 7
Bataille, Georges, 113
Baudrillard, Jean, 42, 52, 57
Bauhaus, 9, 10, 32, 165
Bazin, André, 7
Bellmer, Hans, 112
Benjamin, Walter, 7, 11, 36, 112, 120
Bergman, Ingmar, 50, 95, 96
Bertolucci, Bernardo, 65
Bigger Than Life, 91
black humor: 6, 77–78
Black Lizard Books, 67
Bloch, Ernst, 66
Blue Velvet, 28–47
Boiffard, Jacques-Andres, 113
Brecht, Bertold, 82
Breton, André, 7, 50, 77, 111
Buñuel, Luis, 60, 91, 113, 141

Cahiers du cinéma, 48
camp: 2, 30, 43, 45–46
Cannes Film Festival, 62, 65
Carroll, Noël, 64
Catching the Big Fish, 137
Chareau, Pierre, 9, 10, 165
Chion, Michel, 55, 66, 71, 83, 117, 130, 133
cinema: and cinephilia, 39, 95; and deixis, 101–2; digital, 134–54; as environment; 4–5; as interiorizing technology, 17, 18, 122; as machine, 17–18, 124; and the plastic arts, 4–5, 114–15; the ontology of, 94–95, 106–7, 115, 122; and spectatorship, 4, 7–8, 97, 99, 101–2, 108, 118, 133, 141
cliché: 2, 44, 63, 77, 106, 147
close-up: 26, 74, 89–90, 94, 109, 133, 142–43
Club Silencio, 5, 95, 98, 104, 106–8, 110, 128
Coen, Joel and Ethan, 63, 77
Colomina, Beatriz, 55
comedy: 61, 75–79, 103, 153
Congrès Internationaux d'Architecture Moderne, 31
Contempt/Le mépris, 96, 97
Cruise, Julee, 44, 83

davidlynch.com, 65, 136, 152, 154
"David Lynch Music Factory," 152
Del Rio, Rebekah, 108–11, 128
de Man, Paul, 109, 110
Deming, Peter, 100
Deren, Maya, 141
de Sade, Marquis, 41, 42, 57
design. *See* architecture, furniture, interiors, sound
desire: and cinephilia, 108–9; fetishistic, 41, 43, 50, 54, 58, 76–78, 108, 112; for home, 69; Lacanian, 122; melodramatic, 82–83, 89, 94; vs. anxiety, 66
Desplechin, Arnaud, 63
Discreet Charm of the Bourgeoisie, The, 91
"Distorted Nudes," 112, 143
Doane, Mary Ann 102
domesticity: denaturalization of, 30, 119–24; and *film noir*, 34, 54–55; and gender in *Inland Empire*, 141–54; instability of, 10–20, 35–36; and melodrama, 79–94; mid-century, 2–3, 31–32, 39, 50, 52, 55–56; and sentimentality, 36; small-town, 37–38; and sexuality, 15, 30; theatricality of, 21–22, 24–25, 51, 120–21; and Victorian normalcy, 23–24; virtual, 19–20. *See also* architecture; interiority; interiors
Dune, 28

Eames, Charles and Ray, 31–32, 55–56, 166
Egoyan, Atom, 63
8½, 38
Eisenstein, Sergei, 10
electricity: 19, 38, 88, 128–29, 134–37. *See also* machine; technology
Elephant Man, The, 20–27
Elsaesser, Thomas, 81, 87
Elvis, 76, 78
embodiment: and architectural space, 18; animal, 146; and disfigurement, 20–28, 53; of Dorothy Vallens, 36, 40–41; and femininity in *Inland Empire*, 141–54; hollowness of, 66, 73–75, 109–11; machinic, 128–34, 135; and mesmer-

ism, 134; and sound, 73–74, 108; and stupidity, 67, 77–78
Epstein, Jean, 112
Eraserhead, 10–20

fantasy: cinematic, 39; consumer, 40; vs. desire, 54, 63, 122; of Diane Selwyn, 98–100, 102, 107–8; of humanism, 18–20, 21–28; of Laura Palmer, 89; mass, 111; middle-class, 32, 36, 38, 45, 82; Lynch's interest in, 2, 43–44, 47; melodramatic, 94; pornographic, 59
Faure, Élie, 5, 10
Fellini, Federico, 10, 38, 95
"Fetish," 54, 112
film noir: 37–38, 50, 54, 81
Franklin, Carl, 63
Freud, Sigmund, 32, 41, 81, 82
Fried, Michael, 116
Frost, Mark, 81, 83
Fugitive Kind, The, 76
furniture: and auteurism, 50; and Bauhaus minimalism, 32; Bertoia Diamond Chair, 8; 55–56; and daydreams, 165; designed by David Lynch, 9, 16, 47–49, 52–54, 161–63; Elliptical Table, 55–57; Espresso Table, 48, 162; and femininity, 40–42; 53–55; Floating Beam Table, 48; Herman Miller, 55–56; Knoll Furniture Company, 8, 55–56; in Lynch's home, 8–9; midcentury ensembles of, 38; and politics in *Blue Velvet,* 29–30, 46; and pornography in *Lost Highway,* 50–61; Salone del Mobile, 47, 162; Skank World, 48, 163; Steel Block Table, 48; Wire Mesh Chairs, 56. *See also* design; domesticity; interiority
Fury, 34
Fuss, Diana, 11

Gifford, Barry, 61, 67, 164
Gilda, 100, 102
Godard, Jean-Luc, 65, 95–96
Goodis, David, 67
Grandmother, The, 119–24
Greenberg, Clement, 31–32, 45

grotesque: and aesthetic modernity, 6, 64, 118; as a challenge to bourgeois domesticity, 14–15; comedy of, 76–79; Dorothy Vallens as, 41; and female faces in *Inland Empire,* 141–46, 149; Jingle Dell as, 69–70; and kitsch, 9, 41, 70; and limits of humanism, 20–22, 14–15; and medial impurity, 115–16; as strategy of authenticity, 47; and stupidity of body, 61; 50, 118, 143, 145. *See also* embodiment; organicism
Guattari, Félix, 124
Gunning, Tom, 115

Hagelin, John, 137
Haynes, Todd, 63
Hitchcock, Alfred, 10, 30, 48, 60, 62, 81
Hotel Room, 67
human: animated, 119–24; and dehumanization in *Lost Highway,* 47–51; as displaced by technology, 111–13; formal violations of, 121–22; limits of in *Eraserhead,* 20–28; and Lynch's comedy, 75–79; and Lynch's "inhumanity," 118, 154; and machines, 124–34; and telephonic dispossession, 103–7; and window as technology of, 18–20

Imitation of Life, 82
Industrial Symphony No. 1, 154
Inland Empire, 134–54
interiority: and bourgeois privacy, 11, 24, 51; and the close-up, 21; and industrialization, 11; and Lynch's camera movement, 17, 18, 122; and lyric, 109–10; nineteenth-century evolution of, 10–11; pornographic, 26, 57–61; romantic, 23; theatricality of, in *The Elephant Man,* 20–28; vulnerability of, in *Eraserhead,* 11–20; window as technology of, 26–28
interiors: avant-garde, 20, 31; of Ben's place, 42–47; of the Beverly Johnson House, 8–9, 48; of Deep River Apartments, 29, 37–42; design of in Lynch's films, 5–7; 8–61; of *Inland Empire's* finale, 154; of the Madisons' home in

Lost Highway, 51–58; melodramatic, 81–83, 92; mid-century, 30–31, 50, 57, 81; modernist, 31–32, 50, 81–82; nested, 15, 24, 36; of paintings, 114–15; prosthetic, 15–16; the Red Room, 93–94; the Smithy set, 149–51. *See also* architecture; design; kitsch; furniture; interiority
irony: 6, 30, 62–64, 73, 80, 82

Jameson, Fredric, 2, 29–30, 62
Jarmusch, Jim, 63, 77

Kael, Pauline, 29, 41, 118
Kafka, Franz, 11, 60, 120, 136
Kant, Immanuel, 118
Kaprow, Allan, 4
Kazan, Elia, 81
Kerouac, Jack, 4
kitsch, 3, 6, 30–47, 79, 84, 91, 149
Kline, Franz, 4
Kokoschka, Oskar, 4
Kracauer, Siegfried, 112
Krantz, Tony, 97
Krauss, Rosalind, 112, 117
Kubrick, Stanley, 10

Land Without Bread, 113
Lang, Fritz, 34, 96, 103, 132
Laura, 81
Le Corbusier, 50, 166
Le Studio Canal Plus, 96, 125
Libération, 65
Lost Highway, 47–63
Louboutin, Christian, 54
Lumet, Sidney, 76
Lumière and Company, 80, 95, 169
Lynch, David: and the American Film Institute, 114; architectural interests, 9–10; association with Transcendental Meditation, 137–38; and auteurism, 48–50; cinephilia of, 39, 95; fine arts training, 4–5; 114–15; as furniture designer, 9, 16, 47–49, 52–54, 161–63; and "the Lynchian," 62–63; post-modernism of, 2, 62–63; as surrealist, 111–14
lyric, 6, 64, 78–79, 104, 108–11, 153

M, 132
machine: and animation, 124; and *Eraserhead*'s baby, 17–18; and factory, 12; home as, 60; and human hybrids, 27, 124–34; and industrialization, 27; melo-dramatic, 82, 94; telephones, 103–6
Maddin, Guy, 63
Man Ray, 112
Manual for a Perfect Government, 137
McGowan, Todd, 54, 63, 89, 122
melodrama: in *Blue Velvet*, 6; in *The Elephant Man*, 21, 25; in *Fire Walk with Me*, 79–94; in *The Grandmother*, 119–24; *Lost Highway*'s refusal of, 50–51; Lynch's commitment to, 80–81, 139; modernist, 82–83
Mesmer, Franz Anton, 134, 135
Metz, Christian, 108
Minnelli, Vincente, 81
modernism: and affect, 63–65; and art cinema 94–96; embodied mind of, 135; and *Lost Highway*'s marketing, 50–51; midcentury domestication of, 6, 31–32; and melodrama, 82–83; and medial purity, 116–17. *See also* architecture; interiors; interiority
modernity: affects of, 6, 64–65; cold war, 3; mid-century, 39; nineteenth-century, 11, 23, 37
Mon Oncle, 2
Montgomery, Monty, 67
Moon, Michael, 44
Mulholland Dr., 94–111
Mulvey, Laura, 46, 112

Neale, Steve, 94
Neutra, Richard, 10, 31, 165
Nochimson, Martha, 63

October Films, 48
On the Air, 97
Orbison, Roy, 43, 108, 109
organicism: as aesthetic production, 119; as contaminated by the inorganic, 7, 12, 16, 27, 112–14; in design, 9, 40; and digital cinema, 134–54; domestic fantasy, 54, 57; and finitude, 118–19, 122; of Hollywood continuity editing, 98;

"goodness" of, in *The Straight Story*, 114–34; irrational, 116–19; surrealist, 112–14; and wood, 52–53. *See also* animation; embodiment; grotesque; temporality

Parkett, 62
Peirce, Charles Sanders, 102
Pennsylvania Academy of the Fine Arts, 4, 114, 169
performance: within the home, 20, 22, 24–25, 28; and recording technologies, 107–11; 135–36; scenes of, within Lynch's films, 4, 17, 27, 43, 45, 70, 78, 106–11; and spectacular culture, 20–28; and the tableau, 29, 38, 43–43, 80–81, 85, 89–90, 115–16, 122–23, 149
Persona, 95–97
photography: digital, 143–44; and indexicality, 102, 115; in *The Elephant Man*, 22–23, 25; of Laura Palmer, 79; Lynch's for "Fetish" campaign, 54; surrealist, 112
Polish National Film School, 138
Pollock, Jackson, 4
pornography, 6, 26, 47–61, 74, 118
Preminger, Otto 81
"Premonition Following an Evil Deed," 80, 121
privacy. *See* interiors, interiority
Propaganda Films, 67
Pynchon, Thomas, 62

Quay brothers, 121

Rabbits, 136, 141, 146, 150, 151, 154
radio, 40, 66–79, 81, 135, 136, 154
Ray, Nicholas, 81
Reznor, Trent, 49
Rodley, Chris, 65, 125
Rodowick, D. N., 113
romanticism: 6, 17, 23, 30, 62, 67, 72, 153

Sarde, Alain, 98, 125
Schindler, Rudolf Michael, 10, 165
Scorpio Rising, 45
Secret Diary of Laura Palmer, The, 83
sensation: cinema's capacity for, 108; of

disgust, 47, 118; erotic, 42; and kitschy vicariousness, 30–32; plastic, 41, 43; and transgression, 30
sentimentality: 21, 25, 32, 47, 77, 89–90, 125
sexuality: and Jeffrey Beaumont's maturation in *Blue Velvet*, 28–47; and gay taste, 45–47; and the grotesque in *Eraserhead*, 13–15; and Lynch's politics, 29; and passion in *Wild at Heart*, 67–75; and perversion, 30, 41; and pornographic mystery, 51, 54–61. *See also* camp; domesticity; pornography
Silence, The, 96
Sirk, Douglas, 81, 82, 87
Six Men Getting Sick, 114–19
Sontag, Susan, 58, 61, 94–97
sound: and Alan Splet, 120; and cinematic ontology, 106–8; of domestic unease, 79–80; editing in *Wild at Heart*, 71–72; as interior design, 16, 17, 55; of machines, 26–27; and the mysteries of personality in *Mulholland Dr.*, 103, 105–6; of paintings, 114–15; and sound gags, 71, 75–76, 85, 88; soundtrack of *Lost Highway*, 49; and synchronization, 44–45, 78, 117, 153; and trauma, 69–75. *See also* lyric; radio
Splet, Alan, 120
Straight Story, The, 124–34
Sunset Blvd., 38, 100, 121
surrealism, 50, 111–14, 115, 121, 139, 151, 154
Svankmajer, Jan, 121
Sweeney, Mary, 53, 125

Tarantino, Quentin, 63, 77
Tati, Jacques, 10
technology: digital, 138–54; harmony with, 124–34; and hybridity with organism, 7, 16, 113, 165; of interiority, 16–17; and surveillance, 51–53, 88–89, 92; of the voice, 103–6; of window, 28; wood as defense against, 52–53. *See also* machine
television: as design object, 29; within Lynch's films, 37–38, 51–52, 70, 81, 136, 148, 153; and *Mulholland Dr.*

pilot, 95, 97–99; and *Twin Peaks*, 1, 81–85, 87; vicarious possibilities of, 41; as virtual window in *Eraserhead*, 16

temporality: of anxiety, 65; and art cinema, 97; cinematic, 5; of deixis, 101–2; digital, 140–45; of *film noir*, 54–55; inorganic, 7, 13–14, 81, 113, 117–18, 123; instability of, 51–52, 65, 88, 122; melodramatic, 82–83, 93; of Lynch's comedy, 75–77; of nostalgia, 2–3, 29–30, 88, 110–11; of repetition, 77–79, 115; stalled, 149

That Obscure Object of Desire, 60

Thompson, Jim, 67

Time, 62

Toles, George, 106

tone: deadpan, 61; instability of in Lynch's work, 6, 62–63; of plastic, 3; of rooms, 17, 29, 32, 46–47

Transcendental Meditation, 7, 137–38

Twin Peaks (television series), 1, 2, 36, 52, 54, 81–88, 91, 93, 97, 161, 164

Twin Peaks: An Access Guide to the Town, 83

Twin Peaks: Fire Walk With Me, 79–94

Tworkov, Jack, 4

Unik, Pierre, 113

van der Rohe, Mies, 10, 165

Vertigo, 60, 81

Vertov, Dziga, 112

Vidler, Anthony, 11

Wallace, David Foster, 62–63

Warhol, Andy, 45

Wasserman, H. Barton, 114

Wasteland, 98

Waters, John, 46–47

Wilder, Billy, 38, 100

Willeford, Charles, 67

Wizard of Oz, The, 69–70, 132

Wrapped in Plastic, 1

Wright, Frank Lloyd, Jr., 8, 10, 49, 164–65

Wright, Frank Lloyd, Sr., 9, 10, 164–65

Written on the Wind, 82

Žižek, Slavoj, 2, 63

Justus Nieland is an associate professor of English at Michigan State University, the author of *Feeling Modern: The Eccentricities of Public Life*, and the coauthor of *Film Noir: Hard-Boiled Modernity and the Cultures of Globalization*.

Books in the series
Contemporary Film Directors

Nelson Pereira dos Santos
Darlene J. Sadlier

Abbas Kiarostami
Mehrnaz Saeed-Vafa and
Jonathan Rosenbaum

Joel and Ethan Coen
R. Barton Palmer

Claire Denis
Judith Mayne

Wong Kar-wai
Peter Brunette

Edward Yang
John Anderson

Pedro Almodóvar
Marvin D'Lugo

Chris Marker
Nora Alter

Abel Ferrara
Nicole Brenez, translated
by Adrian Martin

Jane Campion
Kathleen McHugh

Jim Jarmusch
Juan Suárez

Roman Polanski
James Morrison

Manoel de Oliveira
John Randal Johnson

Neil Jordan
Maria Pramaggiore

Paul Schrader
George Kouvaros

Jean-Pierre Jeunet
Elizabeth Ezra

Terrence Malick
Lloyd Michaels

Sally Potter
Catherine Fowler

Atom Egoyan
Emma Wilson

Albert Maysles
Joe McElhaney

Jerry Lewis
Chris Fujiwara

Jean-Pierre and Luc Dardenne
Joseph Mai

Michael Haneke
Peter Brunette

Alejandro González Iñárritu
Celestino Deleyto and
Maria del Mar Azcona

Lars von Trier
Linda Badley

Hal Hartley
Mark L. Berrettini

François Ozon
Thibaut Schilt

Steven Soderbergh
Aaron Baker

Mike Leigh
Sean O'Sullivan

D. A. Pennebaker
Keith Beattie

Jacques Rivette
Mary M. Wiles

Kim Ki-duk
　Hye Seung Chung

Philip Kaufman
　Annette Insdorf

Richard Linklater
　David T. Johnson

David Lynch
　Justus Nieland

The University of Illinois Press
is a founding member of the
Association of American University Presses.

University of Illinois Press
1325 South Oak Street
Champaign, IL 61820-6903
www.press.uillinois.edu